The Big Book of
BEING RUDE

With an Introduction by

JONATHON GREEN

and cartoons by Dan Pearce

CASSELL&CO

Cassell & Co.
Wellington House, 125, Strand, London WC2R 0BB

First Published in 2000

A CIP record for this book is available from the British Library.

ISBN 0 304 35514 3

Distributed in the United States by Sterling Publishing Co. Inc.
387 Park Avenue South, New York NY 10016–8810

Design by Gwyn Lewis

Printed in Great Britain by Mackays of Chatham

The Big Book of
BEING RUDE

Contents

Introduction

What you have here, you dandiprat, you granny-dodger, you mutt-head and you snotnose, to avail myself of what we shall categorize, for lack of anything more specific, as 'terms of general abuse', is what one might term *The Big Book of Filth II*. And, to adopt that old movie sequel cliché, this time it really is personal.

The Big Book of Being Rude returns, unashamed as ever, to the pages of *Cassell's Dictionary of Slang*, tosses in an extra couple of years' research, and returns laden with another six thousand odd head-words, this time pertaining to the fine, and in slang much apos-trophised, art of slagging off (lit. to call someone a *slag*, originally an 18C insult for a coward) one's neighbours. Slang is of course the supreme vehicle of insult. The taxonomy of the slang lexicon may be headed up by sex, drink and drugs, and a round-up of our phys-ical bits and pieces, but insults come high on the list. Slang, as can be seen in any dictionary, takes few prisoners. One may search in vain for the caring, sharing, compassionate end of the vocabulary. There are, on the other hand, nearly one thousand terms for 'fool' (and another 650-plus for 'stupid'). The unsophisticated, the rural, the gauche, the deceitful, the boastful, the self-regarding, the ugly, the fat (and occasionally the lean), the tall and short, the dirty, the crazy, the impotent and the sex-obsessed, the flatterer and the nag, and of course the glutton and the drunkard all get due deserts. And those 'general terms', the scattershot end of the insults market, offer three hundred entries of their own. All these and more will be found in the pages that follow.

Two more areas will also be found below: race and religion. And as one whose earlier book *Words Apart*, a study of the 'language of prejudice' fell generally on shocked ears and provoked the response that while the words existed did it really help for lexicographers to pursue them, I tread these paths with a certain circumspection. The intention of this book is to amuse. Underpinned by serious lexicographical research it undoubtedly is, but these pages are aimed primarily at entertainment rather than enlightenment. So why, one may ask, include the inflammatory lexica of racism, nationalism and anti-clericalism? Like the mountain climber I must answer briefly: because they're there. Insults trade on another's perceived weakness, and into this category fall belief, patriotism or any allegiance to a group. The lexicon of slang insult has a large, we may properly feel far too large, area reserved for just such attacks, whether on the grounds of race – primarily anti-Black, anti-Irish or anti-Asian – or on the grounds of religion – primarily anti-Semitic. The words spawned by this area of vocabulary are rightly regarded as unacceptable by the enlightened majority, but they are slang, they are insults and this is a book of insulting slang. I do not believe in censorship – and in any case, hiding things away is in itself the best stimulus for their discovery. The lexicographer's task, even in an 'entertainment' such as this, is to lay out his or her stall. There is no coercion to 'buy'. As Lenny Bruce once averred: A knowledge of syphilis is not an instruction to contract it.

Thus the serious bit: a necessary health warning as it were. As for the rest, enjoy. Those who would decry slang often claim that its main failing is in the paucity of terms on offer. This book, if it does nothing else, should put paid to that *canard* and hopefully, as well as entertain and amuse, embellish your vocabulary, albeit of a less than wholesome sort. The American socialite and wit Alice Roosevelt Longworth (who said of a leading politician 'You have to know him really well to dislike him thoroughly') owned a favoured pillow, on which were embroidered the words, 'If you haven't anything nice to say about anyone, come and sit by me.' Read *The Big Book of Being Rude* and you too could be her very best friend.

Jonathon Green
JULY 2000

Abbreviations

abbr.	abbreviation
Anglo-Ind.	Anglo-Indian
Aus.	Australia, Australian
Baha.	Bahamas, Bahamian
Bdos	Barbados, Barbadian
Belz.	Belize, Belizean
c.	circa (around)
Can.	Canada, Canadian
dial.	dialect
esp.	especially
fig.	figurative, figuratively
fl.	floruit (flourished)
Gren.	Grenada, Grenadian
Guyn.	Guyana, Guyanese
Hisp. Amer.	Hispanic-American
Ital. Amer.	Italian-American
Jam.	Jamaica, Jamaican
juv.	juvenile
Ling. Fr.	Lingua Franca

lit.	literal, literally
milit.	military
mispron.	mispronunciation
naut.	nautical
N.Z.	New Zealand
orig.	original, originally
poss.	possible, possibly
pron.	pronunciation
rhy. sl.	rhyming slang
S Afr.	South Africa, South African
Scot.	Scotland, Scottish
SE	Standard English
sl.	slang
Trin.	Trinidad, Trinidadian
UK	United Kingdom
Und.	Underworld
US	United States
usu.	usual, usually
W.I.	West Indies, West Indian
WW1	First World War
WW2	Second World War

Languages

Dharuk   an extinct Australian aboriginal language

Fanagalo   a lingua franca developed in the mining areas of
                South Africa

Foulah   The Benue-Congo language of the Fulani people
                of West Africa

Hausa   the Hamitic language of the Hausa people of W
                Africa and central Sudan

Ijo   the Niger-Congo language of the Ijo people of
                southern Nigeria

Kanuri   the Nilo-Saharan language of the Kanuri people
                of Nigeria

Lingua Franca   an Italian-Provençal jargon developed in eastern
                Mediterranean ports

Nguni   a group of Bantu languages spoken by the Nguni
                people of southern Africa

OE   Old English

ON   Old Norse

Polari   an English argot developed among groups of
                theatrical and circus performers derived largely
                from Italian, directly or through Lingua Franca

Romani	a Dardic language spoken by the Gypsies
Shelta	a beggars' and tinkers' jargon composed of Gaelic and Irish formations
Sotho	a group of closely related Bantu languages spoken in Lesotho and South Africa.
Twi	a Ghanaian language
Wemba	an extinct Aboriginal language of South-east Australia
Zulu	a Bantu language spoken by the Zulu people of Natal

How to enjoy

The Big Book of Being Rude

The Big Book of Being Rude presents insulting slang words and phrases under a variety of categories and headings. Each word or phrase is followed by a date in square brackets, [18C], [19C], [late 18C–early 19C] and so on, indicating the period of usage of the word or phrase in question. The '+' sign indicates that the term is still in use, as does the date [2000s] which indicates a recent and current expression.

The round brackets that follow the square brackets contain a range of different types of additional information, including usage labels indicating the geographical usage of the word, e.g. (US) or the social/cultural usage, e.g. (US campus). Where necessary the round brackets also include glosses or etymological explanations for some of the more baffling expressions.

STUPID, IRRITATING
AND CONTEMPTIBLE

GENERAL EXPRESSIONS OF LOATHING

abortion [1940s+] (Aus.)

arsewipe [1950s+]

ass-bite [1970s] (US)

asswipe [1950s+]

ate-your-bun [1990s] (Irish)

baby-raper [1960s+]

barfer [1940s] (US; i.e. they make you vomit)

bastard [late 16C+]

big stiff [late 19C+] (orig. US)

boner [1960s+] (Aus.)

cleatis [1990s]

clotty [1960s+] (Irish)

cock-knocker [1950s+] (US; lit. 'penis-hitter')

cockroach [20C] (US)

come-pot [20C]

crudzoid [1980s] (US)

cudsucker [20C] (US)

cunt's blood [1990s]

dildohead [20C] (US)

dipwad [1970s+] (US)

dirtbag [1940s+] (orig. US)

dirt bird [1940s+]

doos [20C] (S.Afr.; lit. 'box', i.e. 'cunt')

drol [1960s+] (S.Afr.; Afrikaans *drol letjies*, animal droppings)

dykeface [20C]

el sleazo [1970s+] (US)

fart-face [20C]

fart-head [1960s+] (US)

frog [mid-19C+] (US)

gagger [1980s+] (US campus)

germ [1940s–70s] (US)

gluggar [20C] (Irish; *ubh ghlugair*, a rotten egg)

gobeen [1930s+] (Irish; lit. 'little beak')

goorie/goory [1930s+] (N.Z.; Maori *goorie*, a mongrel dog)

grubber [1940s+] (US)

hang-out [1980s+]

hootenanny [1920s+] (US)

jerk [1930s+] (US)

lickskillet [late 19C–1950s] (US)

lobster [1990s] (i.e. 'a tail full of meat and a head full of shit')

lowlife/lowlifer [1910s+] (orig. US)

maggot [1980s+] (Aus.)

malco [1980s+] (*malco*ordinated)

mong [1930s+] (orig. Aus.; *mong*rel)

mongrel [20C] (Aus./N.Z.)

mud turtle [late 19C–1930s] (US)

piss artist [1940s+]

99 99 99 99 99 99 99 99 99 99 99 99 99 99 99 99 99 99 99 99 99 99 99

Sons of bitches

hijo de puta [1950s] (US/PR; Spanish, 'son of
a whore')

sonofabitch [17C+]

son of a bitch [17C+]

whore's melt [20C] (Irish; lit. 'whore's spawn')

66 66 66 66 66 66 66 66 66 66 66 66 66 66 66 66 66 66 66 66 66 66

piss britches [20C] (US Black)

pluke/plook [20C] (Scot. dial. *pluke/plook*, a boil)

pus-bag/puss-bag [20C] (US)

pussbucket [1950s+] (orig. US)

raasclat [1940s+] (W.I./Jam.; lit. 'arse cloth', i.e. a sanitary towel)

ratbag [late 19C+] (orig. Aus./N.Z.)

rat bastard [1950s+] (orig. US)

rat muncher [1980s+]

ratter [1910s] (Aus./N.Z.)

scadger [mid–late 19C]

schlep [1930s+] (orig. US; lit. 'drag')

scud [1960s+] (Ulster; lit. 'jinx')

scuzzbag [1970s+] (US)

scuzzball [1990s+]

scuzzhead [1990s]

skunk [mid-19C+]

slamtrash [19C]

99 99 99 99 99 99 99 99 99 99 99 99 99 99 99 99 99 99 99 99 99 99

Scumbags and spunkgullets

scumbag [1920s+]

scumhead [1990s]

scumpig [1990s]

scumsucker [1960s+] (orig. US)

spunk-bag [1990s+]

spunker [1990s+]

spunk-gullet [20C]

66 66 66 66 66 66 66 66 66 66 66 66 66 66 66 66 66 66 66 66 66 66

99 99 99 99 99 99 99 99 99 99 99 99 99 99 99 99 99 99 99 99 99 99

Cocksucks and scumfucks

cockmunch [1990s]
cocksuck [1960s+] (orig. US)
cocksucker [1910s+] (orig. US)
cunt-lapper [1920s+]
cunt-licker [1940s+] (orig. US)
duck-fucker [1970s+] (US)
feather-plucker [1940s+] (rhy. sl. 'fucker')
fuck [1920s+]
fuckbag [1970s+]
fuckdust [20C]
fucker [19C+]
fuckstick [1950s+]
muff-diver [1940s+] (US)
pig-fucker [1930s+] (US)
rat fuck [1920s+] (US)
rat shagger [1980s+]
scum fuck [1990s]
shag-nasty [20C]

66 66 66 66 66 66 66 66 66 66 66 66 66 66 66 66 66 66 66 66 66

sleaze [1960s+] (US)
sleazo/sleazoid [1970s+] (US)
smeerlap [mid-19C+] (S.Afr.; lit. 'grease cloth')
spud [1980s+] (N.Z. teen)
stinkpot [mid-19C+]
sucka [1990s] (US Black teen)

99 99 99 99 99 99 99 99 99 99 99 99 99 99 99 99 99 99 99 99 99 99

Seminal and faecal stains

dicksplash [1990s] (lit. 'semen stain')

shitstain [1990s] (orig. US)

stains [1980s+] (a misfit, from the semen *stains*
produced by a masturbator)

wankstain [1970s+] (a coward)

66 66 66 66 66 66 66 66 66 66 66 66 66 66 66 66 66 66 66 66 66 66

99 99 99 99 99 99 99 99 99 99 99 99 99 99 99 99 99 99 99 99 99 99

Basticles and cuntocks:
portmanteau insults

basticles [1990s] (*bas*tard + tes*ticles*)

cuntock [1990s] (*cunt* + *cock*)

grimbo [1980s+] (US campus; *grim* + *bimbo*)

ig man [20C] (US Black; *ig*norant *man*)

shed [1920s+] (Aus./N.Z.; *shit* + *head*)

66 66 66 66 66 66 66 66 66 66 66 66 66 66 66 66 66 66 66 66 66 66

swamp breath [1980s+] (US)

swamp-hog [1990s+]

teabag [1990s+]

tithead [1990s+]

toerag [mid-19C+]

trake [1990s] (US Black teen; *trach*eotomy, i.e. someone down
whose throat you want to stick your fingers)

tramp/trampie [1920s+] (orig. US)

trick [1960s+] (orig. US)
tripe-hound [1920s+]
twillip [1940s]
wipe-out [1960s+]
yak [1980s+] (US)

CUNTS, KNOBS AND SCROTES

bollockbrain [1960s+]
cockbite [1960s+] (US)
cockface [1960s+] (US)
cockhead [1970s] (Aus./US)

Miss Dickhead and Mr Cuntface

cunt [mid-19C+]
cuntprick [1990s+]
cuntyballs [1990s+]
Cunty McCuntlips [1990s]
dickhead [1960s+]
fanny rat [1990s]
fuckhole [1980s+]

99 99 99 99 99 99 99 99 99 99 99 99 99 99 99 99 99 99 99 99 99 99

Acronymic insults

a.k. [1930s–70s] (US; *a*ss-*k*isser)

c.s. [1940s+] (orig. US; *c*hicken-*s*hit, lit. 'coward')

d.a. [1970s+] (US campus; *d*umb *a*ss)

d.ph. [1910s+] (US; *d*amned *f*ool, punning on *D. Ph*il, the higher degree awarded for postgraduate research)

k.m.a.! [late 19C–1920s] (US; *k*iss *m*y *a*rse!)

m.f. [20C] (*m*other*f*ucker)

m.h. [20C] (US; a mad person, i.e. *m*ental *h*ealth)

p.i.t.a. [1960s+] (*p*ain *i*n *t*he *a*rse)

r.f. [1920s] (*r*at *f*ucker)

s.a.b. [1980s+] (US campus; *s*ocial *a*irhead *b*itch)

s.o.b./s.b. [1910s+] (*s*on *o*f a *b*itch)

s.s. [early 19C–1930s] (a fool, i.e. *s*ammy *s*oft)

66 66 66 66 66 66 66 66 66 66 66 66 66 66 66 66 66 66 66 66 66 66

hard-on [1960s+] (US)

Joe [1960s+] (N.Z.) (rhy. sl. *Joe Hunt*, cunt)

knob [1990s] (US teen)

monkey dick [1980s+] (US)

muggy-cunt [1990s+] (lit. 'wet vagina')

national front [20C] (rhy. sl. 'cunt')

nobscratch [1990s]

noodle dick [1990s+] (US)

pecker [late 19C+] (orig. US)

plonker/plonk [1960s+]

poes [1960s+] (S.Afr.; lit. 'pussy', i.e. 'cunt')

prannie/pranny [late 19C+] (lit. 'vagina')

prickface [1960s+]

rat prick [1940s+]

scrote [1970s]

twathead [1990s+]

twat-scourer [late 17C]

wormdick [1990s]

wormrod [1980s+] (US)

9 9 9 9 9 9 9 9 9 9 9 9 9 9 9 9 9 9 9 9 9 9 9 9

A pair of smegheads

nob stilton [1990s]

smeghead [1980s+]

6 6 6 6 6 6 6 6 6 6 6 6 6 6 6 6 6 6 6 6 6 6 6 6

MOTHERFUCKERS

mama-huncher [20C]

mama-jabber [20C]

mammy-dodger [1920s–30s] (US Black)

mammy-jammer [20C]

mammy-rammer [20C]

mammy-tapper [20C]

Mary Frances [20C]

Maryland farmer [20C]

Mister Franklin [20C]

mo dicker [1960s+] (US)

mofo/mo-fo [20C]

mofuck [20C]

molly-dodger [1920s] (US)

mother [20C]

mother-flicker [20C]

mother-flunker [20C]

mother-fouler [20C]

motherfucker [1910s+]

mother-grabber [20C]

mother-hubba/mother-hubbard [20C]

mother-hugger [20C]

mother-humper [20C]

mother-jiver [20C]

mother-jumper [20C]

motherlover [20C]

motheroo [20C]

mother-raper [20C]

mother-rubba/mother rubber [20C]

mother-sucker [20C]

motor-flicker [20C]

motor scooter [1960s+] (US)

muddy funster [20C]

mudfucker [20C]

muhfuhkuh [20C]

WANKERS

bag o' wank [1990s]

butt-chuckler [1990s] (lit. 'bottom tosser')

catwanker [1990s]

fist-fucker [1970s] (US)

fuckwank [1990s]

hand job [1980s+] (US)

jack-off [1930s+]

jerk [1930s+] (orig. US)

jerkwad [1990s] (US)

knob jockey [1990s]

knob-shiner [1990s]

99 99 99 99 99 99 99 99 99 99 99 99 99 99 99 99 99 99 99 99 99

Wankers in rhyming slang

> **ham shanker** [1990s]
>
> **Kuwaiti tanker** [1990s+]
>
> **merchant banker** [1980s+]
>
> **oil tanker** [20C]
>
> **Sri Lanka** [1980s+]

66 66 66 66 66 66 66 66 66 66 66 66 66 66 66 66 66 66 66 66 66

meatbeater [1990s]

monkey spank [1990s]

salami slapper [1990s]

spankhead [1990s]

titwank [1990s]

toss-bag/toss-bags [20C]

tosser/toss [1970s+]

toss-off [20C]

tossprick [20C]

wank-bag [1990s+]

wanker [late 19C+]

wrist [1990s]

ARSEHOLES AND BUTTBREATHS

arsehole [19C+]

bum [mid-19C+] (US)

bumhole [mid-19C+]

buttbreath [1980s+] (US)

crap-ass [1970s+] (US)

horse's ass/horse's arse [mid-19C+]

north end of a southbound horse/mule [1960s+] (US; i.e. 'horse's ass')

poopbutt/pootbutt [1960s+] (US Black)

rat-ass/rat arse [1950s+] (orig. US)

rat's asshole [1950s+] (US)

shit ass/shit-arse [20C] (US)

slackarse [1970s+] (Aus)

wedgeass [1940s+]

BAGS OF SHIT

bag of shit [1960s+]
cack/cak [1970s+] (Irish)
cowshit [1960s] (US)
jobbie/jobby [mid-19C+] (orig. Scot.)
piece of shit/pile of shit/pile of shite [1930s+] (orig. US)
scheisspot [1960s+] (lit. 'shit-pot')
scut [late 19C+] (dial. *scutter*, diarrhoea)
shit/shite [late 19C+]
shitbird [1950s+]
shitbum [1970s+]
shiter [1950s+]
shit-for-brains [1970s+]
shithead/shitehead [20C]
shithouse/shitehouse [20C]
shit-stick [20C]
turd in the punchbowl [1990s] (US)

RUDE REJOINDERS AND POTENT PARTING-SHOTS

bag your face! [1980s+] (i.e. bag it up and throw it away)
bah-fungoo/fungoo [1950s+] (US; Italian *vaffanculo*, go fuck yourself in the ass)
bite my ass!/bite my arse! [1950s+] (orig. US)
bite this! [1980s+] (US)
blow it out your ass! [1940s+] (orig. US milit.)
chuck you Farley! [20C] (i.e. 'fuck you, Charley!')
chúpame [1960s+] (US; Spanish, 'suck me')
drop dead! [1930s+] (orig. US)
eat me! [1980s+] (US)

eat shit! [1930s+] (US)

eat the big one! [1980s+] (US)

fire your tail! [20C] (W.I.)

fuck you! [20C]

gaan kak! [1970s+] (S.Afr.; lit. 'go shit!')

get ripped! [1940s+] (Aus.)

get rooted! [1950s+] (Aus.)

get stuffed! [1940s+]

jump up my ass! [1970s] (US)

kiss it/me where the sun don't shine! [1940s+] (orig. US)

orchids to you! [1930s–50s] (punning on *orchidectomy*, castration)

put it in your ear! [1930s+]

ram it!/ram it up your arse/ass! [1930s+] (orig. US)

ride-on-your-back (Aus.)

screw you! [20C] (US)

shit on you! [1960s+] (orig. US)

shove/stick it up your arse/ass! [1970s+]

shove/stick it up your nose! [1920s+] (orig. US)

sit on it and rotate! [1960s+] (US)

smell your monkey! [1990s]

smell your mother! [1990s] (accompanied by waving the middle finger, implying recent sexual activity with the insultee's mother)

stick it in your ear!/up your chimney! [1930s+]

stick it up your arse sideways! [1990s+]

stick it up your cunt! [1930s+] (Aus.)

suck a fatty! [1990s] (US)

suck eggs! [20C] (US)

take a run at yourself! [20C] (Aus.)

take a running jump! [20C]

toast your blooming eyebrows! [late 19C–1910s]
upya! [1940s+] (Aus.)
up you for the rent! [1930s+] (Aus.)
up your arse!/ass!/butt! [1930s+]
up your brown! [20C]
up your dirty skirt! [1940s] (US)
up your flue! [1970s]
up your jumper! [1920s+] (Aus.)
up your pipe! [1930s+]
up your ronson! [1990s] (rhy. sl. *ronson lighter*, 'shiter')
up yours! [1950s+] (orig. US)
work it! [20C] (i.e. *work it* up your arse!)

99 99 99 99 99 99 99 99 99 99 99 99 99 99 99 99 99 99 99 99 99 99 99

The Valley Girl bites back: teen and campus insults

bite me! [1980s+] (US campus)
bite my ass/arse! [1950s+] (orig. US)
bite the ice! [1980s] (US teen, Valley Girls)
burrito on your nose! [1990s] (US Black teen)
eat my shorts! [1990s+] (US campus)
fag your face! [1980s] (US teen)
kiss my tuna! [1980s] (US teen)
lick me! [1970s+] (US campus)
lick my froth! [1980s] (US teen)
lick my love pump! [1980s+] (US campus)
yank on/bite on/eat that! [1980s+] (US campus)

66 66 66 66 66 66 66 66 66 66 66 66 66 66 66 66 66 66 66 66 66 66 66

A short chronology of fruity historical rejoinders

kiss/suck my arse!/ass! [mid-16C+]

pox take you! [late 16C+]

turd in your teeth! [17C]

kiss my parliament! [late 17C]

you are a mouth and you will die a lip! [late 17C–mid-19C]

shit in your teeth! [18C–mid-19C]

go to hell and help your mother make bitch pie [mid-18C–late 19C]

go to hell [mid-18C+]

you are a thief and a murderer and you have killed a baboon and stole his face [late 18C]

fuck you, Charley! [19C]

saw your timber! [mid-19C]

take a carrot! [mid-19C] (used to women, implying potential sexual activity with a carrot)

get fucked! [mid-19C+]

go to hell and pump thunder [late 19C]

bugger you! [late 19C+]

up you! [late 19C+]

up your jacksie!/up your jack! [late 19C+]

66 66 66 66 66 66 66 66 66 66 66 66 66 66 66 66 66 66 66 66 66 66

Go and...

go (and) fuck yourself [mid-19C+]

go and piss up a shutter [1910s+]

go and take a run against the wind [20C]
  (Anglo-Irish)

**go and take a running/crawling/creeping
  jump (at yourself)** [1910s+]

go boil your head [1930s]

go crawl up a hole [1940s+] (Aus.)

go frig yourself [1930s–50s]

go fuck a duck [20C]

go fuck your mother [1930s+]

go jump in a lake [1910s+]

go jump yourself [20C] (orig. US; euphemism
  for 'go fuck yourself')

go milk a duck [20C] (US)

go piss up a rope [20C] (orig. US)

**go shit in your hat/crap in your hat/spit in
  your hat** [1920s+] (US)

go to hell [mid-18C+]

66 66 66 66 66 66 66 66 66 66 66 66 66 66 66 66 66 66 66 66 66

FOOLS AND IDIOTS

airball [1980s+] (US)

arse/ass [20C]

asshole/arsehole [1960s+] (orig. US)

baloney/boloney [1920s+] (orig. US)

bazooka [1940s–50s]

berk/burk/burke [1930s+]

blitherer [20C]

bogue [1970s] (US; i.e. they are 'bogus')

bone [1910s] (US)

bonetop [1910s] (US)

boob [20C] (orig. US)

boofa/boofer [1970s+] (US)

bozo [1910s+] (orig. US)

brainless wonder [1920s] (US)

bunny [1940s+] (orig. US/Aus.)

butt [1990s] (US)

buttmunch [1990s]

chode [1990s] (US; Navajo *choad*, the penis)

chooch [1970s+] (US; Italian dial. *ciucci*, a donkey)

clot [1940s+]

clown [1940s+]

cluck [1920s] (orig. US; i.e. they have the brains of a chicken)

clunker [1950s+]

crazy-ass/crazy-arse [1960s+] (orig. US)

deadneck [1930s]

dialtone [1980s+] (US)

dick [1960s+]

dicklick [1980s+] (US)

dickweed [1980s+] (US)

dildock [1910s+] (US)

dim bulb [1910s+] (US/Can.)

dimmo/dimo [1970s+]

dimwit [1930s+]

dink [1960s+] (i.e. they are small (*dink*y) and inconsiderable)

dipshit [1960s+] (orig. US)

dipstick [1960s+] (orig. US)

dirk [1960s+]

ditz [1970s+] (US; a scatterbrained woman)

div [1970s+]

divvy [1970s+]

clown

A rollcall of 'named' idiots

Boob McNutt [1940s–60s] (US; a strip cartoon character created by Rube Goldberg)

Dilbert Dildo [1960s] (camp gay)

Dumb Dora [1940s–60s] (US camp gay)

Fred [1980s+] (US campus)

Hans Wurst [20C] (US; German proper name *Hans* + *Wurst*, sausage)

Hoople [1920s+] (US; from the US cartoon strip Major *Hoople*)

jackshit/jack shit/jack and shit/jack [1970s+] (US)

Joe Erk [1940s]

Joey [1990s] (US)

Loogan/Loogin/Lugan [1920s–30s] (US; a supposedly typical 'Irish' surname)

McFly [1980s+] (US campus; George *McFly*, a character in the *Back to the Future* films)

right charlie/proper charlie [1960s+]

Thick Dick [1980s]

Willie Lunchmeat/Willie Lump-lump [20C] (US Und.)

dode [1980s+] (i.e. 'dodo')

doobie [1980s+] (US; Scot. *dobie*, a stupid person)

donkey dick [1980s+] (US)

doofus [1960s+] (orig. US Black)

dopey [1930s+]

dork [1960s+] (orig. US; lit. 'penis')

drop-case [1970s] (US)

el dorko [1980s+] (US)

fart [1930s+]

fart-arse/fart-ass [1940s+]

fish-face [1920s+]

fuckface [1960s+] (orig. US)

fucknob [1990s]

fuckwad [1970s+] (US)

fuckwit [1960s+]

gaum(head) [20C] (US; dial. *gaumless*, stupid)

gilpin [1930s] (US)

gimp [1920s+] (US; lit. 'cripple')

glom [1930s+] (US)

gob-lock [1990s] (lit. 'mouth-lock', i.e. an inarticulate person)

gobshite [20C]

goof [1910s+]

goofball [1940s+] (US)

googie/googy [1930s]

goo-goo [1930s] (US)

goombah/gumbah [1950s+] (US)

goomer [1960s+] (US)

goon [1920s+] (US)

goon-child [1940s–70s] (US)

goop/goopy [20C] (orig. US)

grunt [1970s+] (US)

guffy [1900s]

gumby [1960s+]

half-ass [1920s+] (US)

half-bake [1960s]

hodad/ho-daddy/hodag [1980s+] (US; surfing jargon, 'non-surfer')

horse's hangdown [20C] (lit. 'horse's penis')

horse's neck [1920s–70s] (US)

horse's patoot/horse's patootie [1980s+] (US; lit. 'horse's ass')

icky [1930s–40s] (US Black)

ignant [1940s+] (US Black; *igno*rant)

igno [1970s+] (US; *igno*ramus)

imby [1980s] (US; *imb*ecile)

jerk [1930s+] (orig. US)

jerko [1940s+] (US)

jerkweed [1990s] (US)

jumbo [1940s+]

klunk [1940s+] (US)

knobber [1990s] (US)

knucklehead [1930s+]

knucklenob [1950s+] (US)

lame [1950s+] (orig. US Black)

load [1940s+] (US)

log [1990s+]

malarkey/malaky/malarky/mallarkey/mullarkey [1920s+] (orig. US)

meatball [1930s+] (US)

mental midget [1960s+] (US)

mess [1930s+] (orig. US)

missing link [20C] (US)

momo/mo-mo [1950s+] (US; i.e. 'moron')

mouth-breather [1980s+]

nazz [1990s] (US teen)

nerk [1950s+]

nig-nog [1950s–60s] (i.e. 'nigger')

nimwad [1980s+] (US)

nitwit [1910s+] (orig. US)

nucker [1990s] (US Black)

numbnuts [1940s+] (US)

numbwit [1950s+]

nutso [1960s+] (orig. US)

oofus [1930s–60s] (US Black)

palooka [1920s+] (US; a large and stupid person)

pie-face [1920s+]

pillock [1960s+]

poop [20C]

pork [1950s+]

prat/pratte/pratt [1960s+]

prick [1920s+] (orig. US)

pronk [1950s]

rat's head [20C]

shitkicker [1960s+] (US)

short stop [1960s–70s] (US)

simp [20C] (orig. US; *simp*leton)

slappie [1990s] (US)

soppy ha'porth [1930s+]

spaz-wit [1980s+]

stiffy [1950s–60s] (lit. 'corpse')

stupo [1920s] (Anglo-Irish)

tard [1970s+] (US; re*tard*)

tatey farmer [1990s] (lit. 'potato farmer')

thickie [1970s+]

thicko [1970s+]

twit [1920s+]

twizzit [20C]

yasha [1950s–60s] (camp gay; Russian, 'peasant')

zipalid/zipperhead/zipperlid [1970s+] (i.e. their head has been unzipped and the brain removed)

DWEEBS AND CHEESEDONGS: IDIOTS ON CAMPUS

assface [20C] (US campus)

buttlick [1980s+] (US campus)

cheese dong [1980s+] (US campus; lit. 'smegma penis')

dickwad [1980s+] (US campus)

dork [1960s+] (orig. US; lit. 'penis')

dorkmunder [1980s+] (US campus; *dork* + poss. Dort*münder* Union Pils)

dorkus (pretentious) [1990s] (US campus; a pretentious fool)

egg-for-fuck [1990s] (US campus; playing on 'shit-for-brains')

dude [1960s–70s] (US campus)

four-oh-four/404 [1990s] (US teen; in internet use, error number *404* = 'file not found')

hoser [1980s+] (Can./US campus)

lunch/lunchie [1960s+] (US campus; i.e. they are 'out to lunch')

lunchmeat [1950s+] (US campus)

lunchpail [1960s+] (US campus)
mental giant [1980s+] (US campus)
nugget [1980s+] (US campus)
one-eyed yankee [1990s] (US Black teen)
pud [1930s+] (US teen/campus; lit. 'penis')
remo [1980s+] (US campus; *rem*edial)
sped [1980s+] (US campus; *sp*ecial *ed*ucation)

99 99 99 99 99 99 99 99 99 99 99 99 99 99 99 99 99 99 99 99 99 99

Dumbbutts

dumb [1920s+] (orig. US)
dumb-ass/dumb-arse [1950s+] (orig. US)
dumb-bell [1910s+]
dumb bunny [1920s+] (US)
dumbbutt [1950s+] (US)
dumb cluck [1930s+] (orig. US)
dumbellina [1950s+] (camp gay)
dumbfuck/dumb-fuck [1940s+] (orig. US)
dumbnuts [1970s+] (US)
dumbo [1930s+] (orig. US)
dumbshit [1960s+] (US)
dumbski [20C] (US)
dumbsmack [1940s–50s] (US)
dumb sock [1930s+] (US)
dumbwad [1970s+] (US campus)
dumbwit [1930s] (US)
dum-dum/dumb-dumb [1960s+] (orig. US)
dummo [1970s] (US)

66 66 66 66 66 66 66 66 66 66 66 66 66 66 66 66 66 66 66 66 66 66

sub-human [1980s+] (US campus)
wad [1980s+] (US campus)
whack/wack [1980s+] (US campus)
whiz pop [1970s] (US campus; lit. 'dud firework')

IDIOTS IN RHYMING SLANG

RHYMING WITH BERK
Charlie Smirke [1970s+]

RHYMING WITH CHUMP
lump and bump [late 19C–1930s]

RHYMING WITH CUNT
Berkeley hunt/Berkshire hunt/Burlington hunt [1930s+]
Charlie [1940s+] (i.e. *Charlie* Hunt)
Joe Hunt [20C]

RHYMING WITH DILL
Beecham's pill [1950s+] (Aus.)
jack and jill [20C] (Aus.)

RHYMING WITH DOPE
Joe Soap [1930s+]

RHYMING WITH FOOL
lump of school [late 19C]
twelve-inch rule [20C]
two-foot rule [mid-19C]

RHYMING WITH GAY
thirty-first of May [1920s+] (Aus.)

dumb bunny

RHYMING WITH GOON
 egg and spoon [1970s+] (Aus.)

RHYMING WITH LOON
 man in the moon [20C]

RHYMING WITH MUFF
 beery buff [20C]

RHYMING WITH MUGGINS
 Harry Huggins [20C]

RHYMING WITH PLONKER
 Willy Wonka [1970s+]

RHYMING WITH PRAT
 kit-kat [1960s+]
 paper hat [1960s+]
 tin hat [1960s+]
 top hat [20C]
 trilby hat [20C]

RHYMING WITH PRICK
 Hampton (Wick) [late 19C+]
 kiss-me-quick [20C]

RHYMING WITH TWAT
 dillypot [1940s–60s] (Aus.)
 dollypot [1920s+] (Aus.)

RHYMING WITH WANKER
 J. Arthur [1940s+] (i.e. *J. Arthur* Rank(er))

DICKBRAINS AND DICKHEADS

airhead [1970s+] (US, orig. teen)
asshead [1960s] (US)
balloon-head [1930s+] (US)
blockhead [16C]
blubber-head [early 19C–1940s]
bonehead [20C] (orig. US)
boofhead [1940s+] (orig. Aus.)
bottlehead [mid-17C–late 18C]
boxhead [1920s+]
buckethead [20C] (US)
bullet-head [17C–18C]
butthead [1980s+] (US)
cheesehead [1910s+] (US)
chowderhead [19C] (US)
chucklehead [early 18C–late 19C]
cloth-head [1920s+]
cluckhead [1940s+]
corkhead [1940s] (US)
cottonhead [1930s+] (US)
craphead [1950s+] (orig. US)
crudhead [1980s+]
cunthead [1970s+] (orig. US)
deadhead [20C]
dickbrain [1970s+] (US)
dickhead [1960s+]
dopehead [1940s–60s] (US)
dorkbrain [1970s+] (orig. US)
dorkhead [1970s+]

jarhead

dosshead [20C]

dumbhead [late 19C+]

dunderhead [late 17C+]

dur-brain [1990s+]

fat-head [mid-19C+]

fuckbrain [1970s+]

fuckhead [1960s+]

goonhead [1980s+] (US)

grouthead [mid-16C; mid-19C–1900s]

honch-head [1990s]

hosehead [1980s+] (US campus)

jarhead [1940s+] (US Black)

jerkhead [1980s+] (US)

jingle-brains [late 17C–early 19C]

jolterhead/jolthead [late 18C–19C]

99 99 99 99 99 99 99 99 99 99 99 99 99 99 99 99 99 99 99 99

Animal brains

apehead [1920s] (US)

batbrain [1940s–60s] (US)

beetle-brain [17C]

beetle-head [16C–late 18C; 1940s–50s]

birdbrain [1930s+]

bughead [mid-19C+]

mousebrain [1970s+] (US)

mutthead [1940s] (US)

nit-head [1990s+]

66 66 66 66 66 66 66 66 66 66 66 66 66 66 66 66 66 66 66 66 66

jughead [late 19C+] (US)

knobhead/knobknot [1920s+] (orig. US)

knucklehead [1930s+] (orig. US)

lamebrain [1910s+] (orig. US)

lamehead [1970s] (US)

lardhead [1930s+] (US)

linthead/lintbrain [1960s+] (US)

loggerhead [late 17C+]

lop/lophead [20C] (US Und.)

lughead [1950s+] (US)

mallethead [1950s+] (US)

muddle-head [19C]

99 99 99 99 99 99 99 99 99 99 99 99 99 99 99 99 99 99 99 99 99 99 99

Fruit- and vegetable-heads

applehead [1950s+] (US)

bananahead [1940s+] (US)

beanbrain [1950s+] (US)

bean-head [1910s+] (US)

cabbage-head [17C–late 19C]

coconut head [20C] (US)

gourd-head [mid-19C–1970s] (US)

melonhead [1930s+] (Aus./US)

onionhead [1910s–50s] (US)

peabrain/peahead [20C] (orig. US)

potato-head [20C] (US)

pumpkin head [1970s]

66 66 66 66 66 66 66 66 66 66 66 66 66 66 66 66 66 66 66 66 66

mud-head [late 18C–1950s]

mullethead [mid-19C+] (US)

mummyhead [1990s] (US Black gang)

mush-head [late 19C+] (orig. US)

nailhead [1930s–40s] (US)

nibhead [mid-19C–1920s]

noddy head [mid-19C–1900s]

noodlehead/noodlebrain [1910s+] (US)

nubbin-head [1930s+] (US Black)

numbhead [mid-19C–1950s] (US)

nuthead [20C] (orig. US)

pestlehead [19C]

pinhead [1940s+]

plump-pate [19C]

pointed-head/pointy-head/pointhead [1960s+] (US)

poophead [1970s+] (US campus)

prickhead [20C]

propeller head [1990s]

putty-head [1910s+] (US)

rockhead [20C] (US)

rubblehead [20C]

sap-head [early 18C–late 19C]

sockhead [late 18C]

sophead [19C]

spackahead [1990s]

squarebrain [20C]

stupe-head [1950s+] (US)

thickhead [20C]

timber-head [mid–late 17C]

🙶🙶🙶🙶🙶🙶🙶🙶🙶🙶🙶🙶🙶🙶🙶🙶🙶🙶🙶🙶🙶

Meat- and fish-brains

bacon-bonce [20C]
beef-brain [18C]
beef-head [late 18C–early 19C; US mid-19C+]
chickenbrain [1920s] (US)
hamhead/hamburgerhead [1910s–50s] (US)
meatbrain [1980s+] (orig. US)
meathead [1910s+] (US)
mutton-head [mid-18C+]
prawnhead [1960s+] (Aus.)

🙶🙶🙶🙶🙶🙶🙶🙶🙶🙶🙶🙶🙶🙶🙶🙶🙶🙶🙶🙶🙶

toolhead [1970s+] (US campus)
weatherhead [19C]
wetbrain [1970s+]
woodhead [1990s]

ANIMAL …

aardvark [1960s+] (US)
donkey [mid-19C+]
gerbil [1980s+] (US)
giddy goat [20C]
goat [1910s+]
monkey [1940s–50s] (US)
mullet [1950s+] (US)
newt [1920s+] (US campus)

oyster [1940s–70s] (US)
pondlife [1990s]
squid [1980s+] (US campus)

VEGETABLE ...

banana [1910s+] (US)
dill pickle [1900s] (US)
fruit loop [1980s+] (US)
gourd [1970s+] (US campus)
melon [1930s+] (Aus./Can./N.Z./US Black)
nana/narna [1940s+] (orig. Aus.)
nutcake [1960s+] (US)
prune [1940s+]
quince [1930s+] (Aus.)
turnip [mid-19C]

... AND MINERAL

butt plug [1990s] (orig. US; a type of sex aid inserted into
the anus)
dick spanner [1990s]
doorknob [1930s+]
hockey puck [1960s+] (US)
panhandle [1990s]
wingnut [1980s+]
yoyo [1930s+] (US)

THE IDIOT: A HISTORICAL OVERVIEW

TWO LOOBIES: THE MIDDLE AGES

looby [14C–late 19C]

lubber [14C–19C]

NODDIES AND NINNYHAMMERS: THE 16TH CENTURY

bel-shangle [late 16C–early 17C] (lit. 'bell-jangler', i.e. a fool with cap and bells)

buffle [16C] (French, 'buffalo')

clumperton [mid-16C–early 18C]

cuckoo [late 16C+]

doddypoll/dodipol/doddipool [late 16C–mid-17C] (lit. 'doting-head')

goose-cap [16C–mid-18C; 19C] (lit. 'goose-head')

hobby horse [late 16C–early 17C]

hoddy-doddy [16C–18C; US 19C–20C] (dial. 'snail')

hoddy peak [16C] (lit. 'snail-head')

jobbard [16C] (French *jobard*, silly)

jobberknowl/jobbernowl/jabberknowl/jabbernowl [late 16C–late 19C] (lit. 'silly head')

lobcock [16C] (lit. 'flaccid penis')

ned fool [late 16C–early 17C]

ninnyhammer [late 16C–1910s]

nit [late 16C+]

noddy [early 16C–late 19C] (someone who wags their head foolishly)

simpler [late 16C–early 17C] (UK Und.)

sop [late 16C+] (milk*sop*, a weakling)

asinico/asinego [early 17C–early 18C] (Spanish, 'little donkey')

blunderbuss [17C–late 18C; 1960s] (an unwieldy type of gun)

booberkin [early 17C+] (lit. 'little booby')

booby [early 17C+] (Spanish *bobo*, a fool)

clod [17C]

clodpate [late 17C–mid-18C] (lit. 'clod-head')

clodpoll/clodpole [late 17C+] (lit. 'clod-head')

dildo [mid-17C+] (i.e. like a fake penis, they are not autonomously competent)

doodle [early 17C–mid-19C]

dull-pickle [late 17C–18C]

fopdoodle [17C]

gadso [17C–early 19C] (Italian *cazzo*, a penis)

gawk(head) [17C–early 19C] (Scot. *gowk*, a cuckoo)

goose [17C+]

groutnoll [early 17C] (lit. 'grumble-head')

implement [late 17C–18C]

lerricomtwang [mid–late 17C] (from the chorus of a contemporary song)

Mr Nawpost [late 17C–late 18C] (i.e. if hungry they would 'gnaw a post')

nick-ninny [late 17C–early 19C]

dull-pickle

nigit [late 17C–18C] (elison of 'an idiot')

nigmenog/nimenog [late 17C–18C] (dial. *nigmanies*, a trifle)

nincompoop/nincumpoop/nickumpoop [late 17C+]

pig sconce [mid-17C–late 19C] (lit. 'pig-head')

Silly Willy [17C–18C]

simkin/simpkin [late 17C–late 18C]

Sir Quibble-Queer [late 17C–mid-18C] (a trifling fool)

souse-crown [late 17C–18C] (lit. 'drunken head')

Squire of Alsatia [late 17C–early 19C] (a rich fool, from the title of a play by Thomas Shadwell)

tom-farthing [17C] (i.e. they are only worth a *farthing*)

woodcock [early 17C–mid-18C]

woolly crown [late 17C–mid-19C] (lit. 'woolly-head')

COOTS AND SAPSKULLS: THE 18TH CENTURY

addle-cove [18C–mid-19C]

buttered bun [early 18C]

cake/cakey [late 18C–late 19C]

codfish [late 18C–mid-19C] (US)

coot [late 18C+]

country chub [early 18C]

crackbrain [18C]

cunningham/Mr Cunningham [late 18C]

dull swift [late 18C]

gabes [18C] (i.e. they 'gape' vacantly)

gawney [18C] (Midlands dial. 'stare vacantly')

get [18C–19C] (lit. 'bastard')

gooseberry [18C] (punning on the dessert *gooseberry* fool)

gump [18C+] (US prison; Yorkshire dial. 'homely', 'parochial')

hubble-bubble fellow [late 18C–19C] (*hubble-bubble*
  = incomprehensible talk)
jibbernoll [early 18C] (lit. 'silly head')
nocky boy [late 18C–early 19C]
noddipol/noddy pate [18C] (lit. 'noddy-head', i.e. their head
  wags foolishly from side to side)
paper skull/paper scull [late 18C–early 19C]
pig widgeon/pig widgin [late 18C–early 19C]
sap-pate [early 18C]
sapskull [18C]
shallow pate [late 18C–early 19C]
Simple Simon [late 18C+]
spoon [late 18C–late 19C] (i.e. they are 'open and shallow')
stupe/stoop [mid-18C+]
stupid [early 18C–late 19C]
Tom Doodle [18C]
yea and nay man [late 18C–mid-19C] (i.e. they can only answer
  'yes' or 'no' to a question)

DILBERRIES AND DROOLIES: THE 19TH CENTURY

ballocks/bollocks/bollix/bollox [late 19C+]
Billy Barlow [19C] (the name of an 1840s street clown)
bloke [late 19C+] (US)
buffy [mid-19C]
cheese [late 19C+]
chowdar [mid-19C]
clam [mid-19C+] (US)
clift/cleft [late 19C+] (i.e. their brain has been *cleft*)
crock [19C]
cuddy [mid–late 19C] (dial. 'sucking lamb')

cunningberry/cunningbury [early–mid-19C]

daftie [late 19C+]

dead meat [mid-19C+] (lit. 'corpse')

dickey-dido [mid-19C+] (lit. 'vagina')

dilberry [mid-19C+]

dingbat [late 19C+] (orig. US)

dizzy flat [late 19C] (US; lit. 'dizzy peasant')

dope [mid-19C+]

drooly [mid-19C+] (US)

dummy [early 19C+]

flycatcher [19C] (i.e. they could *catch flies* in their gaping mouth)

gag [mid-19C] (US; i.e. they make you laugh)

gawp [early 19C+]

goober/goob [mid-19C+] (US; lit. 'peanut')

gooby [19C]

gooney/goonie/goney [19C+] (US)

goth [mid-19C] (i.e. a 'barbarian')

guddha [mid-19C–1900s] (Anglo-Ind.; Hindi *gadha*, a fool)

guffin [mid–late 19C] (a clumsy fool)

gulpin [mid-19C]

gummy [19C]

horrid horn [mid–late 19C] (Anglo-Irish; Irish *omadhun*, a fool)

horse's ass/horse's arse [mid-19C+]

josser [late 19C–1940s] (Romani, 'outsider')

loon [early 19C+]

loony/looney/loonie/luny/lunie [mid-19C+] (orig. US)

lunk [mid-19C+] (US)

moony [mid-19C]

mopstick [late 19C]

Mr Wiggins [early 19C]

mudcat [mid-19C–1940s] (US)

mudding-face [late 19C–1910s] (*mud* + pud*ding-face*)

muff [19C–1910s]

muffin [mid-19C]

mutt [late 19C+] (US)

neddy [early 19C+] (lit. 'donkey')

nincom/nincum [19C] (*nincom*poop)

nod cock/nodge cock [19C] (lit. 'nod-head', i.e. their head wags foolishly)

oolfoo [late 19C] (backslang, 'fool')

poggle/puggle/puggly [late 19C–1900s] (Hindi *pagal*, a madman)

Sammy (Soft) [early 19C–1930s]

sap [early 19C+]

sate-poll [late 19C] (lit. 'fill-head', i.e. it is filled with nonsense)

shot-clog [mid–late 19C] (a fool who is tolerated for their willingness to pay for drinks (*shots*))

99 99 99 99 99 99 99 99 99 99 99 99 99 99 99 99 99 99 99 99 99 99

Three academic failures

Dublin University graduate [1950s+] (i.e. 'Irish')

flunk [late 19C+] (US; an academic failure)

wooden spoon [late 19C] (from the award given to the person with the lowest result in mathematics at Cambridge University)

66 66 66 66 66 66 66 66 66 66 66 66 66 66 66 66 66 66 66 66 66 66

sillikin [mid-19C–1910s]
Silly Billy/Silly Billie [late 19C+]
sillypop [late 19C]
softhorn [mid-19C] (lit. 'donkey')
squab [19C+] (US)
stump [19C] (i.e. they are 'small and thick')
thick [mid-19C+] (orig./mainly juv.)
tit [19C+]
tool [mid-19C+]
tootledum-pattick [19C] (Cornish dial.)
tosspot/toss-bottle [late 19C+] (lit. 'drunkard')
trunk [19C] (i.e. they have no 'head')

IDIOTS OF THE WORLD

IRISH

binlid [20C] (Ulster)
eejit/eedjit/ijit [20C] (usu. Irish; pron. of 'idiot')
ganch/gaunch [20C] (Ulster; Irish *gaimse*, a fool)
gipe/gype [20C] (Ulster; Scot. 'awkward person')
gom/gawm/goamey/gam/gorm [mid-19C+] (orig. Irish; *gamal*, a simpleton)
gowl [late 19C+] (Irish; lit. 'vagina')
guffoon [late 19C] (Irish)
gunterpake [20C] (Ulster)
head-the-ball [1990s] (Irish; i.e. their brains have become scrambled from using their head in this way)
lig/liggety [1940s+] (Ulster; *lig* = stupid man, *liggety* = stupid woman)
Rodney [mid-19C+] (Irish; dial. 'idler')

80–90 [20C] (from the numeric values ascribed to the Hebrew letters *pay* and *tzadik* which constitute a euphemism for 'putz')

klutz [1950s+] (orig. US; German *klotz*, a lump of wood)

putz/potz/putzo [1930s+] (Yiddish, 'penis')

schlemazel/schlemasel/shlemozzle [late 19C+] (Yiddish *schlimm Masel*, bad luck)

schlemiel/schlemihl/shlemiel [late 19C+] (Yiddish, 'bungler')

schmendrick/shmendrick/shmendrik [1940s+] (a character in an operetta by Abraham Goldfaden)

schmo/schmoe/shmo/shmoe [1940s+] (orig. US; euphemism for 'schmuck')

schmuck/schmock/shmuck [20C] (Yiddish, 'penis')

yock/yok [20C] (backslang, 'goy', a gentile)

yutz [20C] (US; Yiddish, 'penis')

head-the-ball

Billy Muggins [20C] (Aus.)

Blind Freddie [1940s+] (Aus.)

clunk [1940s+] (Aus./US)

dill [1940s+] (Aus./N.Z.; *dill*ypot, the vagina)

dillbrain [1950s+] (N.Z.)

dip [1920s+] (orig. Aus.)

drongo [1940s+] (orig. Aus.)

fuck-knuckle [20C] (Aus.)

galah [1930s+] (Aus.; a cockatoo known for its chattering)

gellyhead/jellyhead [1990s] (N.Z.)

gum-sucker [mid–late 19C+] (Aus.)

gup [1930s–40s] (Aus.)

imbo [1930s–50s] (Aus.; *imb*ecile)

jumbuck [mid-19C+] (Aus./N.Z.; lit. 'sheep')

log of wood [1950s+] (Aus.)

mopoke/morepork [mid-19C+] (Aus.; i.e. 'mope hawk', a species of owl)

ning-nong/ning-nang [early 19C+] (Aus./N.Z.)

nong [1940s+] (Aus.; *non c*ompos mentis)

poon [1940s+] (Aus.)

prawn [late 19C+] (Aus.)

prawn-headed mullet [1930s+] (Aus.)

queer [1920s+] (Aus.)

tonk [1940s+] (Aus.)

tuppence [1940s+] (Aus.; i.e. they are only '*tuppence* in the quid')

warb [1930s+] (Aus.; *warb*le, a type of maggot)

whacker [1960s+] (Aus.; lit. 'masturbator')

wombat [20C] (Aus./US)

WEST INDIAN

batty-wax [20C] (lit. 'arse-shit')

bobo [1940s] (Spanish *bobón*, a clumsy simpleton)

chupidee/chupidie/chupidy/chupiddy [20C] (pron. of 'stupid')

half-(a-)idiot [20C] (W.I./Bdos)

logi-logi/logo-logo [1950s] (i.e. 'log')

maku [20C]

monkey-face [1930s–60s] (a stupid, ugly person)

moo-moo [20C] (Twi *e-mumu*, a deaf-blind person)

nyaams head [1950s] (lit. 'eating head', i.e. they only think of eating)

pistakle/pistarckle [20C] (i.e. they '*piss* about' and cause a 'spec*tacle*')

preke/preky [1940s+] (Spanish *pereque*, an intolerable person)

quashie [1940s+] (Twi *kwasie*, a boy born on a Sunday)

Silly as ...

silly as a bag [1930s+] (Aus./N.Z.)

silly as a chook [1940s+] (Aus./N.Z.; *chook* = chicken)

silly as a cut snake [1930s+] (Aus./N.Z.)

silly as a hatful of arseholes [1940s–50s] (Aus.)

silly as a hatful of worms [1950s+] (orig. Aus.)

silly as a two-bob/Woolworth's watch [1950s+] (Aus.)

silly as a wheel [1950s+] (Aus.)

rass [1940s+] (lit. 'arse')
speng [1990s] (W.I./UK Black teen)
stupidie [20C]

'NOT ALL THERE' ... PHRASES FOR IDIOTS

apartments to let [mid-19C+]

couple of chips short of a fish dinner [20C]

couple of tinnies short of a slab [1980s+] (Aus.; lit. 'couple of cans short of a case of beer')

few bricks short of a load [1960s+]

few snags short of a barbie [1980s+] (Aus.; lit. 'few sausages short of a barbecue')

five annas short of the rupee [19C+]

gates are down, the lights are flashing, but the train isn't coming [1990s+]

have a few of one's pages stuck together [20C]

silly as a
hatful of worms

have a tile loose [mid-19C]

have only fifty cards in one's deck [1920s–40s]

lift doesn't reach the top floor [1990s]

lights on but there's nobody home [1970s+]

no more than ninepence in the shilling [late 19C+]

not all there [mid-19C+]

not having both oars in the water [20C]

not playing with a full deck [1960s+] (orig. US)

not the full cup of tea [1970s+]

not the full dollar [1970s+] (Aus.)

not the full quid [1940s+] (Aus./N.Z.)

one brick short of a load [20C]

one sandwich short of the picnic [1960s+]

one sausage short of a b.b.q. [1990s] (US teen)

only 80 pence in the pound [20C]

only one and ninepence in the florin [1910–70s]

out to lunch [1950s+]

play with 44 cards in the deck [1960s+]

tenpence to the shilling [mid-19C+]

there's a kangaroo loose in the top paddock [1990s] (Aus.)

three bricks shy of a load [20C] (US)

two pence short of a bob [20C]

two sandwiches short of a picnic [1980s+]

two wafers short of a communion [1960s+]

wheel is turning, but the hamster is dead [1990s+]

GULLS AND DUPES (MAINLY FINANCIAL)

alec/aleck [1910s+] (Aus.)

angel [19C] (US Und.; an innocent)

bait [mid–late 19C] (US)

bird [16C] (Und.)

bleeding cully [late 17C–early 19C] (i.e. they 'bleed' money)

bubble [late 17C–19C] (the South Sea *Bubble* of 1721, a prospect which appeared 'shiny' and inviting on the outside but was in fact insubstantial)

bush bunny [1920s+] (Aus.)

cat's paw [late 18C–19C] (from the fable of a monkey using a cat's paw to rake roasted chestnuts out of the fire)

chub [mid-16C–late 18C]

chump [late 19C+]

cod's head [mid-16C–mid-19C]

cod's head and shoulders [19C]

99 99 99 99 99 99 99 99 99 99 99 99 99 99 99 99 99 99 99 99 99

Mugs in rhyming slang

Billy Button [20C] (W.I. rhy. sl. 'gets nutten', i.e. nothing)

hearth rug [1910s–50s]

milk jug [1920s+] (Aus.)

steam tug [1930s+] (Aus.)

stone jug [1920s+]

toby jug [20C]

Tom Tug [19C]

66 66 66 66 66 66 66 66 66 66 66 66 66 66 66 66 66 66 66 66 66

❞ ❞

Wet geese: naïve newcomers

bebopper/bopper/diddybopper [1980s+]
(US Black)

choirboy [1970s+] (US)

codling [early 17C–mid-18C]

cornbread [1950s+] (US Black; a naïve
Southerner)

foo-foo [mid-19C+] (W.I.; i.e. 'fool-fool')

Johnny-come-lately [mid-19C+]

Johnny Raw [19C] (esp. Aus.)

nature boy [1940s+] (US)

never-see-come-see [20C] (W.I.)

old soldier [mid-19C+]

shorthorn [late 19C–1940s] (US)

wet foot [1960s+]

wet goose [20C]

❝ ❝

coniwobble [early 18C]

cony [late 16C–early 18C] (lit. 'rabbit')

cull [late 17C–mid-19C]

cully [mid-17C–late 19C]

doe [1950s–60s] (US Black)

duck [20C] (US Und.)

game [late 17C–early 19C]

hickster [1990s]

jug [late 19C–1950s]

99 99 99 99 99 99 99 99 99 99 99 99 99 99 99 99 99 99 99 99 99

Greenhorns

Dr Green [mid-19C] (US)

green [mid–late 19C]

green apple [1960s–70s] (US)

greenbean [1950s+] (US)

greenbelly [1950s] (US)

greenhorn [late 17C+]

greenie [late 17C+]

green pea [1910s–70s] (US)

greeny [late 17C+]

herb [1990s] (US Black)

66 66 66 66 66 66 66 66 66 66 66 66 66 66 66 66 66 66 66 66 66

juggins [late 19C]

lemon [20C] (punning on 'sucker')

Mr Muggins [late 19C+] (Aus.)

mug [mid-19C+]

natural [late 17C+] (an innocent)

patsy [20C] (*Patrick*, invoking the stereotype of Irish stupidity)

posso-de-luxe/possodeluxe [1930s+] (Aus.; an extremely rich dupe)

possum [1940s+] (Aus.)

puppet-head [1960s+] (US teen; a gullible, conventional person)

rum [1950s–60s] (US Black)

rum cull/rum cully [late 17C–mid-19C] (UK Und.)

rummy/rummie [1910s+]

sucker [early 19C+] (orig. US; lit. 'unweaned animal')
Tom Coney/Tom Cony/Tom Conney [17C–early 19C] (lit. 'Tom Rabbit')
toy [1980s] (US Black teen)

MAD PEOPLE

batshit/batcrap [1960s–70s] (US)
beserko [1980s] (US)
Bess O'Bedlam [mid-19C] (a lunatic vagrant; *Bedlam* = the Hospital of St Mary of Bethlehem, which housed mental patients)
bug [late 19C+]
couch case [1960s+]
cracko [20C]
crazo [1970s+] (orig. US)
crazy [19C+] (orig. US)
crazyhead [1970s] (US)
cuckoo bird [1940s+] (US)
daffy [1980s+] (US)
demento [1970s+] (US)

99 99 99 99 99 99 99 99 99 99 99 99 99 99 99 99 99 99 99 99 99

Retards

muppet [1970s+]
retard [1970s+] (orig. US)
veggie/veggy [1980s+] (Irish; a physically or mentally disabled child)

66 66 66 66 66 66 66 66 66 66 66 66 66 66 66 66 66 66 66 66 66

dingaling/ding-a-ling [1930s+] (orig. US; from the 'ringing' in the sufferer's head)

dingbats [1910s+] (Aus./N.Z.)

5150 [1990s] (the US police code indicating 'an insane person is annoying the public')

flake (artist) [1950s+] (orig. US)

headcase [1960s+]

loco [mid-19C+] (US; Spanish, 'crazy')

looney tune/loony tune [1960s+]

loony/looney/loonie/luny/lunie [mid-19C+] (orig. US)

meat axe [1940s+] (Aus./N.Z.)

mental [1910s+]

psycho [1940s+] (orig. US)

schitz/schiz/skitz/skiz [1920s+] (orig. US)

schizo/shizo [1940s+] (orig. US)

screw-loose [late 19C+] (orig. US)

section eight [1940s+] (US; the US army discharge code covering grounds of mental instability)

wall-hugger [1980s+]

whack-a-doo [20C]

whack job [1970s+] (US)

whacko [1970s+]

99 99 99 99 99 99 99 99 99 99 99 99 99 99 99 99 99 99 99 99 99 99 99

Mad people in rhyming slang

bread and butter [20C] ('nutter')

Mickey Rooney [20C] ('loony')

pound of butter [1980s+] ('nutter')

66 66 66 66 66 66 66 66 66 66 66 66 66 66 66 66 66 66 66 66 66 66 66

99 99 99 99 99 99 99 99 99 99 99 99 99 99 99 99 99 99 99 99 99 99

Nutters

nut [20C] (orig. US)
nutbar/nutbasket/nutbucket [1970s+] (US)
nutburger [1980s+] (US)
nutcake [1960s+] (US)
nutcase [1940s+]
nut roll [1940s+] (US Black)
nutso [1960s+] (orig. US)
nutter [1950s+]

66 66 66 66 66 66 66 66 66 66 66 66 66 66 66 66 66 66 66 66 66 66

ECCENTRICS AND WEIRDOS

arch-duke [late 17C–late 18C] (a
character in Shakespeare's *Measure
for Measure*)
bezark [1920s–40s] (US)
bizarro [1980s]
block ornament [mid-19C] (lit.
'small piece of meat displayed on a
butcher's block')
bombhead [1950s–60s]
buggeroo [1940s+]
caution [mid-19C+]
cockamamie [1930s+] (US)
crank [early 19C+]
cuckoo [late 16C+]

bombhead

cure [mid–late 19C] (*curiosity*)

flip [1950s+] (US)

freak/freako [late 19C+] (US)

fruitcake [1950s+]

funny bird [late 19C]

funny-looking article [20C] (an odd-looking person)

kangarooster [1920s+] (Aus.)

kook/kuke/cook [1950s+] (US)

mad haddock [20C] (Aus.)

martian [1970s+] (US)

moony cove [late 19C]

oddball [1940s+] (orig. US)

odd fish [18C+]

queer bird [mid–late 19C]

queer customer/queer merchant [19C+]

queer fellow [early 18C+]

queer fish [19C+]

quiz [late 18C–mid-19C]

rum touch [early 19C]

screwball [1930s+] (orig. US)

squirrel [1940s+] (US; punning on 'nuts')

trip [1970s+] (US campus)

way-out [1960s+] (US)

weirdie/weirdy [late 19C+]

weirdo [1940s+]

GLOOMY AND BAD-TEMPERED

SHORT-TEMPERED PEOPLE

blowtop [1930s+] (US Black)

blue hen's chicken [20C] (a dominant, aggressive and short-tempered woman; *blue hen* = a hen that breeds first-rate fighting cocks)

feist [20C] (US)

fire-tail [20C] (W.I./Guyn.; a woman who loses her temper easily)

grass-fighter [1950s+] (Aus.; a person who brawls in public, i.e. they *fight* on *grass* rather than in the boxing ring)

hornet [mid-19C]

loose cannon (on a rolling deck) [1970s+] (orig. US)

pepper-fly [1950s] (W.I.)

rattle cap [mid-19C]

Scot [early 19C–1910s]

spit-cat/spit-kitten [late 19C–1910s] (a short-tempered woman)

talking head/talking hairdo [1960s+] (US Black; a person on the verge of a fight)

SORE-HEAD AND SURLY-BOOTS

bear [18C+]

billy-goat [1920s] (US)

crab [late 16C–early 17C; late 19C+]

crab-apple [mid-19C–1920s] (US)

crankpot [20C] (US)

grouch-box/grouch-pot [late 19C+] (US)

grump [20C]

🙶 🙶

Grumpy women

crooked rib [late 18C–early 19C] (an ill-
tempered wife)

hinchinarfer [late 19C] (i.e. 'inch-and-a-halfer',
referring to the length of the disgruntled
woman's husband's penis)

mare [14C–18C; 1930s+]

pickle [late 18C–late 19C]

🙶 🙶

grumpus [1980s+] (US)

grumpy-drawers/gloomy-drawers [1980s+] (usu. juv.)

lemon [mid-19C]

nadger [late 19C+] (Ulster)

patch [19C+]

sore-head [mid-19C+] (US)

surly-boots [late 17C+]

thorny wire [20C] (Anglo-Irish; i.e. they are 'prickly')

DISMAL JIMMY AND OTHER PURTING GLUMPOTS

Calamity Jane [20C] (US; a pessimist)

crape-hanger/crepe-hanger [1920s–40s] (from the hanging of
black to signify mourning)

death's head upon a mopstick [late 18C–early 19C] (a
miserable, impoverished, emaciated person)

dikbek/diklip [1970s+] (S.Afr.; lit. 'thick mouth')

Dismal Jimmy [1920s–40s]

drizzlepuss [1930s–50s] (US)

Gloomy Gus [20C] (US; a comic-strip character created by Frederick Burr Opper)

glum-pot [mid-19C]

hearse(-driver) [late 19C] (US)

mard-arse [20C] (dial. *mardy*, miserable, sulky)

misery [late 18C+]

mope [mid-16C+]

negaholic [1980s+] (US)

poor-me-one [20C] (W.I.; a sympathy-seeker)

purting glumpot [mid-19C] (dial. *purt*, to sulk, to pout)

sad apple [20C] (US; a pessimist)

sad sack [1920s+] (orig. US campus)

sad sack of shit [1920s+] (orig. US)

sheep-biter [late 17C–18C]

stop-the-clock [20C] (Ulster; from the custom of stopping the clocks following a death in the house)

sheep-biter

GROUSER AND GRUMBLE-GUTS

bag-puncher [1900s–20s] (US)
Bawly-Ike [mid-20C] (US)
beefer [late 19C–1930s] (US)
bellyacher [late 19C+]
binder [1930s–40s]
bitcher [20C]
cat-whipper [20C] (Aus.)
crib biter [mid-19C]
croak [1910s] (US)
crusty gripes [late 19C]
drizzle [1930s–40s] (US campus)
dynamiter [1910s] (US)
griper [1930s] (US)
grizzle [early 18C]

99 99 99 99 99 99 99 99 99 99 99 99 99 99 99 99 99 99 99 99 99 99

Drama queens and stress merchants

drama queen [1960s+] (orig. gay)
fret-kidney [mid–late 19C]
performer [1930s+] (orig. naut.)
stress case [1980s+] (US campus)
stress merchant [1980s+]
stress-monger/stress-monster [1980s+] (US campus)
worrit [mid-19C]
worryguts [1930s+]
worry wart [1930s+] (US)

66 66 66 66 66 66 66 66 66 66 66 66 66 66 66 66 66 66 66 66 66 66

grouser [1910s–20s]

grumble-guts [late 19C+]

grumbletonian [late 17C–mid-19C]

grunt [20C] (US)

gum-beater [1940s–70s] (US)

kicker [late 19C–1930s] (US)

kvetch [1960s+]

ma's plaster [20C] (Irish; i.e. they need a *plaster* from their *ma*)

misery-moany [1940s+] (Irish)

moaner [1920s+] (orig. US)

Peter Grievous/Peter Grievance [late 18C–1930s]

sourpuss [1930s+] (orig. US)

Uncle Payther [20C] (Irish; from a character in the play
The Moon and the Stars by Sean O'Casey)

IRRITATING PEOPLE

drink of water [20C] (Ulster)

fleabag [1960s+] (US Black)

gallstone [1960s] (US)

haemorrhoid/hemo [1960s+] (US campus)

menace [1930s+]

mothball [1940s–50s] (US Black/campus)

99 99 99 99 99 99 99 99 99 99 99 99 99 99 99 99 99 99 99 99 99 99 99

Pests in rhyming slang

haddock and cod [20C] ('sod')

string vest [1960s+] ('pest')

woolly vest [1960s+] ('pest')

66 66 66 66 66 66 66 66 66 66 66 66 66 66 66 66 66 66 66 66 66 66

pain in the arse/ass [1960s+]

pain in the butt/backside/bum [1960s+]

pain in the neck [1930s+]

pintle [20C] (Ulster; a small, irritating person, lit. 'penis')

voit [1990s] (US teen)

NOSEY PARKERS

basket [1930s+] (an interfering old woman)

biddy [1980s+] (orig. US campus; an interfering old woman)

botfly [20C] (Aus.; an insect producing parasitic maggots)

Bungo-Bessy [1940s+] (W.I.)

do-gooder [late 19C+] (a well-intentioned but interfering person)

kibitzer/kibbitzer/kabitzer [1920s+] (a person who offers
  unwanted advice)

Meddlesome Mattie [1940s+] (US; the title of a poem by
  Ann Taylor)

meddling duchess [late 19C] (an upper-class woman who
  interests herself, on self-proclaimedly
  philanthropic grounds, in matters that
  do not concern her)

nibshit [1960s+] (US; lit. 'peck shit')

nosey bob [late 19C–1930s] (Aus.)

nosey parker [20C]

FUSSPOTS AND FRIG PIGS

flutterbudget [20C] (US)

frig pig [late 18C–19C]

fussbudget [20C] (US)

fusspot [20C]

Granny Grunt

Granny (Grunt) [20C] (rhy. sl. 'cunt')

manmanpoul [20C] (W.I.; French *maman poule*, mother hen)

old palaver [19C] (Scot.)

NAGGING WOMEN

alarm clock [1920s] (US)

ass-breaker [1960s] (US)

ball-breaker [1970s+] (orig. US)

ball-buster [1950s+] (orig. US)

ball-cutter [1960s+] (US)

ball-tearer [1950s+] (orig. US)

Calamity Jane [20C] (US)

crabber [1930s]

devil's daughter [late 18C–mid-19C]

old hige [1940s+] (W.I.; lit. 'old hag')

sister of the Charterhouse [early–mid-16C] (referring to the silent monks of the Charterhouse, who could not answer back)

tarleather [17C]

yenta [1920s+] (orig. US)

BLATHERGABS AND TATTLE-TALES

blabberguts [1910s] (US)

blabbermouth/blabmouth [1930s+]

blathergab [20C] (US)

bone carrier [20C] (US)

busy-lickum [1940s+]

chaff-cutter [mid-19C]

chatty-chatty [1950s+] (W.I.)

clashbag/clashbeg [20C] (Ulster; *clash* = gossip)

ball-cutter

clatterbrain/clatterbox [19C]

death adder [1930s+] (Aus.; an ill-tempered gossip)

earwig/ear-wigger/wiggin's [1940s+]

gatemouth [1920s–40s] (US Black)

jitterbug [1960s+] (US Black)

mighty mouth [1950s+]

mixer [1930s+] (i.e. they 'stir')

mout-hab-nuttin-fe-do [20C] (W.I.; lit. 'mouth has nothing to do')

muffin-walloper [late 19C] (a woman who dissects her acquaintances over tea and muffins)

news bug [1950s] (W.I.)

rattle bag/rattle-bladder/rattle-brain/rattle-cap/rattle-head/rattle-pate/rattle-skull [19C+]

run mouth [20C] (W.I./Gren.)

sack mouth [1980s+] (US Black)

shit-stirrer [late 19C+]

stewer [1900s–40s] (US Black)

stirrer [1970s+]

storefront preacher [20C] (US Black; a gossip who *preaches* to those who idle away their days outside a small-town general store)

tattle(-basket) [18C]

tattle-box [18C]

tattle-tale [18C]

CHATTERBOXES

alligator [1970s] (US)

bag of wind [19C+]

barber [1920s+] (US; a tediously talkative person, esp. in sports use)

blabberer [mid-18C+]

bladder [late 16C–late 18C]

blowhole [1920s+] (Aus.)

breeze puncher [1910s] (US)

bucketmouth [1970s] (US)

bunny [1950s–60s] (rhy. sl. *rabbit and pork*, to talk)

99 99 99 99 99 99 99 99 99 99 99 99 99 99 99 99 99 99 99 99 99 99 99

Male gossips

chat [1950s] (W.I.)

furphy king [1910s+] (Aus.; *furphy* = rumour)

Miss Lashey [1950s] (W.I.)

Mother Ga-ga [1950s+] (gay; an interfering older homosexual)

66 66 66 66 66 66 66 66 66 66 66 66 66 66 66 66 66 66 66 66 66 66

chaw-mouth [late 19C+] (US; lit. 'chew-mouth')

chickenhead [1990s] (US teen; from the chicken's bobbing head and constant 'squawking')

church-bell [late 19C–1900s] (rural; a talkative woman)

diarrhoea-mouth [1970s+] (US)

ear-basher [1940s+] (orig. Aus.)

ear-bender [20C] (US)

fanny merchant [1910s+] (a person who is 'all talk and no action')

flannel mouth/flannel face [19C+] (US)

flapjaw [20C] (US)

foghorn [20C] (a person who talks too loudly)

gabber [late 18C–mid-19C]

gabberlooney/gobberloony [20C] (Ulster)

gabble [19C]

gabble-grinder [19C]

gabby-guts [1940s] (Irish)

gabster [19C]

gasbag/gasman [late 19C+]

gas pipe [mid-19C–1910s] (US)

alligator

gasser [19C]

hinge-jaw [20C] (US)

jaw-me-dead/jaw-me-dad [late 18C–1900s] (i.e. they 'talk you to death')

jawsmith/jaw-smith [late 19C–1940s] (US)

Johnny Walker [20C] (rhy. sl. 'talker')

long-playing record [1960s+]

man with a paper ass(hole) [1950s+] (US Black)

motormouth [1960s+] (orig. US)
mouth [late 17C–mid-19C]
mouth almighty [mid-19C]
mouthamassy (Liza) [20C] (W.I. ; lit. 'mouth have mercy')
poll parrot [mid-19C+]
prattle-box [early 18C]
ratchet mouth/ratchet jaw [1950s+]
rattletrap [19C]
satch [1900s–40s] (US; *satch*el-mouth)
sheep's head [late 17C–19C] ('like a sheep's head, all jaw')
sputterbudget [20C] (US)
tattlebudget [20C] (US)
wax-borer [1930s+] (Aus.; i.e. they 'bore' through ear wax)
whirling spray [1940s+] (Aus.)
windjammer [1910s–40s] (orig. US)
windy wallets [late 19C–1900s]
yarn-chopper/yarn-slinger/yarn-spinner [late 19C–1920s]

99 99 99 99 99 99 99 99 99 99 99 99 99 99 99 99 99 99 99 99 99 99 99

All mouth and trousers

all gong and no dinner [1970s+]
all mouth and trousers [late 19C+]
all piss and wind [20C]
all prick and breeches [1920s+]
all talk and no cider [19C] (US)
all wind and piss [late 19C+]

66 66 66 66 66 66 66 66 66 66 66 66 66 66 66 66 66 66 66 66 66 66

♥♥ ♥♥ ♥♥ ♥♥ ♥♥ ♥♥ ♥♥ ♥♥ ♥♥ ♥♥ ♥♥ ♥♥ ♥♥ ♥♥ ♥♥

Taciturn people

cup too low [late 17C–early 18C] (i.e. they
need another drink to become more
loquacious)

Dean Maitland [1940s+] (Aus.; from the film
The Silence of Dean Maitland)

like a bump on a log [mid-19C–1930s] (US;
stupidly silent or inarticulate)

mute as a maggot [1920s] (absolutely silent)

**mute as mumchance (who was hanged for
saying nothing)** [late 18C–early 19C] (silent
and miserable)

❝❝ ❝❝ ❝❝ ❝❝ ❝❝ ❝❝ ❝❝ ❝❝ ❝❝ ❝❝ ❝❝ ❝❝ ❝❝

ARROGANT, HAUGHTY AND OVERBEARING PEOPLE

climb-a-pole [mid-19C] (US)

crackerjack [1910s] (US)

the great I am [20C]

high bicycle [1930s] (US)

his nibs [early 19C+]

hooha/hoohah/hoo [1980s+] (US)

hot oil [1980s] (US Black)

jive-ass [1960s+] (orig. US Black)

jive nigger [1960s+] (orig. US Black)

King Shit/King Spit [1940s+] (orig. US)

Mr Nonsuch/Mr Nonesuch [late 19C]

muck [1900s–50s] (US)
muck-a-muck/muckety-muck [mid-19C+] (US)
mugwump [early 19C+] (orig. US)
nibs [early 19C+]
noise [1900s–30s]
stiff-rump [late 17C–19C]
stuffy [1950s+]
top shot [1920s+] (orig. US)
wiffle-woffle [1910s–20s]

BRAGGARTS AND BULLSHITTERS

alligator mouth [1960s+] (US)
baloney bender [1920s+] (orig. US)
bangster [mid-16C–late 18C]

99 99 99 99 99 99 99 99 99 99 99 99 99 99 99 99 99 99 99 99 99 99

A box of big bananas

big banana [1980s+] (US)
big bollocks [1950s]
big bopper [1960s+] (US)
big boy [1920s+] (US)
big dog [19C] (US)
big head [mid-19C+]
big house nigger [20C] (US Black)
big shit [1930s+]
big shot [1920s+] (orig. US)
big stuff [1910s+] (orig. US)
big time [1960s+] (US)

66 66 66 66 66 66 66 66 66 66 66 66 66 66 66 66 66 66 66 66 66 66

big bollocks

bellswagger/belswagger [late 16C–early 19C] (lit. 'belly-swagger')

bigmouth [1930s+]

bilge artist [1920s+] (Aus.)

blowbag [1920s+] (Aus.)

blower [19C]

blowfly [20C] (US)

blowhard [early 19C–1920s]

bosher [1910s–30s]

brag [late 17C–late 18C]

bull artist [1910s+]

bullshipper [1910s+]

bullshitter [1910s+] (orig. Aus)

bull shooter [1920s+] (US)

bull slinger [1930s+] (US)

crap artist [1930s+] (US)

crap slinger [1930s] (US)

double-plated blowhard [late 19C] (US)

fartknocker [20C] (US)

fatmouth [20C] (US Black)

flannel mouth/flannel face [19C+] (US)

flapjaw [20C] (US)

four-flusher [late 19C+] (US; i.e. a bluffer, a real flush requires five cards)

furioso [17C]

grootbek [1940s+] (S.Afr.; lit. 'large beak')

hot-air artist/hot-air merchant [late 19C+] (orig. US)

Jack Bragger [late 16C]

kill-cow [mid-19C–1900s] (i.e. they claim to be able to 'kill a cow at one blow')

line-shooter [1940s+]

mouth-off [1950s+] (orig. US)

puckfist/puckfoist [early 17C] (dial. *puckfist*, a puff-ball)

shitter [1910s+] (orig. US)

swank [late 19C]

swanker [1930s–50s]

swankpot [20C]

swellhead/swelled-head [mid-19C+]

Tooley Street tailor [late 19C] (from the three *tailors* of *Tooley Street*, London, who presented a petition to Parliament carrying only their three signatures but headed 'We, the people of England …')

windbag [19C+]

woofer [1930s+] (US Black)

Loud and fiery

blowgun [20C] (US)

cacafuego [early 17C–late 18C] (lit. 'shit-fire')

fire-eater [mid-19C+]

loudmouth [1930s+] (orig. US)

loudspeaker [1930s] (US)

pump-thunder [19C]

raise mountain [18C]

shitefire [17C]

66 66 66 66 66 66 66 66 66 66 66 66 66 66 66 66 66 66 66 66

SHOW-OFFS

actress [1950s–60s] (US camp gay)

big-note artist [1940s+] (Aus.)

big noter [1940s+] (Aus.)

boasie/boasy [1950s+] (W.I.; lit. 'proud')

boasy-naked [1950s+] (W.I.)

fronter [1970s+] (US Black)

grandstand-artist/-jockey/-player [late 19C+]

hambone [1950s+] (US; i.e. a 'ham' actor)

harlequin Jack [late 19C]

hot-dogger [20C]

Jack the lad [1950s+]

lair/lare [1920s+] (Aus.)

sprig [early 17C]

swanky/swankey [mid–late 19C]

teddy bear [1950s+] (Aus.; rhy. sl. 'lair')
thrasher [1990s] (US campus)

SMART ALECKS

aleck [1900s–30s] (orig. US)
bright boy [1920s–30s] (orig. US)
crackwise [1940s–50s] (US Black)
gospel-sharp/-shooter/-slinger/-whanger [19C+] (US)
know-all [late 19C+]
know-it-all [19C+]
know-it of know-all park [1910s+]
mug aleck [1930s+] (Aus.)
smart alec/smart aleck/wise aleck [mid-19C+] (orig. US)
smart-arse/smart-ass/smartarse/smartass [1930s+] (orig. Aus.)
smart guy [late 19C+] (orig. US)
smartiepants/smarty-drawers/smartipants [1940s+] (orig. US)
smarty [mid-19C+] (orig. US)
smarty-boots [1940s+] (orig. US)
wise guy [late 19C+] (US)

99 99 99 99 99 99 99 99 99 99 99 99 99 99 99 99 99 99 99 99 99 99

Clever dicks

clever boots [20C]
clever dick [19C+]
clever dog [19C+]
cleverguts [19C+]
clever shins [19C+]

66 66 66 66 66 66 66 66 66 66 66 66 66 66 66 66 66 66 66 66 66

UNTRUSTWORTHY PEOPLE

alias man [1960s+] (orig. W.I.)

bluff artist [1930s] (US)

horse thief [1920s+] (US)

kike/kyke [late 19C+] (orig. US; lit. 'Jew')

luokal-mediocal [1950s] (W.I.; an unreliable person; pron. of 'local mediocre')

Mr Hyde [20C] (rhy. sl. 'snide')

no-good [late 19C+]

skanker [1970s+] (W.I.; an untrustworthy, dissolute person)

slippy tit [20C] (Ulster; a sly person)

twister [early 19C+]

yaffner [late 19C–1930s] (US Black)

99 99 99 99 99 99 99 99 99 99 99 99 99 99 99 99 99 99 99 99 99 99

Bad 'uns and wrong 'uns

bad crowd [late 19C–1900s] (US)

bad halfpenny [mid-19C]

bad hat [early 19C–1950s]

bad lot [mid-19C+]

bad penny [early 19C+]

bad 'un [early–mid-19C+]

wrong guy [1940s+] (US Und.)

wrong number [1930s+] (US)

wrong 'un [late 19C+]

66 66 66 66 66 66 66 66 66 66 66 66 66 66 66 66 66 66 66 66 66 66

HYPOCRITES

good young man [late 19C]

Joey [mid-19C] (*Joe* Holy, one who pretends to great religiosity)

sham saint [early 18C]

twin-coat [1970s] (W.I.; i.e. they have two 'coats')

twin-mouth [1970s] (W.I.; i.e. they have two 'mouths')

white-belly rat [1920s–50s] (W.I.; a type of rat which supposedly breathes on its prey after biting to minimize the pain)

INSINCERE PEOPLE

Cynthia [1950s–60s] (camp gay; i.e. 'synthetic')

empty suit [1980s+] (US)

fake [late 19C–1930s] (US)

false face [1970s+] (US campus)

glad-hander/gladhand-shaker [20C]

gusher [mid–late 19C] (a person who makes insincere and sentimental remarks)

handshaker [late 19C–1920s] (US)

jiver [1920s–50s] (US Black)

jive turkey [1970s+] (US Black)

phoney/phony [late 19C+]

jive turkey

♥♥ ♥♥

Back-stabbers

cat in the pan [16C]

dingo [1920s+] (Aus.)

handsupper [1940s+] (S. Afr.; i.e. they 'put their hands up')

rat face [20C] (orig. US)

rotten sheep [late 19C] (Irish; a traitor to the Fenian cause)

shiever [1920s] (US Und.; lit. 'knifer', i.e. they 'stab you in the back')

" " " " " " " " " " " " " " " " " " " "

LIARS

crapper [late 19C+] (US)

fib [late 16C; mid-19C]

fibber [early 18C+]

holy friar [20C] (rhy. sl.)

long-bow man [late 17C–mid-19C]

lyrebird [late 19C+] (Aus.)

one-eyed scribe [1970s] (US Black; a monumental liar)

stibber-gibber [mid-16C] (a habitual liar; elision of *Stephen and Gilbert*, contemporary generic names for lying clerks)

story-teller [mid-18C+]

stretcher case [1940s+] (i.e. they 'stretch the truth')

taradiddler [late 18C–late 19C] (a petty liar)

thumper [mid-17C–mid-19C] (a dedicated liar)

Tom Pepper [early 19C+] (a mythical sailor ejected from Hell for lying)

town crier [20C] (rhy. sl.)
two inches beyond upright [late 19C]
yentzer [20C] (US; Yiddish, 'fucker')

FLATTERERS

con-man [late 19C] (US)
earwig [mid-17C–late 19C]
honeyfoogler [19C+] (US; dial. *connyfogle*, to entice)
oil merchant [1930s–50s] (US)
politician [20C]
schmoozer/schmooser [20C] (Yiddish, 'chat-er')
soft-sawderer [mid–late 19C] (lit. 'soft solderer')
sweetmouth [mid-19C+] (W.I.)

TOADIES

apple-polisher [1920s+]
arsehole-crawler/arsehole-creeper/arsel-creeper [late 19C+]
arse-wiper [20C]
ass-wiper [1950s]
a-wiper [20C] (*arse-wiper*)
back-scratcher [1940s+] (US)
boot [1900s–10s] (US campus; *boot*licker)
booter [1940s] (US campus; *boot*lick*er*)
brown ankle [1970s+] (N.Z. prison; i.e. they are so far 'up the arse' of the authorities that only their ankles are visible)
brown nose/brown-noser [1930s+] (orig. US milit.; i.e. it is *brown* from 'arse-kissing')
bum boy [20C]
bum-creeper [late 19C]

Buster Brown/Busta Brown [1990s] (US Black)
cheese-eater [late 19C+] (US; i.e. a 'rat')
cheesy rider [1960s–70s] (punning on the film *Easy Rider*)
creeper [17C+]
crumb-catcher [1940s–50s] (US)
gat-creeper [1980s+] (S.Afr.; *gat* = anus)
greaser [20C] (US)
lackey-dog [1940s+] (W.I.)
lambe/lambiche [1960s+] (US; Spanish, 'licker')
pickthank [17C] (they 'pick a thank', i.e. curry favour, esp. by informing against someone else)
p.i.p. [20C] (W.I.; *party in power*)
placebo [mid-14C–early 17C] (Latin, 'I will please')
quiller [mid-19C] (*quill* = straw, i.e. they 'suck up')
schloep/shloep/schloop/shloop [1960s+] (S.Afr.; representing the sound of 'sucking')
smoodger [late 19C+] (Aus.; lit. 'kisser')
soap-crawler [mid-19C–1900s] (*soap* = flattery)

99 99 99 99 99 99 99 99 99 99 99 99 99 99 99 99 99 99 99 99 99 99 99

Hangers-on

barnacle [17C]
burr [16C–early 19C]
caboose [19C] (US; a cow-hide container stretched across the back of a chuck wagon)
claw-back [16C–17C]
claw-poll [16C–19C]
drag [20C]

66 66 66 66 66 66 66 66 66 66 66 66 66 66 66 66 66 66 66 66 66 66

ARSELICKERS

a-licker [1990s] (US; *ass-licker*)
arse lick/ass lick [1930s+] (orig. US)
arse-licker/ass-licker [1930s+]
ass-kisser [20C] (US)
ass-sucker [1940s+] (US)
bootkisser [19C]
bootlicker [mid–19C+] (orig. US)
brown-tonguer [20C]
bum-licker [1930s+]
bum-sucker [1930s+]
buttlick [1980s+] (US campus)
cocksucker [late 19C] (orig. US)
fart-sucker [19C–1900s]
foot-kisser [20C] (US)
heel-licker [20C] (US)
kiss-arse/kiss-ass [1910s+] (orig. US)
kisser [1950s+]
kiss my arse fellow [late 18C–early 19C]
kiss-up [1950s+]
lick(-arse)/lick-me-lug [20C] (Irish)
suck [1900s–50s]
suck-around [1950s] (US)
suckbutt [1990s+]
sucker [mid-19C] (US)

bootlicker

suck-hole [1950s+] (Aus./Can.)

suck-off [1920s+] (US)

suck-up [mid-19C+]

toches/tokus-licker/t.l. [20C] (orig. US; Yiddish *tuches*, the buttocks)

FAILURES, LOSERS AND NOBODIES

also-ran [late 19C+] (orig. Aus.)

biscuit-eater/biscuit-hound [20C] (US; a dog that relies on biscuits fed to it by its master)

blob [20C] (mainly Aus.)

bug-eater [19C] (US)

cayuse [1900s–20s] (US; lit. 'undersized horse')

dandiprat/dandyprat [mid-16C–19C] (a small coin worth 1¹/₂ old pence)

deadbeat [mid-19C+] (orig. US)

dirt-dobber/dirt-scratcher [1940s–60s]

dropkick [1980s+] (Aus./N.Z.)

dud [early 19C+] (*dud*man, a scarecrow)

egg-sucker [19C+] (US)

erk [1940s+] (in the Navy, 'lower deck rating'; in the Air Force, 'aircraftsman second class')

fuckup/fug-up [1940s+] (orig. US)

gully dirt [20C] (US)

ha'penny boy [1960s+] (Irish)

Hooley [1960s] (US; the noted millionaire and subsequent bankrupt Mr *Hooley*)

humpty-dumpty [1920s–30s]

Jack with the feather/plume of feathers [late 16C–early 17C]

Joe Crap [1940s+] (US)

Joe Shit (the rag man) [1940s+] (US)

little casino [1900s–50s] (US)

little shot [1930s+] (US)

loser [1950s+] (orig. US)

mullock [late 19C+] (Aus.; dial. 'rubbish')

neb [1920s–40s] (US; Yiddish *nebech*, nothing)

nebbish/nebbich/nebich [late 19C+]

never was/never-waser/never-wozzer [late 19C+] (US)

nickel-and-dimer [1960s+] (US)

niffy-naffy fellow [late 18C–early 19C] (dial. 'trifling fellow')

not in it [19C+]

phlizz [1920s]

pie-eater [1940s+] (Aus. prison; from the free meat pies eaten by WW2 army deserters)

pipsqueak [1910s+]

pissant [1940s+] (*piss* + *ant*)

runt [early 18C+]

schlepper [1930s+] (orig. US; Yiddish, 'dragger')

screw-up [1920s+] (orig. US)

🦛 🦛

Campus losers

brick [1980s+] (US campus)

fluke [20C] (orig. US campus; i.e. they rely on luck rather than ability)

wicked loser [1980s+] (US campus)

Z-bird [1960s+] (US teen)

🦛 🦛

lame-o/lamo [1970s+] (US campus)

lightweight [late 19C+] (orig. US)

limp-dick/limp-prick [20C] [early 19C] (W.I.)

milk [late 19C–1920s]

mollycoddle [mid-19C+]

mollypuff/mullipuff [early 17C–early 18C]

namby-pamby [18C]

noddy [1950s+]

no neck [1950s+]

nosebleed [1950s]

old lady [1930s+]

papbroek [1930s+] (S.Afr.; lit. 'soft trousers')

penny loaf [late 19C] (UK Und.)

percy(-boy)/percy-pants [20C] (orig. US)

piece of chickenshit [1980s+] (US campus)

pill [mid-19C+]

priss [late 19C+]

pudding [late 19C+] (US)

punk [1950s+] (orig. US)

punk-out [1950s–60s] (US)

quake breach/quake buttock [late 16C–early 17C]

ringtail [1920s+] (Aus.)

short stop [1950s–60s] (US Black)

sissie/cissie/cissy/sissy [late 19C+]

sissy-boy [1940s+] (US)

sissy pants [1940s+]

slag [1930s+]

snow [1960s+] (Aus.)

soft [mid-19C+]

soft ha'porth/daft ha'porth [20C]

softy/softie [mid-19C+]

sook/sookey/sookie/sooky [1930s+] (Aus./N.Z.)

sop-can [1950s+]

squib [20C] (Aus.)

three pennorth of God help us [20C] (Aus.)

weed [mid-19C+]

wet smack [1920s+] (US)

99 99 99 99 99 99 99 99 99 99 99 99 99 99 99 99 99 99 99 99 99

Rabbits, chickens and other frightened animals

acorn calf [19C] (US; lit. 'runt', from the belief that eating acorns resulted in giving birth to weak young)

calf [20C] (US)

chicken [early 17C+]

cow-baby [late 16C–18C] (i.e. 'calf')

crawfish [mid-19C+] (orig. US; a crustacean noted for moving backwards)

jellyfish [1930s+]

newt [1920s+] (US campus)

possum [late 19C] (US)

possum-guts [1950s–60s] (Aus.)

pussy [20C]

pussyfoot [1930s]

rabbit [20C]

shy-cock [late 18C–early 19C]

66 66 66 66 66 66 66 66 66 66 66 66 66 66 66 66 66 66 66 66 66

jellyfish

wimp [1960s+]
wimp-guts [1980s+]
wimpo/wimpoid [1980s+]
wuss [1970s+] (orig. US teen)
yellow back [20C]
yellow belly/yellow guts/yellow heel [1910s+]

99 99 99 99 99 99 99 99 99 99 99 99 99 99 99 99 99 99 99 99 99 99

Timid people

cold-footer [1910s–20s] (orig. Aus.)
creeping Jesus [early 19C+]
frighten Friday [20C] (W.I.)
Nervous Nellie [1920s+] (US)
quilt [20C] (Irish)
Ralph [1950s–60s] (camp gay)
rubber sock [20C]

66 66 66 66 66 66 66 66 66 66 66 66 66 66 66 66 66 66 66 66 66 66

99 99 99 99 99 99 99 99 99 99 99 99 99 99 99 99 99 99 99 99 99 99

Cowards in rhyming slang

Charley Howard [1930s] ('coward')
Harris Tweed [1950s] ('weed')

66 66 66 66 66 66 66 66 66 66 66 66 66 66 66 66 66 66 66 66 66 66

THEY COULDN'T ...

beat a carpet [late 19C+]
blow the froth off a glass of beer [1980s] (Aus.)
find a grand piano in a one-roomed house [20C]
get pussy in a cathouse [1970s] (US Black)
knock the dags off a sick canary [1980s] (Aus.)
knock the skin off a rice-pudding [1980s] (Aus.)
fight a bag of shit [20C] (Aus.)
fight their way out of a paper bag [20C] (orig. Aus.)
knock/pull a sick moll off a pisspot [1950s+] (Aus.)
organize a fuck in a brothel [1950s+]
organize/run a piss-up in a brewery [1930s+]
pick a seat at the pictures [20C]
pull the tail out of a peewee [1980s+] (Aus.)
tell the time if the town-hall clock fell on them [20C]
train a choko vine over a country dunny [20C] (Aus.)

MISFITS AND SOCIAL REJECTS

anorak [1980s+]
bodgie [1950s+] (Aus.)
bottom feeder [1970s+] (US teen; a fish that *feeds* from the *bottom* of the sea or riverbed)

dag [1910s+] (Aus./N.Z.; the clotted droppings that stick to the tail of a sheep)

divvy [1970s+]

dweeb/dweebie [1980s+] (orig. US teen)

flop [1900s–30s]

klutz [1950s+] (orig. US)

Melvin/Marvin [1950s+] (US)

nerd/nurd [1950s+] (orig. US)

nob [1970s+]

schlemiel/schlemihl/shlemiel [late 19C+] (Yiddish, 'bungler')

spas/spaz [1960s+] (student/school; *spas*tic)

square in a social circle [1930s–40s] (US Black)

tool [mid-19C+]

wally/wolly [1970s+]

weenie/weener/wiener/weeny/weeney/wienie [1960s+]

womble [1970s+]

woojang [1990s]

SWOTS AND EGGHEADS

beard [1920s+]

bearded weirdie [late 19C+]

bone [late 19C] (US campus; i.e. they '*bone* up')

book-sharp [late 19C+] (US West)

brain [1910s+]

brownbagger [1950s+] (US; from the *brown bag* containing their packed lunch)

cereb [1970s+] (US campus; *cereb*ral)

conch [20C] (US campus; *consc*ientious)

conk-buster/konk-buster [1930s–50s] (US Black)

Misfits on campus

cheddar [1990s]
cheeseman [1980s]
Chester [1990s]
closet case [1950s+]
corndog [1980s+]
cull [1980s+]
donut hole [1990s]
Dudley [1980s]
dweezle [1980s+]
eggo [1980s+]
Fred [1980s+]
gimp [1980s+]
goombah/gumbah [1990s]
gouda, gouda, gouda [1990s]
gweeb/gweep/gweebo [1970s+]
mutant [1980s+]
newt [1920s+]
nimrod [1930s+]
penis wrinkle [1980s+]
puck [1970s+]
social donut hole [1980s+]
sub-human [1980s+]
wet rag [1970s+]
wrinkle [1980s+]
yernt [1980s+]
zonko [1970s+]

66 66 66 66 66 66 66 66 66 66 66 66 66 66 66 66 66 66 66 66 66

culture-hound [1920s–30s]

culture-vulture [1940s+] (US campus)

egg [20C] (US campus)

egghead [20C] (orig. US)

freak [late 19C] (US campus)

geek [1970s+] (US Black/teen)

grind [late 19C+] (US campus)

grubber [late 19C] (US campus)

gunner [1970s+] (US campus)

highbrow [late 19C+]

longhair [1920s+] (orig. US)

mug [late 19C]

number eight hat [1940s+]

pencil geek [1970s+] (US campus)

Poindexter [1980s] (US teen)

pointed-head/pointy-head/pointhead [1960s+] (US)

power tool [1960s+] (US campus)

pseud [1960s+]

sap [late 18C–19C] (school; Latin *sapiens*, wise)

schooly [1980s+] (US Black)

smack [1980s+] (US campus; i.e. they continually *smack* their head in concentration)

smug [late 19C] (teen)

spadet [1980s+] (US campus)

squid [1980s+] (US campus)

swot/swat [mid-19C+]

teach [1950s+] (US Black)

throat [1970s+] (US campus; cut-*throat*)

tool [1970s+] (US campus)

BORING!

clone [1980s+] (US campus)

cold potato [20C] (US)

dead ass [20C]

droop [1920s–60s] (US campus)

dropout [20C] (orig. US)

dilberry [1970s] (US)

dingleberry [1920s+] (US)

droid [1980s+] (orig. US)

flake [1950s+] (orig. US)

Irving [20C] (US)

least [1950s] (US Black)

L-7/l-seven [1950s+] (US Black/teen; i.e. a 'square', formed when 'L' and '7' are put together; the phrase can be accompanied by using thumb and forefinger extended at right angles to form a square)

lunchbucket [1950s+] (US)

moto [1990s] (US campus; *m*aster *o*f *t*he *o*bvious)

mundane [1990s] (US campus)

norm/normal [1980s+] (US campus)

nudnik/noodnik [1920s+] (US; Yiddish, 'bore')

prose [late 17C–late 19C]

sleeping Jesus [1960s+] (US Black)

snore [1970s+]

stick [mid-19C+]

stiff [1950s+]

turkey [1950s+]

yeah man [1980s+] (US campus)

Zelda [1950s+] (US teen; a dull girl)

HORRIBLY FAT AND
PAINFULLY THIN

FAT PEOPLE

barrel [20C]

(Big) Bertha [1920s–40s; 1980s+] (US; the nickname of a large WW1 German gun)

blimp [1930s+] (from the fictitious Colonel *Blimp*)

blimp boat [1980s+] (US campus)

blivet/blivit [1940s+] (US, orig. Aus. milit.; 'ten pounds of shit in a five-pound bag')

bloater [late 19C–1900s]

bowl of jelly [1960s+] (US)

bucket of lard/bucket of blubber [20C]

chabby/chabs [1990s]

chub [20C]

chubbs [1990s] (US Black)

fatso [1940s+] (orig. US)

fattoon [1950s] (W.I.)

fatty [late 19C+]

feather-bed [20C] (US)

flop [20C]

floppy [20C] (US)

heavyweight [1970s] (US)

horse heavy [1940s] (US Black)

lard-bucket [20C]

lardo [1980s+] (US)

load [1940s+] (US)

melting moments [19C] (two fat people having sex)

Michelin (tyre) [1950s+] (W.I.)

porker [late 19C+]

blimp

99 99 99 99 99 99 99 99 99 99 99 99 99 99 99 99 99 99 99 99 99

Large-bellied people

ass-belly [1970s+] (US)

blubber-belly [19C]

bag of guts [late 19C+] (US)

blubber-gut/blubber-guts [1940s+] (US)

buddha belly [1970s+] (US)

double guts [early 19C+]

doughbelly [1940s+] (US)

greasy guts [1940s] (US)

gundiguts [late 17C–early 19C]

gutbucket [1930s+] (US)

guts [late 17C+]

guts and garbage [late 18C–mid-19C]

gutso [1950s+]

guttie/gutty [19C] (Irish)

jelly belly [late 19C+]

kettlebelly [late 19C–1920s] (US)

pudding-belly [late 18C–1900s]

tub of guts [20C]

66 66 66 66 66 66 66 66 66 66 66 66 66 66 66 66 66 66 66 66 66

princod [late 18C–early 19C] (Scot. *preencod*, a pincushion)

ribs [late 19C–1900s]

squab [early 18C] (a type of well-upholstered sofa)

tripe and trillibub [17C–18C]

tub [late 19C+]

tub of lard [20C]

whale [late 19C] (US campus)

99 99 99 99 99 99 99 99 99 99 99 99 99 99 99 99 99 99 99 99 99 99

Nine boozy bellies

bay window [mid-19C+]

beer barrel [1930s] (orig. US)

beer gut [1950s+]

beer muscle [1930s–40s] (US)

beer pot [1980s+]

booze balloon [1970s+] (N.Z.)

booze belly [20C] (US)

German goitre [20C] (US; from the stereotyped German capacity for beer)

limehouse cut [20C] (rhy. sl. 'gut')

66 66 66 66 66 66 66 66 66 66 66 66 66 66 66 66 66 66 66 66 66 66

FAT MEN

Baron George [late 19C] (*George* Parkes, a portly theatrical
landlord)

bartholomew (boar) pig [16C–17C]

bladder of lard [mid-19C+]

buss-belt [1960s+] (W.I.)

copper-belly [late 19C+]

Fat Jack of the bone-house [mid-19C–1900s]

fatymus/fattymus [mid–late 19C]

flanderkin [late 17C–early 19C]

forty-guts [mid-19C]

gutsy [late 19C+]

Jack Weight [late 18C–19C]

Mr Double Tripes [late 18C–early 19C]

puff guts [late 18C–1900s]

FAT WOMEN

bargain bucket [1990s]

b.o.b. [1990s] (US; *b*ig *o*ld *b*itch)

buffalo [1960s] (US)

bundle [early 19C–1950s]

chubette [1950s+]

fatyma/fattyma [mid–late 19C]

feather-bed and pillows [19C]

flahoola [late 19C–1900s] (Irish)

fuss [mid-17C–early 18C]

fussock/fuzzock/fussocks [late 17C–late 19C]

fustilarian [late 16C–early 17C]

heavyweight [1970s] (US)

heifer [late 19C+] (US Black; an unattractive, obese woman)

Judy with the big booty [1970s+] (US Black)

murch [1990s]

pig [20C]

pigger/pigmouth [20C] (US Black)

poultice [late 19C]

Queenie [late 19C] (US)

shuttlebutt [1970s+] (US campus)

sow [late 18C+]

99 99 99 99 99 99 99 99 99 99 99 99 99 99 99 99 99 99 99 99 99

Builders' bottoms

builder's bum [1980s+]

plumber's bum [1980s]

working-man's smile [1980s+] (US)

66 66 66 66 66 66 66 66 66 66 66 66 66 66 66 66 66 66 66 66 66

SPECIALITY FATTIES

Bahama Mama [1980s+] (US Black; a fat, unattractive 'Black Mammy' stereotype)

beer bottle [late 19C–1900s] (a stout, red-faced man)

black-silk barge [late 19C–1900s] (society; a woman whose flattering black silk clothes fail to offset her barge-like proportions)

blood and guts alderman [19C] (a fat, pompous man)

buddley [20C] (Ulster; Irish *bodalach*, a large, ungainly young person)

buffarilla [1960s–70s] (US campus; a plump, homely young woman; *buffa*lo + go*rilla*)

Buxton bloaters [late 19C–1900s] (overweight invalids, wheeling around in bath chairs while they take the medicinal waters)

99 99 99 99 99 99 99 99 99 99 99 99 99 99 99 99 99 99 99 99 99

Large-buttocked people

barrel-ass [1940s] (US)

blubberass [1950s] (US)

blubber-butt [1950s+] (orig. US)

brawny-buttock [early 18C]

broad-gauge lady [late 19C] (a woman with wide hips)

bubblebutt [1980s+]

fat-arse/fat-ass [1930s+]

fatty bum-bum [1950s+] (W.I.)

lard(-ass)/lard-arse [1930s+] (US)

wide load [1990s] (US campus)

66 66 66 66 66 66 66 66 66 66 66 66 66 66 66 66 66 66 66 66 66

cement-mixer [1960s] (an overweight, aggressive woman)

cut puss [1950s] (W.I.; an effeminate fat man, lit. 'castrated cat')

Dutch build [19C] (a stocky, thickset individual)

fat cock [mid-19C] (a fat old man)

German aunt [20C] (US; a fat, frumpy woman)

Miss Piggy [1970s+] (a fat, melodramatic person, from the *Muppet Show* character)

Queen Mary [1980s+] (US gay; an obese gay man)

tent [1970s] (a fat woman in a voluminous garment such as a kaftan)

Whitechapel breed [late 18C] (a woman who is 'fat, ragged and saucy')

THIN PEOPLE

back-and-belly [1950s] (W.I.)

death's head upon a mopstick [late 18C–early 19C]

fence rail [20C] (US)

hairpin [1910s]

hat rack [20C] (Aus./US)

kangaroo [late 19C] (a thin, narrow-shouldered person)

long drink of water [late 19C–1900s; 1930s+]

matchstick [1950s+]

Miss Xylophone [1950s–60s] (camp gay)

monkey on a stick [late 19C–1910s] (a thin person with abrupt, jerky movements)

one of Pharaoh's lean kine [late 16C] (*kine* = cattle)

pair of tongs [late 19C–1900s]

pinner [1980s+] (US campus)

raany/ranny [20C] (Ulster; Irish *ranaí*, thin)

rasher of wind [mid-19C–1940s]

rushlight [late 19C] (lit. 'glimmer')

scaly bloke [1930s] (N.Z.; a thin man)

scarce-o-fat [1950s] (W.I.)

skin-a-guts [1910s–20s]

skin-and-grief [late 19C]

skinned rabbit [late 19C–1910s]

Skinny Lizzie [20C] (a thin woman)

spider-catcher [late 17C–early 18C] (a thin man)

straight up six o'clock girl [1940s] (US Black; a thin woman)

twig [1980s+] (US campus)

wangle [late 19C–1910s] (Irish; a thin man; dial. *wangling*, sickly, weak, delicate)

99 99 99 99 99 99 99 99 99 99 99 99 99 99 99 99 99 99 99 99 99 99

Skin and bone

anatomy [late 19C–1900s]

atomy [late 16C–mid-19C]

bag of bones [early 19C+]

bald-rib [early 17C]

barebones [late 16C–early 19C]

bare-brisket [19C–1900s]

bone [late 19C]

bone-in-a-valley [1950s+] (W.I.)

boneyard [19C]

natomy/nattermy [19C]

snaky-bony [1950s] (W.I.)

66 66 66 66 66 66 66 66 66 66 66 66 66 66 66 66 66 66 66 66 66 66

99 99 99 99 99 99 99 99 99 99 99 99 99 99 99 99 99 99 99 99 99 99 99

Eight small breasts and two titless wonders

chapel hat pegs [20C]

fried eggs [1930s+]

ironing board [20C] (a flat-chested woman)

mosquito bites [1970s+] (US campus)

titless wonder [1930s+] (orig. RAF; a flat-chested woman)

two raisins on a bread board [20C]

66 66 66 66 66 66 66 66 66 66 66 66 66 66 66 66 66 66 66 66 66 66 66

SHORT PEOPLE

dibbi dibbi [1980s+] (W.I./UK Black teen)

dink [1920s+]

duckbutt [1930s+] (US)

dusty butt [1900s–40s] (US Black)

forty-foot [mid-19C]

go-by-the-ground [late 17C–18C]

grundy [16C]

half-pint [late 19C+] (US)

hoddy-doddy [16C–18C; US 19C–20C]

Jack Sprat [late 16C–19C]

kipper [1900s–50s]

lofty [20C]

makeweight [late 18C–early 19C]

half-pint

Mickey Mouse [1940s–70s] (US)

munchkin [1950s+] (US)

muppet [1970s+]

nugget [mid-19C+] (Aus.)

nyiff nyaff [20C]

peewee [20C]

picayune [early 19C+] (orig. US; a small low-value coin)

pikkie [1940s+] (S Afr.; Afrikaans, 'little fellow')

pintle [20C] (Ulster; lit. 'penis')

sawed off [late 19C+] (US)

scrap [late 19C+]

short-arse/short-ass [1940s+]

short 'un [18C+]

🙿 🙿

Tumble-turds: short, fat people

bundletail [late 17C–early 18C] (a short, fat woman)

five by five [1930s+] (Can./US Black; a short fat man, i.e. his girth is the same as his height)

humpty-dumpty [late 18C–late 19C]

lacatan [1950s] (W.I.; a variety of small banana)

podge [mid-19C+]

pudge [early 19C+]

tumble-turd [1940s–50s] (W.I.; a short, stocky person, from a type of large black beetle that rolls and buries pieces of dung)

walrus [1920s+] (US)

🙽 🙽

shorty [20C]

squib [20C] (Aus.)

squirt [mid-19C+] (orig. US)

stub [late 19C]

TALL PEOPLE

longas [1950s] (W.I.; i.e. 'long arse')

long legs [18C+]

Long Meg [late 17C–early 19C] (the noted, if semi-mythical giantess *Long Meg* of Westminster)

long shanks [late 17C–20C]

long streak of misery [late 19C+] (a tall miserable person)

long 'un [18C+]

papa-tree-top-tall [1930s–40s] (US Black)

sky-scraper [mid-19C]

tree [1980s+] (US campus; a very tall woman)

vooter [1990s] (US teen; i.e. '-footer')

LONG THIN STREAKS OF PISS: TALL, THIN PEOPLE

beanpole [mid-19C+]

cornstalk [early 19C] (US)

hop-pole [mid-19C]

lamp-post [late 19C+]

lanky [mid-19C+]

legs [19C+]

lonely in the weather [1950s] (W.I.; i.e. their head is above the clouds)

long slab [20C] (a tall, thin woman)

long thin streak of piss [20C]

rainbow [1950s] (W.I.)

Sahara [1940s] (S Afr.)

Sally B. [late 19C] (US; a tall thin woman, from the actress *Sarah B*ernhardt)

streak [1940s+] (orig. Aus.)

string bean [1930s+]

topper [late 19C–1900s]

whang [20C] (Irish; Scot. 'bootlace')

yard of pump water [late 19C]

UGLY PEOPLE

bear [1950s+] (US Black)

Berkshire hog [1950s+] (W.I.; a type of large, dark-skinned pig)

booger bear [late 19C–1960s] (US Black)

bracket-face [17C–late 18C]

cheese [1980s+] (US campus)

creature [20C] (W.I.)

cuntface [late 19C+]

dog [1930s+]

drack sort [1930s+] (Aus.)

faust [1930s–40s] (US Black)

fish-face [1920s+]

forty miles of bad road [1960s+] (US)

grosser [1970s+] (US)

honker [1970s+] (US campus)

knocker-face/knocker-head [late 19C–1920s]

moose-face [mid-19C–1940s] (US)

mutt [1970s+]

nightmare [1980s+] (US campus)

99 99 99 99 99 99 99 99 99 99 99 99 99 99 99 99 99 99 99 99 99 99 99

Butter-snouts and prunefaces

blubber-mouth [1940s] (US; a person with heavy jowls)

brutus [1980s+] (US campus; a mean, ugly person)

butter-snout [late 19C–1910s] (a person with a noticeably greasy complexion)

closet case [1950s+] (US campus; a socially inept, unattractive person)

farthing-faced chit [1900s] (a small, pinch-faced, insignificant person)

fiddle-face [mid–late 19C] (a person with a miserable, 'long' face)

gibface [mid–late 19C] (a person with a heavy lower jaw; dial. *gib*, a tom-cat)

monkey-face [1930s–60s] (W.I.; a stupid, ugly person)

monkey Jesus [1940s] (W.I.; a very ugly person)

muppet [1970s+] (an unattractive, possibly mentally retarded person)

picklepuss [20C] (US; a sour-faced individual)

pie-face [1920s+] (a person with a round or blank face)

pruneface [20C] (US; a plain or miserable-looking person)

pumpkin head [1970s] (a person with an abnormally large head)

zombie [1930s–50s] (US Black/campus; a bizarre-looking person)

66 66 66 66 66 66 66 66 66 66 66 66 66 66 66 66 66 66 66 66 66 66 66

no oil painting [late 19C+]

no van dyke [20C]

plug-ugly [mid-19C+] (orig. US)

prom date [1980s+] (US campus)

UGLY MEN

babu(-man) [20C] (W.I.; an ugly old man)

Captain Cheddar [1980s+] (US campus)

Dick [1960s+] (US teen)

Eddie [1980s+] (US campus)

india [1950s–60s] (camp gay)

shapes [late 17C–early 18C] (i.e. he is ill-proportioned)

toad [20C] (US gay; an ugly middle-aged gay man)

UGLY WOMEN

antidote [late 17C–early 18C] (i.e. she is an *antidote* against attraction)

bag of smacked twats [1990s]

bat [1920s+]

beast [1940s+] (US, mainly campus)

blind cobbler's thumb [1990s] (the face of an unattractive woman, i.e. its pockmarks resemble needle-pricks)

blister [1960s]

boiler [1920s+] (US)

booger [1980s+] (US campus)

boot [1950s+]

Broomhilda [1980s+] (US campus; a short, unattractive woman, from a US comic strip character, itself a pun on the Wagnerian heroine *Brünhilde*)

bucket [1950s–60s] (US)

bucket of smashed crabs [1990s]

bushbitch [1980s+] (US)

buzzard [late 18C+]

cagmag [late 18C–mid-19C] (dial. 'old goose')

Dracula [1950s+]

faggot [1960s+] (US teen/ campus)

firkin of foul stuff [late 17C–18C]

freezing weather [1930s–40s] (US Black)

genga [1990s] (feminized version of *Genghis* Khan)

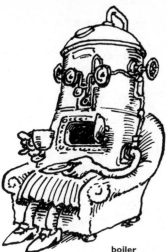

boiler

ghoul [1940s–70s] (US)

gorilla [1970s] (US campus)

hag [1920s–50s] (US campus)

hatchet-face [late 17C–mid-18C]

hedgehog [19C]

hood rat [1990s] (US Black teen)

lobo [1940s] (US Black; lit. 'grey wolf')

moose [1990s]

pitch [1970s+] (US campus; *p*ig + bi*tch*)

roach [1970s+] (US campus)

scab [1960s+] (US Black)

scrag [1940s+] (US campus)

snatch [1990s] (US campus)

99 99 99 99 99 99 99 99 99 99 99 99 99 99 99 99 99 99 99 99 99

Women as farmyard animals

CANINE
   airedale [1950s] (US)
   beagle [1940s–50s] (US)
   bow-wow [1960s+]
   coyote [1980s+]
   mud puppy [1980s+] (US campus)

PORCINE
   bushpig [1980s+] (US campus)
   grunt [1990s]
   hellpig [1980s+] (US campus)
   hog [1970s+] (US campus)
   hogger [1960s+] (US campus)
   oinker [1980s+] (US)
   pig [20C]
   sweat hog [1970s+] (US campus)

BOVINE
   cow [late 17C+]

ASININE
   mule [1950s+]
   swamp donkey [1990s]

GALLINACEOUS
   thunder chicken/thunder chick
     [1970s+] (US Black)

66 66 66 66 66 66 66 66 66 66 66 66 66 66 66 66 66 66 66 66 66

,, ,,

Face like a ...

face like a bagful of spanners [1970s+]

face like a stripper's clit [1990s]

face like the back of a bus [1940s+]

face like the rear end of a cow [1940s+]

face like the side of a house [1940s+]

" "

,, ,,

Baggers: three examples of extreme ugliness

one-bagger [1980s+] (US campus; a woman so ugly one would need to put a bag over her head before having sex)

double-bagger/two-bagger [1980s+] (US; a woman so ugly that prior to sex one would need to place a bag over her head and a bag over one's own head in case hers broke)

double bag and stumper [1990s] (a woman so ugly that one would have to place paper bags over both participants' heads in order to face up to intercourse, and one would, in any case, rather cut off all one's limbs than have sex with her)

" "

stank ho [1970s+] (US campus; lit. 'ugly whore')

stumper [1990s]

troll [1980s+] (US campus)

whammy [1980s+] (US campus)

99 99 99 99 99 99 99 99 99 99 99 99 99 99 99 99 99 99 99 99 99

Don't get too close...

Medusa [1990s] (US Black teen; a woman who is beautiful from the neck down, from the mythical *Medusa*, a gorgon whose hair was made of snakes and who, though a beautiful woman from the neck down, was facially so ugly her gaze would turn a man to stone)

Monet [1990s] (US teen; a woman who resembles the impressionist paintings by Claude *Monet*, i.e. from a distance she looks attractive, but close up she is a mess)

night fighter [1970s] (US campus; a woman who appears attractive by night but not in daylight)

sphinx [1990s] (US Black teen; a woman who is beautiful from the neck up, from the mythical *Sphinx*, a monster with the head of a woman and body of a lion)

strobe-light honey [1990s] (US Black teen; a woman who seems attractive in flickering light but not otherwise)

66 66 66 66 66 66 66 66 66 66 66 66 66 66 66 66 66 66 66 66 66

99 99 99 99 99 99 99 99 99 99 99 99 99 99 99 99 99 99 99 99 99 99

Too much make-up

crusty-beau [late 17C–late 18C] (a dandy
who takes especial care of his complexion,
often with cosmetics)

doughface [20C] (US; a woman who wears
an excess of cosmetics)

easter egg [20C] (US; a woman wearing too
much make-up.

mind the paint [late 19C] (used to refer to a
passing woman who is considered to be
wearing too much make-up)

slap queen [1950s–60s] (gay; a male homosexual given to the heavy use of make-up)

66 66 66 66 66 66 66 66 66 66 66 66 66 66 66 66 66 66 66 66 66 66

Wilma [1980s+] (US campus; the character *Wilma* in the
cartoon and film *The Flintstones*)

wing commander [1990s] (punning on 'RAF', i.e. *r*ough *a*s *f*uck)

UGLY AND MISERABLE FACES

baboon-faced [1940s+] (very ugly)

bacon-faced [late 17C–early 19C] (fat-faced, heavily jowled)

bracket-mug [19C] (an ugly face)

burying face [late 19C–1900s] (a miserable face)

Friday face [late 16C–19C] (a miserable or dour face, from
Friday's traditional status as a day of abstinence)

fuckfaced [1940s+] (having an ugly, miserable face)

jack-knife face [mid-19C+] (US; a thin, pointed face)

like an owl in an ivy-bush [late 18C–19C] (describing a person with a narrow face and a large wig or very bushy hair)

marriage face [late 19C] (middle-class; a miserable face)

muffin-face/muffin-countenance [mid-18C–early 19C] (an expressionless or miserable face)

pumpkin-face [late 19C] (US; a round, expressionless face)

rogers [late 19C] (society; a ghastly face)

rum phiz/rum phyz [late 18C] (an odd-looking face)

splatter face [late 19C] (a broad face)

Tyburn collop [16C] (a miserable face)

ugly plug [19C] (US; an ugly face)

SMEGS AND HOG-GRUBBERS: DIRTY AND UNKEMPT PEOPLE

clip-nit [early 18C] (a dirty ruffian; *nit* = louse egg)

crud [1940s+] (orig. US milit.)

crudball [1960s+] (US)

crumbo [1930s+] (orig. US)

๑๑ ๑๑ ๑๑ ๑๑ ๑๑ ๑๑ ๑๑ ๑๑ ๑๑ ๑๑ ๑๑ ๑๑ ๑๑ ๑๑ ๑๑ ๑๑ ๑๑ ๑๑ ๑๑

Drabs and dishclouts: dirty women

dirty puzzle [late 17C–early 19C]

dishclout [late 18C]

drab [early 16C–19C]

queer mort [late 17C–19C]

rubacrock/rubbacrock [19C] (a dirty, lazy woman)

๒๒ ๒๒ ๒๒ ๒๒ ๒๒ ๒๒ ๒๒ ๒๒ ๒๒ ๒๒ ๒๒ ๒๒

❧❧ ❧❧ ❧❧ ❧❧ ❧❧ ❧❧ ❧❧ ❧❧ ❧❧ ❧❧ ❧❧ ❧❧

Grubs and snotnoses: dirty children

ash-cat [19C] (US)
Ash-cat Sam [mid-19C–1900s]
grub [mid-19C+]
mucky pup [20C] (Aus.)
salop [20C] (W.I.)
snotnose [1940s+] (orig. US)
wet nose [1940s+] (orig. US)

❦❦ ❦❦ ❦❦ ❦❦ ❦❦ ❦❦ ❦❦ ❦❦ ❦❦ ❦❦ ❦❦ ❦❦

dirtball [1970s+] (US)
dirty bundle [1940s+] (W.I.; an untidy person)
droopy-drawers [1930s+] (an untidy, sloppy or depressing person)
flipper [20C] (Irish; a messy, untidy man)
fright [mid-18C+] (a person of grotesque or unkempt
   appearance)
grot [1960s+] (Aus.)
hog-grubber [late 17C–18C]
preke/preky [1940s+] (W.I.; Spanish *pereque*, an intolerable person)
ragmop [1940s–50s] (US Black; an unkempt person)
scruff [mid-19C+]
slobber-slobber [1950s] (W.I.)
smeg [1980s+]
snotter [20C] (Ulster)
snotty-nose [19C+]
something the cat brought in [1920s+]
warb [1930s+] (Aus.; *warb*le, a type of maggot)

PHYSICAL IMPERFECTIONS

BOILS, ZITS AND PLUKES

boo-boo [1950s+] (US; a minor scar, bruise, or acne spot)

can of oil/canov [late 19C+] (rhy. sl. 'boil')

chorb [1970s+] (S Afr. teen; Bantu *chubaba*, a skin blemish)

Conan Doyle [late 19C+] (rhy. sl. 'boil')

custards [1920s+] (Aus.)

dohickey/doohickey [1910s+] (orig. US; a love-bite or pimple)

gin bud [19C] (a facial spot or ulcer resulting from excessive gin-drinking)

goober/goob [1970s+] (US campus; a small mole, spot or similar skin blemish)

goopheads [1940s+] (US)

jack bumps [1960s+] (US; acne, allegedly caused by masturbation)

pimgenet/pimginnit [late 17C– early 18C] (a prominent, red pimple)

pluke [20C]

Randolph Scott [20C] (rhy. sl. 'spot')

Selina Scott [20C] (rhy. sl. 'spot')

zit [1950s+] (orig. US teen)

99 99 99 99 99 99 99 99 99 99 99 99 99 99 99 99 99 99 99 99 99 99

Two freckled faces

bran-faced [late 18C–early 19C]

christened by the baker [late 18C–early 19C]

66 66 66 66 66 66 66 66 66 66 66 66 66 66 66 66 66 66 66 66 66 66

SPOTTY AND POCK-MARKED PEOPLE

carbuncle face [late 17C–late 18C]
craterface [1980s+] (campus/teen)
crumpet-face [mid–late 19C]
frosty face [late 18C–19C] (a person whose face is pitted with smallpox scars)
mockered [mid-19C+] (marked with small-pox scars)
pimply [1970s+]
pizza face [1980s+] (US teen)

99 99 99 99 99 99 99 99 99 99 99 99 99 99 99 99 99 99 99 99

Three red faces

beetroot mug [late 19C–1910s]
grog blossom [18C+] (a red face caused by the bursting of blood-vessels through excessive, long-term drinking)
toddy blossom [19C]

66 66 66 66 66 66 66 66 66 66 66 66 66 66 66 66 66 66 66 66 66

99 99 99 99 99 99 99 99 99 99 99 99 99 99 99 99 99 99 99 99 99

Three pale faces

ashy [20C] (US Black; pale, ashen-faced)
calf's head [late 19C] (a white-faced man with a large head)
underdone [late 19C] (having a pale complexion)

66 66 66 66 66 66 66 66 66 66 66 66 66 66 66 66 66 66 66 66 66

SQUINTS, SQUINTERS AND OTHER OCULAR ODDITIES

banjo-eyes [1920s–70s] (US; a person with large, wide-open eyes)

bog-eyed [1940s+] (having tired eyes, the result of too little sleep or too much alcohol)

boss-eye [late 19C+] (a person who squints or has an injured eye)

buck-eyed [20C] (US Black; having eyes considered out of the ordinary, cross-eyed, squinting, protruding etc.)

bug-eye [20C] (a person with round or bulging eyes)

chaney-eyed [17C] (small-eyed)

cranberry eye [late 19C] (US; a bloodshot eye from excessive drinking)

cunt-eyed [1910s+] (US; having narrow, squinting eyes)

eyes like cod's ballocks [20C] (popping eyes)

eyes like pissholes in the snow [20C] (orig. milit.; deeply sunken eyes, often bloodshot, poss. as a result of an excess of alcohol)

goggler [early–mid-19C] (a person with bulging 'goggle' eyes)

gooseberry-eyed [late 18C–late 19C] (having eyes that look like boiled gooseberries, i.e. grey and lifeless)

gravy-eyed [late 18C–19C] (bleary-eyed, having mucus-filled eyes)

moon-eyed hen [late 18C– early 19C] ('a squinting wench')

mutton-eye [20C] (a person with a squint)

queer ogles [late 17C–mid-19C] (Und.; cross eyes)

craterface

queer peepers [18C–19C] (Und.; squinting or short-sighted eyes)

squinny-eyes [late 17C–mid-19C] (squinting eyes)

squint-a-pipes [late 18C–mid-19C] (a squinting man or woman)

squinters [late 19C] (squinting eyes)

swivel-eye [mid-19C] (a squint)

wapper-eyed [late 18C–early 19C] (sore-eyed, squinting)

99 99 99 99 99 99 99 99 99 99 99 99 99 99 99 99 99 99 99 99 99 99

Bags under the eyes

coal [1990s] (Aus.)

commercial traveller [1930s] (i.e. they carry 'bags')

luggage [1970s] (US teen)

66 66 66 66 66 66 66 66 66 66 66 66 66 66 66 66 66 66 66 66 66

99 99 99 99 99 99 99 99 99 99 99 99 99 99 99 99 99 99 99 99 99 99

Spectacle-wearers

four-eyes [mid-19C+]

gig [late 19C] (*gig*-lamps, the lights on either side of a carriage)

glass eyes [late 18C–19C]

glaze-ons [1960s]

goggles [20C]

like whelks behind a window-pane [1890s–1910s] (describing the eyes of a person who wears very thick glasses)

specky twat [1990s+]

66 66 66 66 66 66 66 66 66 66 66 66 66 66 66 66 66 66 66 66 66

99 99 99 99 99 99 99 99 99 99 99 99 99 99 99 99 99 99 99 99 99

One-eyed people

Freney [late 18C–early 19C] (Irish; the 18C
one-eyed highwayman James *Freney*)

one and a peppermint-drop [late
19C–1900s]

seven-sided animal [late 18C–late 19C] (i.e.
they have 'a right side and a left side, a fore
side and a backside, an outside, an inside
and a blind side')

seven-sided son of a bitch [19C] (US)

single peeper [late 18C–early 19C]

66 66 66 66 66 66 66 66 66 66 66 66 66 66 66 66 66 66 66 66 66

LARGE AND MISSHAPEN NOSES

banana-nose [1920s+] (US; a long or hooked nose)

bottle-nose [late 19C–1900s] (a person who has a large,
prominent nose)

briar-root [late 19C] (an ill-shaped, battered nose)

cheese-cutter [mid-19C] (an aquiline nose)

cherry-picker [20C] (US; a large, hooked nose)

conk [early 19C+] (someone who has a large nose)

conky/konky [mid-19C+] (someone with an especially
prominent nose)

dook [mid–late 19C] (i.e. 'duke', from the Duke of Wellington,
known for his large nose and nicknamed 'Conky')

muzzle-chops [17C] (a man with a prominent nose and
mouth)

needlenose [1940s–70s] (US; a person with a pointed nose)

nutcrackers [late 19C–1900s] (a hooked nose and a prominent chin, à la Mr Punch)

parish pick-axe [late 19C] (a prominent nose)

pugified [late 18C–mid-19C] (snub-nosed)

snipe [20C] (Ulster; a person who has a long nose, from the bird's long beak)

RED NOSES

Bardolph [1990s] (the Shakespearean character)

beacon [late 19C]

copper-nosed [late 17C–18C]

danger light/danger signal [20C]

fiery snorter [mid-19C]

geranium [late 19C]

nose to light candles at [late 16C–early 17C]

old raspberry [1910s–20s] (an old person with a notably red nose, presumably a drunkard)

rarzo/rahzo [late 19C+] (a red-nosed man)

Rudolph [1990s]

strawberry [late 19C] (a broken-veined, bloated nose)

DOUBLE CHINS AND OTHERS

Andy Gump [1920s+] (US; a conspicuously receding chin, from the chinless cartoon character created by Sidney Smith)

chillers [20C] (Irish; a double chin)

chisel-chin [20C] (US; a person whose lower jaw protrudes)

saving chin [late 18C–mid-19C] (a protruding chin, i.e. it catches food)

BUCK TEETH AND THEIR OWNERS

able to eat corn-on-the-cob through a picket fence [20C]
(buck-toothed)

bread-and-butter teeth [20C]

butter bean teeth [20C]

dominoes [late 19C] (yellow and rotten teeth)

Franklin teeth [1920s–30s] (Can.; from the protruding grille of
the *Franklin* automobile)

gravestones [20C] (US; prominent front teeth or false teeth)

out-mouthed [20C] (Ulster; having protruding teeth)

rabbit tooth [early 19C]

snag [1910s+] (Aus.; a jagged tooth)

snaggle-tooth [1900s] (a woman with poor, uneven teeth)

tombstone [mid-19C–1900s] (a crooked tooth)

LARGE EARS

bakore [1970s+] (S Afr.; Afrikaans, 'owl ears')

cabbage leaves [20C] (US)

flaps [1960s+]

jug-handles/jug-lugs [20C] (sticking-out ears)

🙶 🙶

Wearers of orthodontic braces

laser lips [1970s+] (US campus)

metal mouth [1970s+] (US campus)

tin grin [1970s+] (US campus)

tinsel teeth [1970s+] (US campus)

twinkle teeth [1970s+] (US campus)

🙶 🙶

99 99 99 99 99 99 99 99 99 99 99 99 99 99 99 99 99 99 99 99

Dick breath: people with halitosis

death breath [1980s]

dick breath [1990s] (US)

dog-breath [1940s+] (orig. US)

dragon [1980s+] (US campus; i.e. they 'breathe fire')

jungle mouth [1970s+] (US campus)

king death [20C] (rhy. sl. 'bad breath')

lend us your breath to kill Jumbo [late 19C] (said to a halitosis sufferer, the idea being that their breath is strong enough to kill an elephant)

rotten guts [1910s–20s]

swamp breath [1980s+] (US)

trumpeter [late 18C–early 19C]

66 66 66 66 66 66 66 66 66 66 66 66 66 66 66 66 66 66 66 66 66

lend us your breath to kill Jumbo

LESS THAN PERFECT LEGS

badger-legged [mid-17C–early 18C] (having one leg shorter than the other)

baker-legged [18C–19C] (knock-kneed)

ballocks in brackets [20C] (a bow-legged man)

bench-legged [19C] (US; bow-legged)

bottle legs [20C] (crooked legs)

cat sticks [late 18C–19C] (very thin legs)

cheese-cutters [mid-19C] (bandy legs)

chicken-hammed [18C] (bandy-legged)

cowboy [1950s+] (a bow-legged man, i.e. his legs are bent from sitting on horses)

crookshanks [late 18C–19C] (a bandy-legged person)

gander-legged [19C] (US; thin-legged)

Irish arms [20C] (thick legs)

Irish legs [late 18C–19C] (heavy female legs)

queer gams [early 19C] (bandy legs)

spiddock-pot legs [17C] (ungainly legs; northern dial. *spiddock*, a spigot)

spider-shanked [late 18C–early 19C] (having very thin legs)

tampon braces [1930s–40s] (US Black; a woman with unattractive legs)

trapsticks [early 18C–mid-19C] (thin legs)

HAIRDOS AND HAIRDON'TS

BLONDES: REAL AND FAKE

bale of hay/bale of straw [1920s+] (orig. US.; a blonde woman)

bleached mort [late 18C] (a fair-haired woman)

bottle baby [1940s+] (orig. US; a woman with dyed blonde hair)

bottle blonde [1940s+] (a woman with dyed blonde hair)

coal-scuttle blonde [1930s–50s] (US; a Black woman with a blonde wig)

skillet blonde [1920s–30s] (US Black; a Black woman with a blonde wig)

snow [1960s+] (Aus. school; a blond-haired weakling)

straw [1920s+] (a person with light blond hair)

suicide blonde [1930s+] (orig. US; a woman with dyed blonde or peroxide blonde hair)

turnip-pate [late 17C–18C] (a very fair head of hair)

REDHEADS

blossom-top [mid–late 19C] (US)

bluey [20C] (orig. Aus.)

brass-head [20C] (W.I.; a Black person who has a reddish tint to their hair due to lack of protein)

bricktop [19C] (US)

brickyard blonde [20C] (US)

bushfire blonde [1940s+] (Aus.)

carrothead/carrot-top [mid-19C–1930s]

carrots [late 17C+]

copper-nob/copper-knob [mid-19C+]

copper-top [late 19C–1910s]

flames [19C+]

ginger [late 19C+]

ginger-nob [20C]

jersey [late 19C–1910s] (Aus.)

Jessie [1940s] (US Black; a red-haired girl or woman)

mahogany top [mid–late 19C]

poison-pate [late 17C–mid-19C]

Rufus [1950s] (Latin *rufus*, red)

rusty [20C]

sorrel-top [late 19C–1910s]

BLACK HAIRSTYLES

b.b. head [20C] (US Black; a boy with a tight-curled, knotty head, i.e. his hair resembles *b.b.* shot)

black-pepper brain/grains [1960s+] (W.I.; very short hair)

chemical head [1930s+] (US Black; hair that has been chemically straightened)

crinkle top [1970s] (US Black; a Black woman with unstraightened hair)

duckhead [1970s+] (US Black; a woman with short, nappy hair)

99 99 99 99 99 99 99 99 99 99 99 99 99 99 99 99 99 99 99 99 99 99 99

Ginger pubic hair

c.c.c. [1990s] (*c*opper *c*oloured *c*unt)

copper crack [1990s]

Davy Crockett's hat [1990s]

ginge minge [1990s]

rusty bucket [1990s]

66 66 66 66 66 66 66 66 66 66 66 66 66 66 66 66 66 66 66 66 66 66 66

gas-head [20C] (US Black; a person who has had their hair straightened)

kinky [1920s–40s] (US; a person with kinky hair, usu. a Black person)

kinkyhead [mid-19C–1950s] (US Black; a person with kinky hair)

nailhead [1970s] (US Black; an unattractive woman with short, tightly curled hair, resembling nail heads)

nappy-ass [1990s] (US Black teen; a person with tightly curled hair)

nappy head/naphead [1930s+] (US Black; a person with tightly curled hair)

nigger-head [1950s+] (W.I.; a Black person's naturally kinky hair)

nigger knots [20C] (W.I.; thick, tough Black hair)

short nail [1960s–70s] (US Black; a Black woman with short tightly curled hair)

tackhead/tackyhead [1960s–80s] (US Black; an unattractive woman with ill-kempt hair)

BUSHY, UNMANAGEABLE AND UNTIDY HAIR

brillohead [1980s+] (US campus; a person with very coarse hair)

bull's wool [1900s–40s] (Aus.; a young man with a mop of bushy hair)

bush-head [1980s] (US; a person with bushy hair)

cootie garage [1920s] (US; elaborately styled hair, lit. 'louse garage')

duck's butt [1970s] (US Black; a woman with unkempt hair)

messy attic [1950s] (US Black; hair in need of dressing)

pubehead [1980s+] (US teen; a person with short, curly hair)

sponge hair [1930s–50s] (US Black; hair that resists combing)

99 99 99 99 99 99 99 99 99 99 99 99 99 99 99 99 99 99 99 99 99 99

Long hair

hairhead [1970s+] (US; a long-haired man, a
   hippie)

where's your violin? [1940s+] (Aus.; said a
   person whose hair is seen as over-long, from
   the traditional identification of violin-playing
   with 'long-haired' intellectuals)

who robbed the barber? [late 19C–1910s] (said
   to a person whose hair is seen as over-long)

66 66 66 66 66 66 66 66 66 66 66 66 66 66 66 66 66 66 66 66 66 66

CURIOUS COIFFURES

bogbrush [1960s+] (a cropped, spiky haircut)

bokdrol [1970s+] (S Afr.; a hairstyle that resembles a pile of
   goat droppings; Afrikaans, 'goat droppings')

bugger's grips [20C] (orig. Naval; 'wings' of hair that adorn the
   temples of upper-class Englishmen, imputed by coarse rumour
   to be handholds for those who are positioning such partners
   ready for anal penetration)

duck's arse/duck's ass [1950s+] (a type of hairstyle, adopted by
   teddyboys and rockers, in which the back of the hair is turned
   upwards in a manner similar to a duck's tail)

farmer's haircut [20C] (US; a short haircut that leaves a white
   strip of skin showing between the bottom of the hair and the
   tanned portion of the neck)

idiot fringe [late 19C] (a contemporary hairstyle popular with
   girls and young women)

louse walk [mid-19C] (a back-hair parting)

pineapple cut [20C] (Aus.; a rough haircut, leaving the hair shaggy and irregular)

woof [1980s+] (US campus; an extremely unfashionable hairdo)

WIGS

divot [1930s]

fur [1950s–60s] (US Black; a woman's wig)

head-topper [mid-19C]

Indian rug [1960s+] (gay; a cheap wig done in braids)

Irish jig [20C] (rhy. sl.)

louse bag [late 18C–early 19C]

Mr Wigsby/wigsby/wigster [late 18C–early 19C] (a man wearing a wig)

noddle case [18C]

queer topping [late 17C–18C] (Und.; a second-rate or worn-out wig)

rat [1930s] (US Black)

rug [1940s+] (orig. US)

scandalous [late 17C–early 19C]

store-bought hair [1900s–30s] (US Black)

syrup [20C] (rhy. sl. *syrup of figs*)

toup [1950s+] (*toup*ee)

CHROME DOMES AND TURRET-TOPS: BALD MEN

bacon-bonce [20C]

baldfaced stag [mid-19C]

baldie/baldy [mid-19C+] (orig. US)

bladder of lard [mid–late 19C]

bonehead [1950s+]

chrome dome [20C] (orig. US)

cue-ball [1940s] (US)

curly [1910s+] (Aus.)

dry-head [1940s+] (W.I.)

Dutch cheese [19C] (i.e. their head resembles a round, shiny, wax-covered cheese such as Edam)

egghead [20C]

eggshell blonde [1940s+] (Aus./N.Z.)

ivory dome [20C]

cat-smellers

Marquis of Granby [mid-19C] (the British commander-in-chief at the Battle of Warburg (1760), whose hat and wig fell off as he led a cavalry charge)

onionhead [1930s–1970s] (US)

scaldy [20C] (Irish; ON *scalle*, a bald head)

skinhead [1950s+] (orig. US)

slap-head [1980s+]

turret-top [1940s] (US)

worf [1990s] (US teen; a bald man who combs his hair to hide the fact that he is bald)

FACIAL HAIR AND ITS OWNERS

FACIAL HAIR

bum-fluff [late 19C+] (adolescent facial hair)
cat-smellers [mid-19C] (US)
face fittings [20C] (Aus.)
face fungus [20C]
feathers [20C] (Aus.)
gritty whiskers [20C] (stubble)
Newgate ring [mid-19C] (a moustache and beard, but no
side-whiskers)
pez [1940s–50s] (US Black)
scraper [late 19C] (society; a short beard or moustache)

BEARDS

alfalfa [late 19C–1920s] (US)
chin-splitter [1900s] (US; a narrow goatee beard)

99 99 99 99 99 99 99 99 99 99 99 99 99 99 99 99 99 99 99 99 99 99 99

Bearded weirdies

bearded weirdie [1940s+]
beardie [late 19C+] (Aus.)
beaver [late 19C+]
billy-goat [19C]
frilled lizard [20C] (Aus.)
fungus(-features) [1920s+]
old whiskers [late 19C]

66 66 66 66 66 66 66 66 66 66 66 66 66 66 66 66 66 66 66 66 66 66 66

doormat [mid–late 19C] (a short cropped beard)

goat [late 19C+] (US; *goat*ee)

lace curtains [1910s–30s] (US)

mattress [1920s] (US)

muff [1940s–50s] (US)

muzzle [late 17C–early 19C]

soul patch [1990s] (a single tuft of hair worn beneath the lower lip)

spinach [late 19C+] (US)

MOUSTACHES

brush [1940s] (US Black)

coffee-strainer [20C] (US; a bushy moustache)

cookie-duster [1930s+] (US)

cowcatcher [mid-19C] (US; a full moustache)

cricket team [1940s–50s] (Aus.; a small, sparse moustache, i.e. it has only eleven (hairs) on each side)

cunt-tickler [1960s] (US)

99 99 99 99 99 99 99 99 99 99 99 99 99 99 99 99 99 99 99 99 99

Strangely weird: rhyming slang beards

Charley Sheard [1970s+]

just as I feared [20C] (from the Lewis Carroll limerick: 'There was an old man with a beard/Who said "It is just as I feared/Two owls and a hen/Four larks and a wren/Have all built their nests in my beard"')

strangely weird [20C]

66 66 66 66 66 66 66 66 66 66 66 66 66 66 66 66 66 66 66 66 66

face fins [20C] (a large moustache)

football team [1940s–50s] (Aus.; a small, sparse moustache, i.e. it has only eleven (hairs) on each side)

lip rug [1970s] (US Black)

misplaced eyebrow [1910s–20s] (US)

mouser [1930s–40s] (US)

mush/moosh [1960s]

pussy tickler [1940s–50s] (US Black)

soup-strainer [1930s+] (a large moustache)

stache [1940s+] (US campus)

third eyebrow [1990s]

walrus [1910s–50s] (a large, bushy moustache)

weeper [late 19C] (a long, sweeping moustache)

whip and lash [20C] (rhy. sl.)

SIDEBURNS

earguards [1940s] (Aus.; a short sideburn)

grogans [1910s–20s] (US; muttonchop side-whiskers)

hackles [late 19C–1920s]

lilacs [late 19C–1910s] (US)

louse traps [late 18C–mid-19C]

Piccadilly weepers [mid–late 19C] (long side-whiskers)

sausages [mid–late 19C]

side-levers [1920s+]

side-scrapers [late 19C] (short sideburns)

side-wings [late 19C–1900s]

sidies [1960s]

sluggers [late 19C+] (US; whiskers that extend from the ear to the chin)

🙊 🙊

Whiskerando and Van Dyke

Van Dyke [1960s+] (US gay; a lesbian with a
moustache on her upper lip, punning on
'dyke, lesbian' + the 17C portraitist Anthony
Van Dyke who was thus bearded)

whiskerando [early 19C–1920s] (a man who is
heavily whiskered)

whiskers [mid-19C+] (a term of address to a
noticeably bewhiskered man)

🙈 🙈

HANDICAPPED PEOPLE

DEAF AND BLIND PEOPLE

blink [1920s+] (US; a blind person)

dum-dum/dumb-dumb [1940s] (a deaf mute)

groper [late 17C–mid-19C] (a blind man)

groperess [mid-19C] (a blind woman)

puppy [mid-19C] (a blind man, from the blindness of
new-born puppies)

stumer [1910s+] (a deaf-mute, i.e. they keep 'shtum'))

CRIPPLES

basket case [1910s+] (orig. a quadriplegic, who, bereft of all
four limbs, would be carried around in a basket)

crip [1910s+]

gimper [1970s+] (US)

hodmandod [late 17C–19C] (a crippled or deformed person, lit. 'snail')

raspberry [1970s+] (rhy. sl. *raspberry* ripple)

scrammy [mid–late 19C] (Aus.; a person with a withered or defective hand or arm; dial. *scram*, withered)

strawberry (ripple) [1980s+] (rhy. sl.)

wingy [late 19C+] (Aus./US; a one-armed man)

THE LAME AND THE LIMPING

flat-wheel [20C] (US)

gammy [mid-19C]

hip at the clinch [20C] (Ulster)

Hopkins/Mr Hopkins [late 18C–19C]

hopping Giles [late 18C–19C] (St *Giles*, patron saint of cripples)

hopping Jesus [mid-19C–1920s]

hoppy [late 19C–1900s] (US)

limping Jesus [19C]

tip-an-pawn [1950s] (W.I.)

99 99 99 99 99 99 99 99 99 99 99 99 99 99 99 99 99 99 99 99 99 99

One-legged people

half-a-foot [1920s+] (W.I.; a person with a wooden leg)

limbie/limby [1910s+] (N.Z.)

peggy [20C]

peg-legger [1930s–40s]

timber-toe [late 18C–1900s] (a person with a wooden leg)

66 66 66 66 66 66 66 66 66 66 66 66 66 66 66 66 66 66 66 66 66 66

GROSSLY
SELF-INDULGENT

barfly and boozehound

GLUTTONS

belly-gut [mid-16C–mid-18C] (a greedy, lazy person)

belly-paunch [mid-16C–17C]

chow hound [1910s+]

eating midden [19C] (Scot.; lit. 'eating dunghill')

fang artist [1970s+] (Aus.)

fresser [20C] (US; Yiddish *fress*, to eat)

gannet [1920s+] (orig. naut.)

gobble-gut [early–mid-17C]

gorb/gorby-guts [late 19C+] (Irish)

gorge [19C]

greedy-gut/greedy-guts [16C+]

grubber [19C]

gully-gut [mid-16C–19C; 1930s+]

guts [late 17C+]

hash hound [1910s–40s] (US)

hungarian [early 17C]

long-mouth [20C] (W.I.)

oinker [1980s+] (US)

pig [mid-16C+]

99 99 99 99 99 99 99 99 99 99 99 99 99 99 99 99 99 99 99 99 99 99 99

Propping up the bar

barfly [20C] (orig. US)

bar-hog [1930s] (US)

barprop [1980s] (US)

barstool jockey [1980s]

66 66 66 66 66 66 66 66 66 66 66 66 66 66 66 66 66 66 66 66 66 66

pig dog [1980s+] (US campus)
scruncher [late 19C+]
stodger [late 19C–1920s]
sweet-lips [late 19C–1900s]

DRINKERS AND DRUNKARDS

alko [20C]
alky [1950s+]
bloat [mid-19C–1910s] (US)
boozer [late 19C+]
boozy [1920s+] (Anglo-Irish)
bottle-boy [1930s–40s] (US)
dipso [late 19C–1970s] (*dipso*maniac)
draftpak [20C] (Scot.)
dredge-head [1970s+]

greedy-guts

99 99 99 99 99 99 99 99 99 99 99 99 99 99 99 99 99 99 99 99 99

Four drunk women

fairy [19C] (a drunken old hag)

f.o.b.b. [1970s] (US; *f*ucked *o*ut *b*oozy *b*itch)

haybag [19C+] (US; a slovenly, drunken, fat old woman)

lady from the ground up [late 19C] (US; a woman who is drunk and disorderly)

66 66 66 66 66 66 66 66 66 66 66 66 66 66 66 66 66 66 66 66 66

dronkie [1930s+] (S Afr.; Afrikaans *dronk*, drunk)

drunken piece [1910s–20s]

drunkie/drunkman [1950s+] (orig. W.I.)

elbow bender [20C]

fish [1910s+] (US)

heavy hitter [1980s] (US; i.e. they 'hit' the drink)

hoisting engineer [1910s–30s] (US)

hollow leg [1920s+] (orig. US)

juicer [1960s+] (US)

oiler [1910s; 1960s+] (*oil* = alcohol)

old soak [early 19C+]

piss artist [1940s+]

pisspot [1920s+]

piss-tank [20C]

royal boozer [mid-19C–1930s]

shicker/shick/shicka/shikkar/shikker/shikkur [1910s+] (Yiddish *shikor*, drunk)

skimisher/skimmisher [20C] (usu. tramp; Shelta *skimis*, to drink)

snorter [1930s]

soak [early 19C+]

sod [1920s+] (US campus)

souse [20C]

stew [mid-18C+] (US)

stewie [1940s] (US Black)

still [late 19C] (US; a quiet drunkard)

tanker [1930s]

waste case [1980s+] (US campus)

waste product [1980s+] (US campus)

99 99 99 99 99 99 99 99 99 99 99 99 99 99 99 99 99 99 99 99 99 99

Gin-soaks and rumpots: spirit-drinkers

brandy-face [late 17C–early 19C]

brandy-shunter [late 19C–1900s]

dog's nose [mid–late 19C] (a whisky drunkard)

gin-bottle [late 19C]

gin-soak [1930s+] (US)

pegger [late 19C] (a drinker of brandy and soda)

rum-dum/rum-dumb [1930s+] (US)

rumhead [late 19C+]

rum hound [1910s–50s]

rummer/rummarian [1940s] (W.I.)

rumpot [1930s+]

soul [late 17C–mid-18C] (a brandy drunkard)

waterman [1950s] (W.I.; *water* = white rum)

66 66 66 66 66 66 66 66 66 66 66 66 66 66 66 66 66 66 66 66 66 66

99 99 99 99 99 99 99 99 99 99 99 99 99 99 99 99 99 99 99 99 99

Grape-cats and plonk-dots:
wine-drinkers

grape-cat [1940s] (US Black)
plonk-dot [1910s+] (Aus.)
plonko [1960s+] (Aus.)
vintner [mid-17C]
winebag [late 19C]
wine-dot [1950s+] (Aus.)
winehead [1960s+] (US)
wino [1910s+] (orig. US)

66 66 66 66 66 66 66 66 66 66 66 66 66 66 66 66 66 66 66 66 66

'HOUNDS' AND 'HEADS'

barhound [1920s+]
booze-head [1960s–70s] (US)
booze hound [1920s+] (US)
bottlehead [mid-17C–late 18C]
brewhound [1980s+] (US campus)
jarhead [1980s]
jughead [1940s–70s]
juice-head/juice-hound [1920s+] (US)
liquorhead [1920s+] (US)
lush-head [1930s–60s] (US)
lush hound [1930s–40s]
piss-head [20C]
sauce-hound [1940s+] (US)
slophead [20C] (Aus./US)

TAVERN-DRINKERS OF GOOD OLDE ENGLAND

afternoon man [early 17C+]

alecan [late 19C–1910s]

artilleryman [late 19C–1910s] (i.e. their talk and actions are 'explosive')

bang-pitcher [mid–late 17C]

bib-all-night [early 17C]

Billy born drunk [late 19C–1900s] (a life-long drunkard)

borachio/borarco [late 17C–early 19C]

borrachio/borracho [17C–19C] (Spanish *borracho*, a drunkard)

brewer's horse [late 16C+]

bubber [17C–18C] (Latin *bibere*, to drink)

bum-boozer [late 19C–1900s]

common sewer [19C] (i.e. everything is poured into them)

cupman [mid–late 19C]

English bearer [late 18C] (a red-faced drunkard, from the red of the St George's Cross)

🙶 🙶

Beerskins and hop-heads: beer-drinkers

beer barrel [1940s]

beer-eater [late 19C–1900s]

beerhead [1970s] (US)

beerskin [1990s] (Aus.)

corn [mid-19C+] (US)

hop-head [20C] (US/N.Z.)

🙶 🙶

🙶🙶🙶🙶🙶🙶🙶🙶🙶🙶🙶🙶🙶🙶🙶🙶🙶🙶🙶🙶🙶🙶

Alderman Lushington and friends

Alderman Lushington [early 19C] (from the brewer *Lushington*)

lush [mid-19C+]

lushing-man [mid-19C–1900s]

Lushington/lushington [19C]

lush merchant [late 19C+] (Aus.)

lushwell [1960s+] (US)

lushy/lushie [1940s] (US Black)

🙷🙷🙷🙷🙷🙷🙷🙷🙷🙷🙷🙷🙷🙷🙷🙷🙷🙷🙷🙷🙷🙷

ensign-bearer [mid-17C–early 19C] (a red-faced drunkard)

five or seven [late 19C] (from poss. sentences for drunkenness, a *five*-shilling fine or *seven* days in prison)

fuddlecap [late 17C–18C]

jerry wag [mid-19C] (*jerry* = tavern)

love-pot [19C]

maltworm [early 18C]

nase nab/nazy nab [late 17C–early 19C] (lit. 'red face')

old soaker [late 18C–early 19C]

old toast [late 17C–early 18C]

one of the faithful [17C]

piss-maker [late 18C–early 19C]

pot-walloper [late 19C]

ring pigger [mid–late 16C]

rinse pitcher [mid-16C]

sink [mid-19C–1910s]

spewterer [mid-17C]

Aristocrats of the bottle

admiral of the narrow seas [early 17C–mid-19C] (a drunkard who vomits over his neighbour at table)

ale-knight [late 16C–17C]

master of misrule [mid-17C] (an uproarious drunkard)

master of the novelties [mid-19C] (a playful drunkard)

knight of the brush and moon [mid-19C]

sportsman for liquor [late 19C–1900s] (a dedicated drinker)

surveyor of the highways [late 18C–early 19C] (someone so drunk that they fall over)

tenant in tail [mid-17C] (an affectionate drunkard)

Two drunken 'Scotsmen'

queen of Scotch [1970s] (US gay; an alcoholic gay man)

whisky-bottle [late 19C] (a Scottish drunkard)

sponge [late 16C+]
swill tub [early 18C–early 19C]
tickle-pitcher [late 17C–18C]
wet hand/wet 'un [late 19C]

THINK AUSTRALIAN, DRINK AUSTRALIAN

beer-chewer [late 19C+] (Aus.)
booze artist [1920s+] (orig. Aus.)
booze-fighter [1910s+] (Aus./US)
booze-rooster [1960s] (N.Z.)
boozician [late 19C–1930s] (Aus.)
boozington/Mr Boozington [mid-19C–1910s] (Aus.)
grog artist [1990s] (N.Z.)
nebo [1960s] (Aus.) (*ineb*riated)
pisso [1940s+] (Aus.)
squiff [1920s+] (Aus.)
swipington/swippington [20C] (Aus.)

99 99 99 99 99 99 99 99 99 99 99 99 99 99 99 99 99 99 99 99 99 99

Five inadequate drinkers

one-pot screamer [1950s+] (Aus.; a person
who cannot drink without becoming
obstreperously drunk)
two-pot screamer [1950s+] (Aus.)
middy screamer [1950s+] (Aus.)
pint screamer [1950s+] (Aus.)
schooner screamer [1950s+] (Aus.)

66 66 66 66 66 66 66 66 66 66 66 66 66 66 66 66 66 66 66 66 66

tid [1920s+] (Aus.; *tid*dly)

tiger [20C] (Aus.; i.e. they have a 'bite')

EXTREME DRUNKARDS AND ALCOHOLIC VAGRANTS

alky stiff [1910s] (US; an alcoholic tramp)

bag lady [1970s+] (orig. US)

belch [1930s] (US; a drunken vagrant)

bottle baby [1920s+] (orig. US; an alcoholic tramp who has become insane and whose mental age is that of an infant)

brother-where-are-you? [1920s] (a visually impaired drunk)

cot-case [1930s+] (Aus./N.Z.; an alcoholic who is confined to bed)

gin-and-tatters [late 19C] (a heavy drinker whose clothing has been reduced to rags)

sclerry [1990s] (a terminal alcoholic, i.e. one who has *scler*osis of the liver)

soakapee [1940s] (W.I.; an alcoholic who fouls their clothes)

speck bum [20C] (a very decrepit alcoholic tramp)

stew bum [20C] (a down-and-out alcoholic)

stinko [1930s–40s] (US; an alcoholic tramp)

SMOKERS

butt fiend [20C] (US)

chimney [late 19C]

coffin-dodger [1900s] (US campus)

esquire of the pipe [17C]

Fag-ash Lil [late 19C+] (a woman who smokes heavily)

fag-hag [1950s] (Can.; a woman who smokes excessively)

gentleman of the whiffe [17C]

hard-up [mid-19C+] (a smoker of cigar or cigarette ends)

knight of the vapour [17C]

Norma Jean Nicotine [1950s–60s] (camp gay)

smoke-eater [1930s+] (US)

DRUG ADDICTS

a.d. [1930s–70s] (US drugs; *a*ddicted to *d*rugs)

all star [1980s+] (drugs; a user of multiple drugs)

back-door artist [1940s–50s] (US Black; a drug addict who preys on fellow addicts for money or drugs)

burnout [1960s+] (drugs)

crispy [1980s+] (US teen; someone whose faculties are impaired by an excess of drug-taking)

99 99 99 99 99 99 99 99 99 99 99 99 99 99 99 99 99 99 99 99 99 99

Needle fiends: intravenous drug-users

joy-popper [1930s+] (drugs; an occasional injector of narcotics)

mainliner/mainline [1930s+] (orig. US drugs)

needle artist [1920s+] (US drugs)

needle fiend [1920s+] (US drugs)

needle jabber/needle pumper [1920s+] (US drugs)

needle man/needleman [1920s–50s] (drugs)

pin-jabber [1920s+] (drugs)

popper [1960s] (drugs)

railroader [1970s+] (drugs)

66 66 66 66 66 66 66 66 66 66 66 66 66 66 66 66 66 66 66 66 66

dope fiend [1950s+] (drugs)

dopehead [1900s–60s] (drugs)

doper [1960s+]

druggie/druggy [1960s+]

drughead [1960s] (US)

dustie [1950s] (US drugs; *dust* = heroin/cocaine/phencyclidine)

fiender [1990s] (US)

glass eyes [1940s–50s] (drugs)

gowster [1930s–60s] (US drugs)

hop/hops [late 19C+]

hop fiend [late 19C–1920s]

hypo [20C] (drugs)

joy-rider [1930s–60s] (US drugs; an occasional narcotic drug user)

juggle/juggler [1960s+] (drugs; an addict who sells drugs to help finance their own addiction)

monkey

junk buzzard [1970s] (US; *junk* = opiate)

junkhead [1960s–70s] (US drugs)

junko [1970s+] (US)

kite [1970s+] (US campus; i.e. they are always 'high as a *kite*')

lifer [1960s+] (US; an addict for *life*)

loadie [1970s+] (US campus; i.e. they are always 'loaded')

monkey [1970s] (US Black/drugs)

monkey-meat [1950s] (drugs; a heavily intoxicated drug user)

mooch [1940s–50s] (drugs)

narco [1950s+] (US drugs; *narco*tics)

period hitter [1960s] (drugs; an occasional drug user)

saffers/saffron [1990s] (a person who is very intoxicated by a drug)

stoner [1970s+]

student [1930s–50s] (drugs; an inexperienced or novice drug-taker)

toxic waste dump [1980s+] (US campus)

99 99 99 99 99 99 99 99 99 99 99 99 99 99 99 99 99 99 99 99 99

Downheads: depressant users

down freak [1970s+] (drugs)

down head [1960s+] (drugs)

ludehead [1970s+] (US drugs; a habitual user of methaqualone, or other depressant drug, from the brandname *Quaalude*, manufactured until 1983)

66 66 66 66 66 66 66 66 66 66 66 66 66 66 66 66 66 66 66 66 66 66

99 99 99 99 99 99 99 99 99 99 99 99 99 99 99 99 99 99 99 99 99

Speedfreaks: stimulant users

meth freak [1960s–70s] (US drugs)

meth-head [1960s+] (drugs)

Miss Flash [mid-20C] (camp gay)

pill-head [1960s+] (drugs)

pill-popper [1930s+] (drugs)

pinhead [1960s]

speed freak [1960s+] (drugs)

66 66 66 66 66 66 66 66 66 66 66 66 66 66 66 66 66 66 66 66 66 66

wall-banger [1960s+] (US teen/drugs; someone who is so intoxicated by drugs that they cannot walk straight)

weekend habit [1970s+] (drugs; an irregular drug user)

zone/zoner [1980s+] (US drugs)

zonker [1950s+]

HEROIN ADDICTS

birdcage hype [1930s–50s] (US drugs; the lowest class of heroin addict)

geezer [1960s+] (US)

greasy junkie [1960s] (US drugs; a heroin addict who maintains their own supplies by running errands for dealers or by prostitution)

horse-head/horse jockey [1950s] (US; *horse* = heroin)

hype [1920s+] (US drugs/Und.; a heroin or morphine addict)

jones [1960s+] (US drugs)

junkette [1960s+] (drugs; a young female heroin addict)

junk hawk [1970s+] (US drugs; a heroin user whose entire existence centres on the drug)

junkie/junky [1920s+] (drugs)

scag hag/skag hag [1960s+] (gay; someone who enjoys associating with heroin addicts)

shitbird [1950s+]

smack freak [1970s+] (drugs)

smackhead [20C] (drugs)

spook [1900s–10s] (drugs)

tecato [1960s+] (US drugs; a morphine or heroin addict; Spanish *tecata*, heroin)

OPIUM ADDICTS

barber's cat [1930s] (drugs; an emaciated opium addict)

fiend [late 19C+]

gong-kicker/gong-beater [1930s–70s] (US)

gowhead [1930s] (US; *gow* = opium)

hop-fighter [1910s] (US drugs; *hop* = opium)

hop jockey [20C]

ice-cream eater [late 19C–1930s] (US drugs; a person who uses opium occasionally rather than being addicted to it)

pill cooker [1920s] (drugs)

pipe-fiend [1910s–30s] (US)

puffer [1970s+] (drugs)

COCAINE ADDICTS

base-head [1970s+]

coke fiend [1910s+] (drugs)

cokehead [1920s+] (drugs)

cokehound [1930s] (drugs)

Cokie Joe [1930s–50s]

cokie/cokey [1910s+] (drugs)

happy duster [1910s+] (orig. US drugs; *happy dust* = cocaine)

joneser [1980s+] (US)

sleighrider [1900s–50s] (US drugs; punning on 'snow', i.e. cocaine)

sniffer [1920s+] (drugs)

snow bird [1910s–60s] (drugs)

CRACK ADDICTS

beamer [1980s+] (drugs)

carpet patrol [1980s+] (drugs; smokers of crack cocaine searching the floor for any grains of the drug they may have dropped)

chickenhead [1990s] (US teen; from the bobbing of the user's head over the crack pipe stem and their 'squawking' when intoxicated)

crack bitch [1990s] (Black; a female crack addict)

cracker jacks [1980s+](drugs)

crack-head [1980s+]

garbage heads [1980s+] (drugs; users who buy crack cocaine from street dealers instead of cooking it themselves)

geekers [1980s+] (US drugs; *geek* = a mixture of crack cocaine and marijuana)

gick monster [1980s+] (drugs)

hit head [1980s+]

hitter [1980s+] (drugs)

hubba pigeon [1980s+] (US drugs; a user of crack cocaine reduced to searching for small pieces of the drug, left lying on the floor after a police raid; rhy. sl. *hubba, I am back* = crack)

klingon [1980s+] (drugs)

non-toucher [1980s+] (drugs; a smoker of crack cocaine who recoils from physical contact while experiencing the drug's effects)

pipe-head [1980s+] (drugs)

piper [1990s] (drugs)

pipero [1980s+] (drugs)

pullers [1980s+] (drugs; users of crack cocaine who pull at parts of their bodies excessively)

rock star [1980s+] (drugs; a woman who trades sex for crack or money to buy crack)

smokehead [1980s+]

thirst monster [1980s+] (drugs)

tweaker [1980s+] (drugs; a crack cocaine user searching desperately for drugs after a police raid)

zombie [1970s+] (US Black)

MARIJUANA USERS

bo-bo jockey [1940s] (US drugs)

cadet [1970s+] (drugs; i.e. 'space cadet')

Cap'n Toke [1980s+] (US campus)

chronic [1980s+] (drugs; a person who smokes cannabis everyday)

dirt-devil [1980s+] (US drugs; an individual who, on most occasions, has poor-grade dope)

goof [1930s–60s] (US)

grasshead [1960s] (drugs)

hash-head [1950s+] (US)

hay burner [1930s+] (US)

hayhead [1940s–50s] (US)

James Bong [1980s+] (US drugs; the person in a group who is the most intoxicated or most visibly intoxicated by cannabis)

Mr Warner [1960s–70s] (drugs)

m.u. [1960s–70s] (drugs; *m*arijuana *u*ser)

mugglehead [1920s–70s] (US drugs)

muggler [1930s] (drugs)

muggles/muggie [1920s–70s] (orig. US drugs)

pothead [1960s+] (drugs)

puller [1950s] (US drugs)

reefer [1920s+] (drugs)

roach bender [1930s] (drugs)

roker/rooker [late 19C+] (S Afr.; Dutch *roken*, to smoke)

space cadet [1970s+] (drugs; a heavy user of cannabis)

tea-head [1940s–60s] (drugs)

tea-man [1930s–50s] (US)

twister [1930s–50s] (drugs)

viper [1930s–50s] (drugs)

weedhead [1950s+] (drugs)

space cadet

IDLERS AND LAZY PEOPLE

ass-scratcher [1930s] (US)

backseat driver [1960s+] (rhy. sl. 'skiver')

baker [mid–late 19C] (US Und.; the image is of a *baker* waiting for dough to rise)

beat [mid-19C–1930s]

blow off [1980s] (US campus)

bludger [1940s] (Aus.)

charge [20C] (Irish)

coaster [late 19C–1950s+] (Aus.)

coffee cooler [19C]

crow-eater [late 19C+] (Aus./S Afr.)

dead ass/dead butt [1950s+] (US)

deadbeat [mid-19C+] (orig. US)

deadhead [20C]

do-little [19C+] (US)

doodler [20C]

dress-and-breath [1920s–30s] (US Black; a very lazy woman, i.e. the most she will do is get *dressed* and *breathe*)

dying duck in a thunderstorm [late 19C+]

fart-off [1940s+] (US)

feather-merchant [1930s+] (orig. US milit.; i.e. they do not 'pull their weight')

flunk [late 19C+] (US)

fuck-off/fug-off [1940s+]

funker [mid-18C+]

goldbrick/goldbricker [mid-19C+] (US)

goof-off [1940s+] (US)

ha'porth of liveliness [late 19C]

hard bargain [mid-19C+]

heavy-arse [late 19C+]

Houdini [20C] (US; Harry *Houdini* the US escape artist)

house-plant [1910s+] (US)

jerk-off [1930s+] (US)

❞ ❞

Loiterers

Collins Street squatter [1960s] (Aus.; a youth who gossips and wastes time in bars and cafés, from *Collins Street* in Melbourne)

corner boy [late 19C+] (orig. US)

corner-ender [1920s+]

corner man [late 19C] (UK Und.)

cowboy [1920s+] (US; a youth who gossips and wastes time in drugstores)

crawler [early 19C+]

dock-walloper [mid-19C+] (US; an idler who frequents the waterfront)

drugstore cowboy [1920s+] (US; a youth who gossips and wastes time in drugstores)

hogger [late 19C+] (Irish; a street-corner idler)

mall rat/mallie [1980s+] (US; a young person who hangs around shopping malls)

Yarra banker [late 19C+] (Aus.; an idler on

❝ ❝

lag(-a-bag)/lag-lost [20C] (Ulster)

lard(-ass) [1930s+] (US)

lassitudinarian [late 19C]

lazybones [late 16C+]

lazyboots [19C]

lazy-legs [19C]

legume [1980s+] (US campus; French *légume*, a vegetable)

limer [1970s+] (W.I.)

loafer [19C] (orig. US)

lollop [late 19C]

London fog [1960s+] (Aus.; a manual worker who does not perform their share of the work, i.e. they 'will not lift')

lump [1980s+] (US campus)

maggot [1980s+] (US campus)

miker [late 19C+]

moegoe [1960s+] (S Afr.; Afrikaans)

mooch [mid-19C+]

moocher [mid-19C+]

neversweat [19C+]

no load [1920s+] (US)

office worker [20C] (rhy. sl. 'shirker')

Paddy Ward's pig [mid-18C–mid-19C]

piker [1940s+] (orig. US)

pointer [mid-19C+] (Aus./N.Z.)

poopbutt/pootbutt [1960s+] (US Black)

prosser [mid–late 19C]

quisby [mid-19C]

sack artist [1940s+] (US)

sack rat [1940s+] (US)

screw-off [1940s+] (US)

shif-man [1950s] (W.I.)

skiver [1910s+]

sleeper [1970s] (US campus)

slob [mid-19C+] (orig. US)

slobber-slobber [1950s] (W.I.)

sloth [1980s+]

slousher [1900s] (N.Z.)

slowpoke [mid-19C+] (US)

slug [1980s+]

sooner [late 19C+] (Aus.; i.e. they would *sooner* do nothing)

spinebasher [1940s+] (Aus.)

taildraft [20C] (Ulster)

waffles [mid-19C]

wanker [late 19C+]

SEXUALLY DEPRAVED

HETEROSEXUALS

b.m. [1950s–60s] (S Afr. gay; *b*aby *m*aker)

breeder [1970s+] (gay)

citizen [1940s+] (US)

civilian [1940s+] (US)

commoner [1940s–60s] (US)

jam [1960s+] (gay; *just a m*an)

Norma [1940s–60s] (US)

normal [1950s–60s] (gay)

one-way [1960s] (US gay)

peasant [1940s+] (US)

pussy pusher [1950s+] (US)

square [1950s+] (gay)

straight [1950s+] (orig. gay)

straight arrow [1950s+] (US)

straightnik [1950s–60s] (US)

PHWOOAAR!: WOMEN AS SEX OBJECTS

bag of snakes [1950s+] (Can.)

beef [20C] (W.I./Jam.)

brush [1930s+] (Aus./N.Z.)

bush [1920s+] (Aus.)

cottontail [1960s+] (US)

chicken dinner [1940s] (US Black)

crumpet [1930s+] (W.I.)

fleshpot [1970s+] (US Black)

fluff [1910s+]

freshwater trout [1940s] (US Black)

funbag [20C]

💕 💕

Heterosexuals: a specialist gay lexicon

Carlotta [1940s–60s] (camp gay; a heterosexual who interferes in the gay world, either as a homophobe or as a 'tourist')

cleavage queen [1940s–60s] (gay; a woman with a prominent cleavage)

Daisy Dumpling [1950s–60s] (camp; a middle-class, heterosexual housewife)

fag-hag [1940s+] (orig. US; a heterosexual woman who courts and indulges the company of male homosexuals)

fish [1940s+] (US gay; a heterosexual woman)

fruit fly [1940s–60s] (US; a heterosexual woman who enjoys the company of homosexual rather than heterosexual men)

grand duchess [1950s+] (a heterosexual woman who occupies pride of place in a homosexual male coterie)

half-iron [1940s+] (a man who enjoys the company but not the specific predilections of homosexuals; rhy. sl. *iron hoof*, poof)

sappho daddy-o [1950s] (US gay; a heterosexual man who socializes extensively with lesbians)

" "

gig [late 17C–18C] (i.e. she is 'ridden')

growl [1940s+] (Aus.; rhy. sl. *growl and grunt*, cunt)

grummet [1960s+] (orig. N.Z.)

head [1930s+] (US)

hogans [1960s+] (US)

hole [1940s+] (US)

mink [late 19C; 1960s+]

muslin [early 19C–1920s]

number [late 19C+] (orig. US)

patootie [1920s+] (US)

placket [17C] (the slit at the top of an apron or petticoat, facilitating dressing and undressing)

99 99 99 99 99 99 99 99 99 99 99 99 99 99 99 99 99 99 99 99 99 99

Arm candy

all tits and teeth [20C] (a superficial young woman with a large smile and large breasts)

arm candy [1990s] (a pretty girl whose role is merely to adorn the arm of her male companion)

bowhead [1980s+] (US campus; a superficial young woman who cares only for her looks, dress and general image)

Fifi [1980s+] (US campus; a sexy but superficial young woman)

Heather [1980s+] (US campus; a superficial young woman, pretty but lacking in intelligence)

66 66 66 66 66 66 66 66 66 66 66 66 66 66 66 66 66 66 66 66 66 66

99 99 99 99 99 99 99 99 99 99 99 99 99 99 99 99 99 99 99 99 99 99 99

White and dark meat

dark meat [late 19C] (Black people seen as sex objects)

white meat [1930s+] (US Black/W.I.; a White woman seen as a sex object)

66 66 66 66 66 66 66 66 66 66 66 66 66 66 66 66 66 66 66 66 66 66

poon [1920s+]

poontang [1920s+]

pork [18C–1900s]

pouch [1940s–50s] (Aus.)

poundcake [1930s+] (US)

prat/pratte/pratt [20C]

punda/pundah [1980s+] (S Afr.)

pussy [20C]

quiff [20C]

ride [1930s+] (orig. Irish)

rort/roart/wrought [1970s+] (Aus./N.Z.)

skirt [late 19C+]

slithery [1930s+]

snatch [1920s+]

spanners [1950s+] (Aus.; i.e. she 'tightens your nuts')

split [1910s+] (Aus./US)

split-whisker [1940s+] (Aus.)

spoofie [1970s] (Aus.; *spoof* = semen)

spunk bubble [1970s] (Aus.)

spurter [1990s]

Bits and pieces

bit [1920s–50s]

bit for the finger [19C]

bit/little bit of all right [late 19C+]

bit of brush [1950s]

bit of crackling [1940s+]

bit of cuff [late 19C–1900s]

bit of fluff [20C]

bit of goods [mid-19C+]

bit of meat [early 18C+]

bit of muslin [mid–late 19C]

bit of stuff [late 19C+]

bit of tickle [1920s+]

bit of tit [1920s+]

downy bit [late 19C]

hairy bit [mid-19C+]

piece of arse/piece of ass [1910s+]

piece of flesh/piece of skin [20C] (W.I.)

piece of magnolia [1960s+] (Can.)

piece of meat [20C]

piece of mutton [late 17C–early 19C]

piece of skirt [17C+]

piece of tail [1940s+] (US)

stukkie [1970s+] (S Afr.)
tail [mid-19C+]
tart [mid-19C+]
tot [1990s+]
tottie/totty [late 19C+]
whisker [1940s+] (Aus.)

SIX CENTURIES OF SLAPPERS

LATE MEDIEVAL TICKLE-TAIL
tickle-tail [late 15C–late 18C]

ELIZABETHAN BAGGAGE
baggage [16C+]
mutton [early 16C+]
twigger [mid-16C–late 17C] (a ewe that is a prolific breeder)
leather [mid-16C+]
hobby horse [late 16C–early 17C] (i.e. she is 'ridden')
pug [late 16C–early 18C]

hobby horse

17TH-CENTURY GOBBLEPRICKS

flap [early–mid-17C] (lit. 'vagina')

gobbleprick [late 17C–18C]

pugnasty [late 17C–18C]

strum [late 17C–18C] (*strum*pet)

tom rig [late 17C–18C]

tickle-toby [late 17C–19C]

HANOVERIAN LIGHT HEELS

barber's chair [18C] (i.e. she is 'used by all-comers')

light heels [early 18C–19C]

horns-to-sell [18C–mid-19C] (a promiscuous wife; *horns* = cuckoldry)

athanasian wench [late 18C] (from the *Athanasian* Creed, which begins *quicumque vult*, whoever wishes)

short-heeled wench/short heels [late 18C–early 19C]

VICTORIAN POKES

grubber [19C]

hot beef [19C]

hot mutton [19C]

meat [19C]

pintle-fancier/pintle-ranger [early 19C–1900s] (lit. 'penis-fancier')

lift skirts [mid-19C]

pullet-squeezer [mid–late 19C] (a woman who prefers younger partners)

loose bit of goods [late 19C]

banbury [late 19C–1910s] ('she rides a cock horse to Banbury Cross')

pig meat [late 19C–1940s] (US Black)

bag [late 19C+] (US)
poke [late 19C+]
tart [late 19C+]

20TH-CENTURY FREE-FOR-ALLS
alley bat [20C] (US)
charity girl [20C] (US)
floozie/floosie [20C] (orig. US)
free-for-all [20C] (US)
hot-bot [20C]
jamette [20C] (W.I.; French sl. *jeanette*, a whore)
letching-piece [20C]
teazy-whacker [20C] (Irish; *teazle* = vagina)
two-bit hustler [20C]

EDWARDIAN NYMPHOS
dirty neck [1910s–60s] (US)
notch [1910s+] (US; lit. 'vagina')
nymph [1910s+] (*nymph*omaniac)
nympho [1910s+] (orig. US; *nympho*maniac)

JAZZ-AGE ALLEY CATS
hot pot [1920s–30s] (US Black; i.e. she is always 'on the boil')
charity ass [1920s–50s]
party girl [1920s–60s]
alley cat [1920s+] (US)
roundheel/roundheeler/roundheels [1920s+] (US)
tramp [1920s+] (orig. US)

DEPRESSION-ERA HOT BOXES

thoroughfare [1930s] (US Black)

zipper [1930s] (US)

jump [1930s–40s] (US)

streetcleaner [1930s–50s] (US Black)

wolverine [1930s–50s]

hot box [1930s–60s] (US)

charity dame [1930s+] (Aus.)

SLAPPERS OF THE AGE OF SWING

stuk [1940s] (S Afr.; Afrikaans, 'piece')

jing-bang [1940s+] (W.I.)

leg [1940s+] (US)

leggo-beast [1940s+] (W.I.; lit. 'wild beast')

charity cunt [1940s+] (US)

charity worker [1940s+] (US)

dirt-bag [1940s+] (orig. US)

wolfess [1940s+]

99 99 99 99 99 99 99 99 99 99 99 99 99 99 99 99 99 99 99 99 99 99

Dirty Gertie and friends

Dirty Gertie [1920s–40s] (US)

Good-time Jane [1940s–60s] (US)

Lady Hot-bot [20C]

Little Miss Roundheels [1950s+] ('she's
always falling on her back')

Melvyn Bragg [1990s] (rhy. sl. 'slag')

Sal Slappers [late 19C] (lit. 'Sally the Slapper')

66 66 66 66 66 66 66 66 66 66 66 66 66 66 66 66 66 66 66 66 66 66

ROCK 'N' ROLL SCRUBBERS

goer [1950s+]

lossie [1950s+] (S Afr.; lit. 'loose one')

punchboard [1950s+] (US campus)

puta [1950s+] (Hisp. Amer.; Spanish, 'whore')

scrubber [1950s+]

slack [1950s+] (W.I.; i.e. she is 'loose')

slag [1950s+] (lit. 'slack person')

sleepytime girl [1950s+] (US)

SIXTIES GIN AND FUCK-ITS

gin and fuck-it [1960s] (a woman, usu. an au pair or tourist, who can be seduced for the price of a drink in a pub)

chicken-head [1960s+] (US Black)

dirty leg [1960s+] (US)

freak [1960s+] (US Black)

low rent [1960s+] (US campus)

mattressback [1960s+] (US)

99 99 99 99 99 99 99 99 99 99 99 99 99 99 99 99 99 99 99 99 99 99

Three highly offensive Australianisms

box of assorted creams [1990s] (Aus.; *box* = vagina, *cream* = semen)

turtle [20C] (orig. Aus.; 'once she's on her back, she's fucked')

walk-up fuck [20C] (Aus.; i.e. a man need only *walk up* and ask)

66 66 66 66 66 66 66 66 66 66 66 66 66 66 66 66 66 66 66 66 66

paper doll [1960s+] (rhy. sl. 'moll')

pig [1960s+] (US campus)

sloppy seconds [1960s+] (a woman who has had sex with one man and is about to have sex with another)

SEVENTIES SCUZZBAGS

hoozie/hosie [1970s] (US; *ho* + fl*oozie*)

hosebag [1970s] (orig. US campus)

sweat hog [1970s] (US campus)

lust dog [1970s+] (US campus)

mount [1970s+] (US Black)

pump [1970s+]

scuzz [1970s+] (orig. US teen)

scuzzbag [1970s+] (US campus)

slapper [1970s+]

town pump [1970s+]

whore [1970s+]

EIGHTIES SLEAZOIDS

butter [1980s+] (US Black; lit. 'vagina')

dickhound [1980s+] (US Black)

99 99 99 99 99 99 99 99 99 99 99 99 99 99 99 99 99 99 99 99 99 99

Bicycles for riding

bicycle [1940s+]

bike [1940s+]

motorcycle [1950s] (US Black)

town bicycle [1920s+] (orig. Aus.)

town bike [1940s+]

66 66 66 66 66 66 66 66 66 66 66 66 66 66 66 66 66 66 66 66 66 66

Women of easy virtue

cinch [1940s+] (US)
easy game [late 19C+]
easy lay [1930s+]
easy make [1940s+] (US)
easy mort [mid-17C–early 18C]
easy ride [1980s+] (US)
easy stuff [1980s+] (US)
pushover [1920s+]

66 66 66 66 66 66 66 66 66 66 66 66 66 66 66 66 66 66 66 66 66 66

hoochie/hootchie/hootchy mama
  [1980s+] (US Black)
hose (queen) [1980s+] (US campus;
  hose = penis)
hyperdrive whore [1980s+] (US
  campus)
psycho hose beast [1980s+]
skeeza/skeeger/skeezer [1980s+]
  (orig. US Black; lit. 'frolicker')
sleaze [1980s+] (US campus)
sleazo/sleazoid [1980s+] (US campus)
slut-puppy [1980s+] (US campus)
third-legger [1980s+] (US Black; *third
  leg* = penis)
wench [1980s+] (US campus)
whoredog [1980s+] (US campus)

easy mort

   dildo [1990s] (Irish)

   garden tool [1990s] (US campus; punning on 'hoe')

   hosebeast [1990s] (US)

   shed [1990s] ('a place to put your tools')

   slorch [1990s] (US campus; *sl*ut + wh*ore* + bit*ch*)

   slusher [1990s] (i.e. she's always damp with desire)

   spunk-bucket [1990s]

   spunk-dustbin [1990s]

   stinker [1990s]

   stoinker [1990s]

   team hole [1990s]

LADIES' MEN: A CHRONOLOGY

FRIGBEARD AND LUSTY-GUTS

   mutton-monger [early 16C–early 18C]

   frigbeard [16C]

   lusty-guts [16C]

   Lusty Lawrence [16C]

   holer/holemonger [16C+]

   fishmonger [17C] (*fish* = vagina)

   goat [late 17C+]

HANOVERIAN MEAT-MONGERS

   whisker splitter [late 18C–early 19C]

   meat-monger [late 18C–19C]

VICTORIAN QUIM-STICKERS

   belly bumper [19C]

   fleece-monger [19C]

ladies' tailor [19C]
ling-grappler [19C] (*ling* = vagina)
gulley-raker/gully-raker [19C]
quim-sticker [19C]
clapster [19C+] (i.e. he risks
'the clap')
wolf [mid-19C+]
girl-trap [late 19C]
hair-monger [late 19C]

EDWARDIAN LOUNGE LIZARDS
rump-splitter/split-rump
[19C–1900s]
lizard [1910s+]
lounge lice [1910s+] (Aus.)
lounge lizard [1910s+]

belly bumper

JAZZ-AGE ASS-HOUNDS
tea-hound [1920s] (US)
chicken inspector [1920s+] (US)
tom cat [1920s+] (orig. US)
chicken-butcher [1930s–40s] (US campus; *chicken* = young woman)
ass-hound [1940s] (US)
cunt-hound [1940s+]
fox [1940s+]

ROCK 'N' ROLL TOUGH CATS
cocksmith [1950s–60s] (US)
whore-chaser [1950s–60s] (US Black)
dog [1950s+] (US Black)
tough cat [1950s+] (US Black)

ball clanker [1960s] (US; a man who boasts groundlessly of his sexual prowess)

cum-freak [1960s+]

pants man [1960s+] (Aus.)

rogue [1960s+] (US Black)

shag artist [1960s+]

BOUDOIR BANDICOOTS

fang artist [1970s+] (Aus.; *fang* = penis)

gash-hound [1970s+]

boudoir bandicoot [1980s] (Aus.)

hoser [1980s+] (Can./US campus; *hose* = penis)

SEX MAD

come-freak [1950s+]

fuckaholic [1980s+]

🙶 🙶

Speciality ladies' men

beastmaster [1980s+] (US campus; a man who consistently dates unattractive women)

chubby-chaser [1970s+] (a man who prefers plump or fat women)

fat-fancier/fat-monger [19C] (a man who prefers plump women)

flower fancier [late 19C–1900s] (a man who specializes in 'flowers', i.e. virgins)

🙶 🙶

99 99 99 99 99 99 99 99 99 99 99 99 99 99 99 99 99 99 99 99 99 99 99

Sickos

berry [1990s]
kink [1960s+]
sicko/sicksicksick [1950s+]
slab boy [1970s+] (a necrophiliac)

66 66 66 66 66 66 66 66 66 66 66 66 66 66 66 66 66 66 66 66 66

hormone [1980s+] (US campus)
hornbug [1950s] (US)
pussy bandit [1950s+] (US)
pussy-hound [1950s+]
sexo/sexoh [1950s+] (N.Z.)
table-end man [late 19C+] (i.e. he cannot wait to reach the
  bedroom)

EFFEMINATES AND PRETTY BOYS

auntie-man [1940s+] (W.I.)
bamsie man [20C] (W.I.; *bamsie* = buttocks)
b. & p. [late 19C–1900s] (the initials of two young men involved
  in a contemporary homosexual scandal)
beanpea [late 19C–1900s] (i.e. 'b. & p.')
birdie [1960s+]
boygul [1980s+] (US gay; playing on 'bagel', and *boy* + *girl*)
butterbox [1960s+] (from the 'softness' of butter)
girl-getter [late 19C–1900s] (i.e. he is unable to father
  'macho' boys)
lizzie/Lizzie [late 19C+] (orig. US)

lollipop [1920s–60s] (US)

manicou man [20C] (W.I.; *manicou*, a type of nocturnal rodent whose young cling on to their mothers for transportation)

Miss Molly/molly(-boy) [early 18C–1920s]

moffry [20C] (W.I.; her*maphro*dite)

mother [1930s+] (US Black)

pantyman [20C] (W.I.)

99 99 99 99 99 99 99 99 99 99 99 99 99 99 99 99 99 99 99 99 99 99 99

The 'nancy boy': a two-part symposium

HISTORY

nan boy [late 17C–late 19C]

Miss Nancy [early 19C–1920s]

Nancy Dawson [late 19C] (a legendary 18C prostitute)

nancy [late 19C+] (orig. US)

nance [20C]

nanny [1940s+] (US)

nancy boy [1950s+]

GRAMMAR

nance [1960s] (US; 'to speak or act effeminately')

nancified [1910s+]

nancifully [1910s+]

nancyism [early 19C–1920s]

66 66 66 66 66 66 66 66 66 66 66 66 66 66 66 66 66 66 66 66 66 66 66

pantywaist [1930s+] (orig. US)
pee-willy [1920s+] (Can.)
pood [1910s+] (*poodle*)
pretty-boy [20C]
quilt [20C] (Irish)
sissie/cissie/cissy/sissy [late 19C+]
sissy pants [20C]
sissy soft sucker/soft sucker [1980s+] (US Black)
spoony/spooney [mid-19C]
twiddlepoop [late 18C–early 19C]

BOYS WHO LIKE FLOWERS

buttercup [20C]
daffodil [1930s–70s] (gay)
lemon sucker [1920s–60s] (US; suggesting lips pursed in a
  camp manner)
lily [1920s+]
pansy [20C]
streak of lavender [1930s]

99 99 99 99 99 99 99 99 99 99 99 99 99 99 99 99 99 99 99 99 99

Gussie and percy-pants

Gussie [1900s–1940s] (US)
Percy [20C] (US)
percy-boy [20C] (US)
percy-pants [20C] (US)
Ralph [1950s–60s] (camp gay)

66 66 66 66 66 66 66 66 66 66 66 66 66 66 66 66 66 66 66 66 66

BOYS WHO LIKE TEA-PARTIES

bun-duster [1920s] (US)
cake eater [1910s+] (US)
cookie-pusher/cookie-dipper [1930s+] (US)

MEN ABOUT THE HOUSE

Betty [19C]
cot [late 17C–late 18C]
cotbetty [19C+]
cotquean [late 16C–early 19C] (lit. 'housewife')
hen-hussy [20C] (US)
kitchen-bitch/kitchen-crumb/kitchen-key [20C] (W.I.)
mama-man [1940s+] (W.I.)
Sheela [late 19C–1910s] (Irish)
slop-pail [1920s]

🙶 🙶

Macho homosexuals

bull [1960s–70s] (US)
butch [1930s+] (orig. US)
butch number [mid-20C]
Hairy Mary [1960s+] (US gay)
jailhouse daddy [1950s–60s] (US prison)
macho [1970s+] (orig. US campus)
pitcher [1960s+]
steamer [1950s–60s]
truck-driver [1950s+] (US Black)

🙶 🙶

HOMOSEXUALS

badger [1990s] (US)

bender [1930s+]

bowler from the pavilion end [1990s]

broken wrist [1960s–70s]

butterfly [1940s] (US Black)

camp [1930s] (orig. US)

chemise-lifter [1960s+]

cream puff [1960s+]

daisy [1940s+]

faddle [late 19C] (lit. 'fussy person')

fag [1920s+] (orig. US)

faggamuffin [1980s+] (Black; a Black homosexual)

fagola [1960s] (US)

fairy [late 19C+] (orig. US)

fembo [1980s+] (US campus; *fem*ale + Ram*bo*)

foop [20C] (backslang, 'poof')

99 99 99 99 99 99 99 99 99 99 99 99 99 99 99 99 99 99 99 99 99 99

Fruit

fruit [1930s+]

fruitcake [1930s+]

fruit-fly [1950s+]

fruit for monkeys [1930s+] (US)

fruit loop [1980s+] (US campus)

juicy fruit [1930s] (US Black)

pineapple [1960s–70s]

tooti-frooti [1960s+] (US Black)

66 66 66 66 66 66 66 66 66 66 66 66 66 66 66 66 66 66 66 66 66

foxy lady [20C]

freak [20C] (orig. US Black)

funny man [1970s+]
   (US Black)

gay boy [1950s+] (US)

gayola [1980s+] (US)

hen [20C] (W.I.)

Hollywood hustler
   [1950s+] (US)

homo [1920s+]

Jesuit [mid-16C]
   (from the contem-
   porary suspicion
   of Jesuits)

lavender cowboy

john-and-john [late 18C–mid-19C]

joy boy [20C] (US)

knick-knack/nick-nack/nic-nac [1960s+] (US; lit. 'trinket')

lavender boy [1920s+]

lavender cowboy [1990s]

limp wrist/limp wrister [1950s+] (orig. US)

madge-cove [early 18C–mid-19C]

man-eater [1940s+]

mole [late 19C–1910s] (i.e. he 'burrows')

morphodite/morphodyte/morphodyke [18C+] (mispron. of
   'hermaphrodite')

one [1930s–60s]

one of those [late 19C]

oofterpa [1940s] (Pig Latin, 'poofter')

Oscar [1900s–50s] (US; *Oscar* Wilde)

perv/perve [1940s+] (orig. Aus.)
poofter/poofdah/poofta [late 19C+] (orig. Aus.)
puff [20C]
punk [20C]
queer [1920s+]
rabbit [1940s+] (S Afr.)
shirtlifter [1960s+] (orig. Aus.)
smockface [19C] (lit. 'smooth face')
sod [mid-19C+]
soft [mid-19C+]
soft boy [1980s+] (Black)
sweet [1970s] (US Black)
swish [1930s+] (orig. US)
three-legged beaver [20C]

99 99 99 99 99 99 99 99 99 99 99 99 99 99 99 99 99 99 99 99 99 99

Younger gay men

capon [1930s–40s]
cupcake [1960s+] (US)
gal-boy [late 19C+] (US)
ganymede [1910s–40s] (US)
lilywhite [late 19C–1900s]
pretty [1930s+]
queerbait [1950s+]
rent boy [1960s+]
tart [1930s+] (gay)
twinkie [1970s+] (US gay)
woman [1960s+] (US prison)

66 66 66 66 66 66 66 66 66 66 66 66 66 66 66 66 66 66 66 66 66 66

99 99 99 99 99 99 99 99 99 99 99 99 99 99 99 99 99 99 99 99 99 99

Older gay men

Athenian [1950s–60s] (gay)

auntie [1930s+] (US gay)

boy buster [1940s–50s] (Aus.; a man, esp. a
prisoner, who specializes in seducing young
men)

chicken queen [1980s+] (an older homosexual
male who prefers sex with teenage boys)

chicken rustler [1960s+] (US gay; a
homosexual who has been placed in charge
of underage boys, e.g. a scoutmaster or
choirmaster)

Colonel Sanders [1960s+] (gay; punning on
the Colonel's internationally franchised fried
chicken and 'chicken' i.e. a young person
viewed sexually)

egg-sucker [1950s+] (US gay)

geriatricks [1950s+] (gay; ageing or old
homosexuals)

hawk [1960s+] (US; an older male homosexual
with a preference for young boys)

over-ripe fruit [1950s–60s]

66 66 66 66 66 66 66 66 66 66 66 66 66 66 66 66 66 66 66 66 66 66

undercover man [20C]

waffle [1970s+] (US Und.)

weirdie [1960s]

99 99 99 99 99 99 99 99 99 99 99 99 99 99 99 99 99 99 99 99 99 99

Homosexuals in rhyming slang

RHYMING WITH QUEER

    ginger [1920s+]

    King Lear [20C]

    shandy [20C] (i.e. *chand*elier)

RHYMING WITH POOF OR POOFTER

    cloven hoofter [20C] (Aus.)

    horse's hoof [1950s+]

    iron (hoof) [1930s+]

    jam duff [20C]

    Nellie Duff/Nelly Duff [20C]

    nice enough [20C]

    woofter/woolly woofter [1980s+]

RHYMING WITH QUEEN

    haricot [1960s+] (Aus.; i.e. *haricot* bean)

    in-between [20C] (Aus.)

    pork and bean [1960s+] (Aus.)

RHYMING WITH NANCE

    song and dance [1910s–30s]

RHYMING WITH CATAMITE

    dyna [1960s] (i.e. *dyna*mite)

RHYMING WITH COCK

    hock [20C]

RHYMING WITH BENT

    Stoke on Trent [1970s+]

66 66 66 66 66 66 66 66 66 66 66 66 66 66 66 66 66 66 66 66 66 66

99 99 99 99 99 99 99 99 99 99 99 99 99 99 99 99 99 99 99 99 99 99

Ugly older gay men

dirty dowager [1950s–60s] (an unkempt, ill-
preserved older gay man)

ill piece [1950s+] (gay)

Mary Worthless [1940s+] (US)

toad [20C] (US gay)

troll [1980s+] (US gay)

66 66 66 66 66 66 66 66 66 66 66 66 66 66 66 66 66 66 66 66 66 66

99 99 99 99 99 99 99 99 99 99 99 99 99 99 99 99 99 99 99 99 99 99

Three camp jockeys

chocky jockey [1990s]

jacksy jockey [1990s]

sausage jockey [1990s] (US)

66 66 66 66 66 66 66 66 66 66 66 66 66 66 66 66 66 66 66 66 66 66

BUM BOYS

anal astronaut [1990s]

arse pirate [1990s]

ass boy [1990s] (US)

ass burglar [1970s+]

back-door commando [1990s]

back-door kicker [1990s]

battie-boy [20C] (orig. W.I.)

battyman [1950s+] (W.I.; lit. 'bottom man')

b.b. [20C] (*b*um-*b*oy)

beachcomber [1990s] (punning on 'log-pusher')
booty-buffer [1990s]
boretto-man [early 18C] (Italian, 'little borer')
bottom man [1950s+]
breechloader [1910s]
buftie/bufty [20C]
bufty-boy [20C]
bufu [1980s+] (orig. US; *buttfu*cker)
buggeranto [early 18C]
bum boy [19C+]
bum chum [1990s]
bummer [1970s]
bum plumber [1990s]
bum-robber [late 19C+]
bunny boy [1940s+] (S Afr.)
cackpipe cosmonaut [1990s]
chuff adder [1960s] (playing on 'puff adder')
chuff chum [1990s]
colon choker [1990s]
dinner masher [1990s]
dirt-tamper [1970s]
donut-puncher [1990s] (US)
eye doctor [1950s+]
freckle-puncher [1960s+]
haemorrhoid hitman [1990s]
hole-filler [1990s]
hoop stretcher [1990s]
hula raider [1990s]
indorser [late 18C–19C]
inspector of manholes [1930s+]

jobby jouster [1990s]
kisser [20C] (ass *kisser*)
log-cabin raider [1990s]
log-pusher [1990s]
manhole inspector [1990s]
mud-packer [20C] (US)
navigator of the windward passage [1990s]
nudger [1990s] (US)
pile-driver [1960s–70s]
poo-packer [1990s]
poo percolator [1990s]
poo pusher [1990s]
poo-stabber [1990s]
prune-pusher [1950s–60s]
putty pusher [1990s]
rear seat gunner [1990s]
rectal ranger/rectum ranger
  [1990s]
rimadona [1960s]
ring master [1990s]
ring raider [1990s]
rump ranger [1950s+]
scatman [1990s]
shit-stabber [1960s+]
shunter [1990s]
skid-pipe plumber [1990s]
stem-wheeler [20C] (US)
stir-shit [late 19C–1900s]
sweetcorn shiner [1990s]

trouser bandit

tailgunner [1960s+] (US)
tan-track rider [1930s+] (orig. Aus.)
turd-burglar [1960s+] (orig. Aus.)
uphill gardener [1990s]
windjammer [20C] (Aus.)

99 99 99 99 99 99 99 99 99 99 99 99 99 99 99 99 99 99 99 99 99 99

Brown dirt cowboys

brown artist [1950s+]
brown dirt cowboy [1990s]
brownie [1940s+] (US gay)
browning queen [1940s+] (US gay)
Cadbury's canal boat cruiser [1990s]
Cadbury's canal engineer [1990s]
chocolate runway pilot [1990s]
chocolate speedway rider [1990s]
chutney farmer [1990s]
cocoa-shunter [1990s]
fudge-nudger [1990s]
fudge-packer [20C] (US)
hitchhiker on the Hershey highway [20C] (US)
Marmite driller [1990s]
Marmite miner [1990s]
peanut buffer [1990s]
peanut-packer [1950s+] (US)
pilot of the chocolate runway [1990s]
sausage smuggler [1990s]
visitor to Vegemite valley [1990s]

66 66 66 66 66 66 66 66 66 66 66 66 66 66 66 66 66 66 66 66 66 66

99 99 99 99 99 99 99 99 99 99 99 99 99 99 99 99 99 99 99 99 99 99

Bum-bandits

arse bandit/ass bandit [20C]

arse brigand [20C]

arse pirate [20C]

balloon-knot bandit [1990s] (*balloon knot* =
the knot tied in a used condom)

blue-arsed bandit [20C]

booty bandit [20C] (US)

bum bandit [20C]

butt pirate [20C]

pisshole bandit [1960s+]

short-arm bandit [1960s–70s] (*short arm* = penis)

trouser bandit [20C]

66 66 66 66 66 66 66 66 66 66 66 66 66 66 66 66 66 66 66 66 66 66

99 99 99 99 99 99 99 99 99 99 99 99 99 99 99 99 99 99 99 99 99 99

Blow-boys and sperm burpers

blow-boy [1930s+] (US)

bone smuggler [1990s]

bone-stroker [1990s]

cocksucker [1940s+]

pickle kisser [1990s]

pipe smoker [1990s]

pole pleaser [20C] (US)

semen demon [20C] (US)

sperm burper [1990s]

66 66 66 66 66 66 66 66 66 66 66 66 66 66 66 66 66 66 66 66 66 66

99 99 99 99 99 99 99 99 99 99 99 99 99 99 99 99 99 99 99 99 99

Butt sluts and mattress munchers: passive homosexuals

bitch [1930s+]

butt slut [20C] (orig. US)

candy-bar punk [1960s] (US prison; a prisoner who has become a passive homosexual while in prison, from the gifts or payments of candy bars that he receives for his services)

cat [1950s+] (Aus.; *cat*amite)

flip [1980s+] (i.e. he *flips* over)

fuckboy [1970s+]

gump [18C+] (US prison; a passive homosexual, the target of predatory prison homosexuals; dial. 'awkward', 'well-meaning')

half a man [1970s+] (US Black)

huckle [1900s] (US; dial. 'bend over')

letterbox [1990s]

mattress-muncher [1960s+] (orig. Aus.)

pillow-biter [1960s+] (orig. Aus.)

pussyboy [1950s]

receiver [20C]

66 66 66 66 66 66 66 66 66 66 66 66 66 66 66 66 66 66 66 66 66

POWDER PUFFS AND SCREAMING QUEENS

brilliant [20C]

fantail [1960s] (US prison; a promiscuous prison homosexual, lit. 'buttock-shaker')

femme/fem [1960s+] (US)

flamer [19C+] (US campus)

flower [20C]

hair fairy [1960s+] (US; an effeminate gay man with long or styled hair)

Joan of Arc [1950s–60s] (camp gay; punning on the 'faggots' with which St Joan was burned)

minty/mintee/mintie [1910s–70s] (US gay; *mint* = effeminacy)

Nellie/Nelly [1910s+]

99 99 99 99 99 99 99 99 99 99 99 99 99 99 99 99 99 99 99 99 99 99

Girls

Annie [1950s]

Ethel [1920s+]

Gladys [1950s–60s] (camp gay; a fat, aggressive, ostentatious male homosexual)

Margery [mid-19C+]

Mary Ann [late 19C+]

Maud [1940s+] (a dowdy male homosexual)

Nola [1930s–60s] (US)

Sheena [1950s–60s] (camp gay; a Black homosexual, from the cartoon character *Sheena, Queen of the Jungle*)

66 66 66 66 66 66 66 66 66 66 66 66 66 66 66 66 66 66 66 66 66 66

99 99 99 99 99 99 99 99 99 99 99 99 99 99 99 99 99 99 99 99 99 99 99

Girl-Boys

broad boy [20C] (lit. 'girl-boy')
gal-boy [late 19C+] (US)
girl-boy [late 19C+] (US)
hesh [20C] (*he-she*)
himmer [1950s] (*him-her*)
she-male [20C]
she-man [20C]
shim [20C] (*she-him*)
woman-man [20C] (W.I.)

66 66 66 66 66 66 66 66 66 66 66 66 66 66 66 66 66 66 66 66 66 66 66

99 99 99 99 99 99 99 99 99 99 99 99 99 99 99 99 99 99 99 99 99 99 99

Transsexuals

Copenhagen capon [1960s+] (gay; from the pioneering sex-change operation undergone in Denmark by Christine Jorgensen)
Danish pastry [1950s–60s] (gay)
something's rotten in Denmark [1950s+] (gay; a jibe at someone who is presumed to have had a sex-change, from a line in Shakespeare's *Hamlet*)

66 66 66 66 66 66 66 66 66 66 66 66 66 66 66 66 66 66 66 66 66 66 66

piss elegant [1950s+]
powder puff [1920s+]
princess [1960s]
queen [late 19C+]
screamer [1960s+] (gay)
screaming fairy [1940s+]
screaming queen [1940s+]

clam smacker

LESBIANS

Amy-John [20C]
bean flicker [1990s]
bull bitch [1960s+] (US)
carpet-muncher [1980s+] (US campus)
clam smacker [1990s] (US)
clithopper [1960s] (a promiscuous lesbian)
donut-bumper [20C] (US)
Dutch girl [1930s+]
dyke [1930s+]
fairy lady [1940s–50s] (US)
finger artist [1940s–70s] (US Black)
fuzz bumper [1980s+] (US campus)
gusset-nuzzler [1990s]
harpy [1970s] (US Black)
Jasper [1950s+] (US prison/Black)
lady-lover [1930s+]
lemon [1980s+] (Aus.)
lemonade [1980s+] (Aus.)
Leslie [1950s+] (Aus.)
muffer [1960s+] (US)

raleigh bike [20C] (rhy. sl. 'dyke')
rug-muncher [1980s+] (US campus)
Sappho [1950s+]
she-he [1940s–60s] (US)
slut-puppy [1980s+] (US campus)
thespian [1970s]
tootsie [20C] (Aus.)
tunaface [1990s]
vegetable [1980s+] (US gay)
wicker [1980s+]
zamie [1950s+]

BISEXUALS

bicycle [1970s+]
bipe [1960s+] (US)
combo [1980s+] (US campus)
double-life man [20C]
dunt [1980s+] (US campus; *d*ick + c*unt*)
flip-flop [20C] (US prison)
switch-hitter [1950s+] (US)

SEXUAL INADEQUATES

VIRGINS AND CELIBATES

b.a.v. [1980s+] (US campus; *b*orn *a*gain *v*irgin, i.e. someone who has not had sex in a long time)
buss beggar [18C–early 19C] (an aging roué who still wants sex but cannot persuade young girls to go to bed with him, lit. 'kiss beggar')

canned goods [1910s–30s] (US)

charity case [mid-20C+]

cherry-boy [1970s] (US; a male virgin)

cherry prick [20C]

cherry tree [1980s+] (US campus; a tall virgin)

Irish virgin [20C] (US; someone who is a virgin and is likely to remain one, from the traditional propensity of pious Irish virgins to become nuns)

lackanooky/lakanuki [1940s+] (US; ill-health caused by lack of sexual activity, i.e. 'lack of nookie')

never squedge [late 19C] (a passionless youth, lit. 'never squeeze')

n.g.b. [1980s+] (US campus; *n*ice *g*uy *b*ut, i.e. a pleasant person, but not one with whom one wishes to have a sexual relationship)

raw sole [1950s+] (US Black; a virgin Black woman)

virgie [1930s–60s]

wretch [1980s+] (US campus; an involuntary celibate)

❞ ❞

Six men with extremely small penises

bugfucker [1970s] (US)

drip-dry lover [1960s+] (US gay; i.e. his penis is too small to shake)

hung like a (field)mouse [1960s+] (US)

hung like a stud mosquito [1960s+] (US)

needle dick [1960s+] (US)

pencil dick [1980s+] (US)

❝ ❝

IMPOTENT MEN

broken arrow [1960s] (US)

dry balls [1930s–40s] (US)

flapdoodle [19C] (someone who is either too young or too old for sex)

flapper [19C] (an impotent old man)

fuck-beggar [18C]

fumbler [late 17C–18C]

mugwump [mid-19C]

mule [1950s+] (W.I.)

yitney [1990s+] (*yitten*, frightened)

PREMATURE EJACULATORS

creamer [1990s]

dress-messer [1990s+]

easter queen [1960s+] (US gay; i.e. he comes 'quick as a rabbit')

fast fuck [20C]

Flash Harry [20C]

two-minute brother [1990s] (US Black)

FRIGID PEOPLE

deep-freezer [1960s]

fridge [1990s]

frozen fruit [1960s] (gay; a frigid homosexual)

icebox [late 19C+] (US)

ice maiden [1950s+]

mummy pussy [1970s+] (US Black; i.e. her sexual organs are 'embalmed')

nun [1980s+]

PRICKTEASERS

ball-breaker [1970s+] (orig. US)
ball-buster [1970s+] (orig. US)
cockteaser/c.t. [late 19C+]
cunt-teaser [20C] (a male tease)
dickteaser [1960s+]
pricktease/prickteaser/p.t. [1950s+]
scammer [1980s+] (US campus)
tease [mid-19C+]
teaser [late 19C+]
trap [1980s+] (US campus)

FRIGSTERS AND FLIPWRECKS: THE OBSESSIVE MASTURBATOR

beat-nuts [1970s] (US)
bone stroker [1990s]
doodle-dandler [19C]
flipwreck [1940s+] (Aus.; a person who has (supposedly) masturbated themselves into physical and mental decline)
frigster/frigstress [late 16C–17C]
fuck-fist/fuck-finger [late 19C–1900s]
milker [late 19C+]
milkman [1990s]
milk-woman [late 19C–1900s] (a female masturbator)
pencil-squeezer [1970s+]
peter-beater [1980s+] (US)
pudpuller [1950s+] (US)
rod walloper [1950s+] (orig. Aus.)
taffy-tugger [1990s]

virtuoso of the skin flute [20C]
whacker/wacker [1980s+] (US)
wire-puller [late 19C+]

CRADLE SNATCHERS AND DIRTY OLD MEN

baby-farmer [20C]
baby-snatcher [1920s+]
chicken-hawk [1960s+]
cradle-robber [1920s+] (orig. US)
cradle-snatcher [20C] (orig. US)
dirty old man [1930s+]
d.o.m. [1950s+] (*d*irty *o*ld *m*an)

TOO YOUNG, TOO OLD
... AND TOO CLOSE
TO HOME

THE FAMILY

PARENTS

oldies [1970s+]
olds [late 19C+]
parental units/units [1980s+] (US campus)
pazzers [1990s] (teen)
peeps [1980s+] (US Black/campus; i.e. 'people')
p.'s [1980s+] (US campus)
relics [mid-19C+]
rental units/rents [1970s] (US campus)

MOTHERS

o.g. [late 19C–1970s] (US Black; *old girl*)
old and bitter [1920s–30s] (a mother-in-law)
old cheese [1990s] (Aus.)
old grabem pudden [late 19C]
strangle and smother [20C] (Aus.; rhy. sl.)

FATHERS

finger [1920s] (N.Z.)
governor [early 19C+]
old strike-a-light [late 19C] (i.e. he cries *strike a light!* when asked
  for yet another 'loan')
relieving officer [late 19C] (i.e. he supplies financial relief)
zoo daddy [1970s+] (US; a divorced father who rarely sees his
  children, alluding to zoo trips on 'visiting days')

BROTHERS

blah [1950s+] (S Afr.)
bratty [1990s] (US teen)
bubba [19C+] (US)
manhole cover [20C] (rhy. sl.)
one and t'other [late 19C+] (rhy. sl.)

SISTERS

black man kissed her [20C] (rhy. sl.)
blood blister [20C] (Aus.; rhy. sl.)
kid blister [20C] (Aus.; rhy. sl.)
moose [1940s+] (US; a little sister; Japanese *musume*, daughter, girl)
skin-and-blister [1920s+] (rhy. sl.)

HUSBANDS (MOSTLY HEN-PECKED)

egg [20C] (US; a henpecked husband)
gaffer [18C]
gander [late 18C–19C]
fuckpump [20C] (from the monotonous regularity of his sex life)
h.d. [1980s+] (US campus; a man who lives off a woman; *h*usband *d*ependent)
homebird [mid–late 19C] (a hen-pecked husband)
horn-grower/horn-merchant [18C] (a married man, from the likelihood of his being eventually cuckolded)
Job/Jobe [late 19C] (a hen-pecked husband, from the biblical *Job*, who received a lengthy telling-off from his supposed 'comforters')
lapful [19C–1920s]

mama's boss [1930s–40s] (US Black, usu. male usage)

monkey man [1920s–60s] (US Black; a man dominated by his wife or girlfriend)

n.n. [late 19C] (society; *n*ecessary *m*uisance)

pinch-wife [late 19C–1900s] (a mean, boorish husband, who does not trust his wife)

tenant at will [late 18C–early 19C] (a man whose wife arrives at the alehouse to make him come home, the 'will' being that of the wife)

yellow gloak [early–mid-19C] (a jealous husband)

99 99 99 99 99 99 99 99 99 99 99 99 99 99 99 99 99 99 99 99 99 99 99

Cuckolds

buck [mid-18C–early 19C] (from the horns of the male animal)

gilt-horn [18C] (a complacent cuckold who is paid for the use of his wife)

hoddy peak [16C] (lit. 'snail head')

holy Moses [early 17C] (from paintings of Moses displaying him with a part-halo, the curves of which resemble horns protruding from his head)

member for horncastle [late 18C–early 19C]

one of livery [late 17C] (i.e. he wears a mark of his position – the horns)

stay [early 19C] (i.e. something a woman casts off to enjoy sex)

tup [late 16C+] (lit. 'ram')

66 66 66 66 66 66 66 66 66 66 66 66 66 66 66 66 66 66 66 66 66 66

99 99 99 99 99 99 99 99 99 99 99 99 99 99 99 99 99 99 99 99 99

Spouses

bitter half [20C]

humdrum [17C–early 19C]

66 66 66 66 66 66 66 66 66 66 66 66 66 66 66 66 66 66 66 66 66

WIVES

anchor (and chain) [20C] (US)

apron [17C+]

ball and chain [1920s+] (orig. US Black)

bit of tripe [late 19C]

blade/old blade [19C] (US)

dutch [late 19C+]

evil [early 19C]

headache [1930s] (US)

her [1990s] (US)

her indoors [1970s+]

lawful blanket [19C]

lawful jam [late 19C–1900s]

little woman [mid-19C+]

load of mischief [late 18C–early 19C]

mat [1940s] (US Black; *mat*tress)

mount [mid-19C]

old curiosity [late 19C–1930s]

old geezer [1910s–20s]

old saw [late 19C–1940s] (US Black)

old woman [late 18C+]

ordinary [late 19C–1900s]

99 99 99 99 99 99 99 99 99 99 99 99 99 99 99 99 99 99 99 99 99

Storm and strife: wives in rhyming slang

RHYMING WITH WIFE

bubble/old bubble [1930s+] (rhyming with
  'trouble', i.e. 'trouble and strife')
carving knife [20C]
Duchess (of Fife) [mid-19C+]
fork and knife [late 19C+]
old dutch [late 19C+] (i.e. 'Duchess of Fife')
'pon my life [late 19C]
sporting life [20C]
storm and strife [20C]
struggle and strife [20C]
trouble and strife [20C]
war and strife [1920s–30s]
worry and strife [1930s]

RHYMING WITH WOMAN

gooseberry pudding/gooseberry pudden
  [mid-19C]

66 66 66 66 66 66 66 66 66 66 66 66 66 66 66 66 66 66 66 66 66

peculiar [early 17C]
poker-breaker [19C–1900s]
she [1990s] (US)
sperrib [late 19C] (middle class; i.e. 'spare rib', from which the
  Bible claims Eve was created)
tiger [late 19C] (US)

99 99 99 99 99 99 99 99 99 99 99 99 99 99 99 99 99 99 99 99 99 99

Dominant and nagging wives

boss-lady/boss-woman [20C] (US)

grey mare [late 18C–19C]

plaster [20C] (Irish; i.e. she 'sticks to you like a plaster')

white serjeant [late 18C–late 19C]

whither-go-ye [late 17C–early 19C] (from the questioning of a nagging wife)

66 66 66 66 66 66 66 66 66 66 66 66 66 66 66 66 66 66 66 66 66 66

CHILDREN

breadsnapper [late 19C+] (Scot./Glasgow; 'a child who can eat their weight in groceries')

bub [early 19C+] (US; a boy)

bubba [20C] (Aus.)

chip [late 17C–early 19C]

chitty-face [early 17C–late 18C] (lit. 'baby-face')

dribble-puss [1940s+]

half-pint [late 19C+] (US)

heads [1990s] (US Black; one's children)

infantry [mid-19C]

lightie/laaitie/lighty [1940s+] (S Afr.; *light*weight)

littlie [1960s+] (Aus./N.Z.)

lullaby-cheat [late 17C–early 19C] (lit. 'lullaby thing')

muppet [1970s+]

nadger [late 19C+] (Ulster)

short [1980s+]

sprog/sproglet [1940s+]

sprout [1930s+] (US)

squirt [mid-19C+] (orig. US)

stone fruit [late 19C–1900s] (*stone* = testicle, i.e. the 'fruit of one's loins')

sympathy generator [1990s] (US; from the use of children by beggars etc. to elicit sympathy)

tail-fruit [late 17C+] (i.e. the 'fruit of one's loins')

whore's ghost [1990s] (Irish; a whore's child)

yuppie puppie [1990s] (a child of the generation for whom children were seen as something of a fashion accessory in the early 1990s)

🙶 🙶

Children in rhyming slang

RHYMING WITH BRAT
Jack Sprat [20C]

RHYMING WITH KID
dustbin lids [20C]

gawd forbid [late 19C+]

God-forbids [late 19C+]

saucepan lid [1960s+]

teapot (lid) [20C]

tin lid [20C] (Aus.)

🙶 🙶

teapots

LITTLE PERISHERS

bisom [20C] (Aus.; *besom*, a witch)

chatter-basket [mid-19C] (US; a small, noisy child)

cherubim [late 18C] (a whinging child, from the line in the Te Deum 'To Thee cherubim and seraphim continually do cry')

cross-patch [late 18C+] (lit. 'cross clown')

gawdelpus/gordelpus [late 19C+] (pron. of 'God help us')

godfer [late 19C] (*godfor*saken)

little perisher [late 19C+]

nose picker [1960s+] (US; a child with offensive habits)

rattle can [20C] (Ulster; a noisy child)

tackle [1980s+] (Ulster)

ILLEGITIMATE CHILDREN

alley cat [1920s+] (US)

bachelor's baby [mid-19C+]

backyard cousin/backyard relation [20C] (US)

brush colt [20C] (US; a horse that has not been deliberately bred)

butter-print [17C–early 18C]

catch colt [20C] (US; a horse that has not been deliberately bred)

colt over the fence [20C] (US)

doorstep child [20C]

fence-corner child [20C] (US)

field colt/field rabbit [20C] (US)

fitz [late 19C–1900s] (the patronymic *Fitz* given to the bastard offspring of royal princes)

get [mid-18C–mid-19C] (lit. 'bastard')

gitlet [20C] (US Black; lit. 'little bastard')

goose egg/gooser [20C] (US)

horn-child [20C] (W.I.; the offspring of an adulterous relationship)

jacket [20C] (W.I.)

99 99 99 99 99 99 99 99 99 99 99 99 99 99 99 99 99 99 99 99 99 99

'Ill-conceived' children

baby in the bushes [1970s+] (US)

bantling [late 18C–mid-19C] (German *Bänkling*, a baby conceived on a bench)

brierpatch child [20C] (US)

bushwhacker [19C] (US)

haystack kid [20C] (US)

outside child [20C] (US, mainly southern Black)

phone booth baby [1960s–70s] (US Black)

66 66 66 66 66 66 66 66 66 66 66 66 66 66 66 66 66 66 66 66 66 66

99 99 99 99 99 99 99 99 99 99 99 99 99 99 99 99 99 99 99 99 99

Early varieties

come-too-soon [20C] (US; i.e. *too soon* for the
parents to get married)

early variety [20C] (US)

hasty pudding [mid–late 19C] (i.e. the couple
have been *hasty*)

sooner [20C] (US; i.e. *sooner* than the
wedding)

66 66 66 66 66 66 66 66 66 66 66 66 66 66 66 66 66 66 66 66 66

quaegemes [early 18C–early 19C] (Latin *quaegemes?*, of what
marriage?)

squeaker [late 17C–18C]

stall-whimper [late 17C–mid-19C] (UK Und.)

trick baby [1930s+] (orig. US Black)

woods colt [late 19C+] (US)

MISTAKES

accident [late 19C+]

by-blow [16C–early 19C]

chance child [mid–late 19C]

come-by-chance [18C+]

fly-blow [mid–late 19C]

incident [late 19C] (orig. US)

misfortune [19C]

mistake [1950s+]

99 99 99 99 99 99 99 99 99 99 99 99 99 99 99 99 99 99 99 99 99

Two last shakes of the bag

afterthought [1910s+] (the youngest child of
a family, conceived long after its siblings)

last shake of the bag [19C+] (a youngest
child; *bag* = scrotum)

66 66 66 66 66 66 66 66 66 66 66 66 66 66 66 66 66 66 66 66 66

YOUNG AND IMMATURE PEOPLE

baby child [1970s] (US Black)

half-baked [late 19C–1930s] (Aus.; an immature person)

melkpens [1970s] (S Afr.; Afrikaans, 'milk stomach')

milk bar cowboy [1950s+]

pup [late 19C+]

teether [1960s]

young, dumb and full of cum [1970s+] (US; used to describe a
teenager whose enthusiasm for life and sex outweighs their
intelligence)

young pup [late 19C+]

YOUNG MEN

candy-butt [1970s+] (US Black)

cub [late 18C+]

kitty [1950s–60s] (US)

quat [early 17C] (lit. 'pimple')

smacker [1930s+] (Aus.)

snork [1940s+] (Aus./N.Z.; lit. 'piglet')

walyo/Wally-O/wallio [20C] (US; Italian *uaglio*, a young one)

yout/yoot [1950s+] (W.I./UK Black; i.e. 'youth')

YOUNG WOMEN

bantam [1940s–50s] (US Black)

beazel [1930s+]

bint/binty [mid-19C+] (Arabic, 'daughter')

bitty [1990s] (US Black)

chick [20C]

chickadee [1930s–70s] (US)

chickie [1940s+] (orig. Aus.)

chicklet [1920s+] (orig. US)

fairy [mid-19C–1930s] (orig. US)

frying size [19C+] (US)

gazelle [late 19C–1940s] (US)

lizard [1980s+] (US Black)

99 99 99 99 99 99 99 99 99 99 99 99 99 99 99 99 99 99 99 99 99 99 99

A short chronology of wenches

wench [13C]

pigeon [16C+]

filly [17C+]

quail [late 17C+]

drozel [early 18C]

chicken [late 18C+]

chickabiddy [19C]

titter [19C]

grouse [mid-19C+]

66 66 66 66 66 66 66 66 66 66 66 66 66 66 66 66 66 66 66 66 66 66

nina [1990s] (US Black; Spanish *niña*, a young girl)

pharaoh [19C–1920s] (US Black; Kanuri *fero*, a girl)

polone/palone/paloney/pollone [1930s+] (Ling. Fr./Polari; Italian *pollone*, a chick)

Richard (the Third) [1940s+] (rhy. sl. 'bird')

sis/siss [late 19C+] (US)

slim-dilly [1920s+] (Aus.)

sninny [1920s+] (Aus.)

squab [1920s] (US; lit. 'unfledged bird')

OLD PEOPLE

RELICS AND WRINKLIES

buster [20C]

coffin-dodger [20C]

creaker [1900s–40s] (US Black)

crumbly/crumblie [1970s+] (society)

dusty [1980s+]

fungus [mid–late 19C] (an old man)

geri/gerri/gerry [1970s+] (*geri*atric)

grayhair [1980s+] (US campus)

relic [mid-19C+]

vet [1930s+] (*vet*eran)

wrinkly [1970s+]

fungus

OLDIES

   old bird [mid-19C+]
   old coot [late 18C+] (a foolish or cantankerous old person)
   old dear [1950s+]
   oldie [late 19C; 1970s+] (usu. teen or youth)
   oldo [1950s]
   oldster [mid-19C+] (orig. and still mainly US)
   old thing [20C]
   old 'un [early 19C+]

WOMEN

   old bag [1920s+] (orig. US)
   old bat [1920s+] (an unattractive older woman)
   old boiler [1920s+] (US)
   old boot [1950s+]
   old cat [late 18C+] (an unpleasant, gossiping old woman)
   old crow [1920s+]
   old dragon [1950s+]
   old hen [20C]
   old moo [late 19C+]
   old mother slipper-slopper [1910s–20s]
   old trot [late 17C+]
   old trout [late 19C+]

MEN

   old cocker [20C] (orig. US)
   old codger [18C+]
   old fragment [1900s]

old geezer/old geyser [late 19C+]

old goat [1940s+] (US)

old moustache [late 19C]

old ram [late 19C+]

old toast [late 17C–early 18C]

A CLUTCH OF CANE TOADS

apple-john [17C] (a foolish old man, from a kind of apple said to keep for two years and to be perfect when shrivelled and withered)

badger [early 19C+] (US; a supposedly ill-tempered animal)

baldhead [early 19C–1900s] (orig. US)

cane toad [1990s] (Aus.; a rich old man)

dads [18C]

fat cock [mid-19C] (a fat old man)

Father Christmas [20C]

frying pan [20C] (rhy. sl. 'old man')

granddad/grandpa [20C]

rustyguts [late 17C–early 19C] (a surly, unpleasant old man)

schfatzer [1930s+] (German *Schwatzer*, a bore)

splodger [mid-19C] (rhy. sl. 'old codger')

square-toes [late 18C–early 19C] (from his old-fashioned footwear)

whiskers [mid-19C+] (US)

A CHOICE SELECTION OF BOILED RAGS

artichoke [19C] (a debauched old woman)

aunt [18C+] (an old Black woman)

basket [1930s+] (an interfering, nosy old woman)

battle-axe/battle-ax [late 19C+] (orig. US; a formidable older woman)

biddy/old biddy [19C+] (an irritating, interfering old woman)

bluehair [1980s+] (US campus)

boiled rag [1940s] (US; rhy. sl. 'old hag')

bubber [19C] (US; an old woman with large pendulous breasts)

granny/grannie [late 18C; 1970s+]

gunpowder [late 17C–early 19C] (a cantankerous old woman, i.e. she 'goes off with a bang')

preterite [late 19C] (lit. 'pertaining to former times')

rag-and-bone shop [1910s–20s] (a decrepit old woman)

stewer [1900s–40s] (US Black; a malicious, gossiping old woman)

sucker [1950s] (W.I.; a nagging old woman; dial. *old suck*, a demon in the form of an old woman)

tabby [late 18C+]

99 99 99 99 99 99 99 99 99 99 99 99 99 99 99 99 99 99 99 99 99 99

Mutton dressed as lamb

m.d.l. [1990s] (*m*utton *d*ressed as *l*amb)

mutton-cove [19C]

mutton dressed as lamb/lamb-fashion [late 19C+]

n.d. [late 19C] (society; *n*o *d*ate)

old ewe dressed as lamb [late 18C]

old fowl [20C] (W.I.)

Peg Puff [19C] (i.e. she is 'puffed up')

phizgig [19C] (lit. 'frivolous woman')

66 66 66 66 66 66 66 66 66 66 66 66 66 66 66 66 66 66 66 66 66 66

SOCIALLY
UNACCEPTABLE

THE RICH, THE POOR AND THE MISERLY

RICH PEOPLE

cornucopia [late 19C] (US)

goldfinch [late 17C–early 19C]

gotrocks [20C] (US; *rocks* = precious stones)

grandma change [1930s–40s] (US Black)

his dibs [1920s–30s] (*dibs* = money)

jillionaire [1930s+] (orig. US)

lombard [1980s] (*loads of money but a right dickhead*)

Mr Money [1950s]

moneybags [early 19C+]

moneybugs [late 19C] (US; millionaires)

money's mammy [1930s–40s] (US Black)

phat pocket [1990s] (US Black)

plute [mid–late 19C] (*pluto*crat)

silk stocking [1950s–70s] (US Black)

turkey-buyer [late 19C] (*turkeys* being beyond the pockets of the poor)

zillionaire [1940s+]

POOR PEOPLE

alley rat [1910s+] (US; a villainous and impoverished person)

bald-coot [early–mid-19C] (an old man who has lost all his money on gambling)

breadfruit swapper [20C] (W.I./Bdos.; i.e. they barter rather than paying with money)

broker [late 19C+] (orig. Aus.)

brokie [1950s] (Aus.)

dead-broker [late 19C+] (Aus.)

dirt-dobber/dirt-scratcher [1940s–60s] (a poor farmer)

gentleman of three outs [late 18C] (i.e. he is 'without money, without wit, and without manners')

hard-up [late 19C–1900s] (Aus.)

light pockets [1940s+] (US)

low-downer [mid–late 19C] (US Black; a poor White person)

muck-snipe [mid-19C] (someone who has lost all their money)

nincum noodle [early 19C] (*no* + *income*; *noodle* = fool)

sub [1970s]

BEGGARS

asker [mid-19C]

cadge-cloak/cadge-gloak [18C–early 19C] (UK Und.)

croaker [mid–late 19C]

cruiser [late 17C–18C] (UK Und.; i.e. they *cruise* the streets)

cup rattler [late 19C] (US)

HUNGRY HOMELESS AND HUMAN TO FEED

dog

curbstone canary/kerbstone canary [1930s] (US tramp; a whingeing beggar)

ding [1930s] (*ding*bat, a vagrant)

dog [20C]

downrighter [1930s] (*downright* = begging)

gagger [mid-19C+] (i.e. they force you to 'swallow' their tale of woe)

grubber [1900s] (US; *grub* = unkempt person)

kedger [19C]

latch [1960s–70s] (US Black)

master of the black art [16C]

maunder/maunderer [late 17C–mid-19C] (Latin *mendicus*, a beggar)

❞ ❞

Gimps and stumpies: maimed and handicapped beggars

crawler [1920s] (US; a legless beggar, usu. moving with the aid of a small wheeled platform)

gimp [1920s+] (US; a crippled beggar)

halfy [1910s–50s] (US; a legless beggar)

joy-rider [1920s–30s] (US; a legless beggar who transports themselves on a skateboard)

single-jack [20C] (US tramp; a one-legged, one-armed or one-eyed beggar)

stumpy [late 19C+] (US; a crippled beggar, esp. one with a leg missing)

❝ ❝

moocher [mid-19C+] (lit. 'skulker')

needy [mid-19C]

needy mizzler [early–mid-19C]

ninny [late 16C–18C] (a whining beggar)

padder [16C] (*pad* = road)

panhandler [19C+] (US)

peg-legger [1930s–40s] (rhy. sl.)

schnorrer [20C] (Yiddish)

shooler/shoolman/shuler [mid-19C] (dial. *shool*, to go about
  begging)

storm-buzzard [1930s–40s] (US Black)

stroller [1980s+] (S.Afr.; Scot. 'vagabond')

touch artist [1940s] (US)

SCROUNGERS

back-row hopper [late 19C–1900s] (a tavern scrounger hoping
  to find someone to buy them a drink)

biter [1950s+] (Aus.)

bot [1910s] (Aus./N.Z.)

botfly [1940s+] (Aus.)

cadger [late 19C+]

dole-bludger [1970s+] (Aus.; a person who claims unemploy-
  ment benefit while work is available or while actually working
  in the 'black' economy)

ear-biter [1930s–50s] (US)

ear-lugger [20C] (Aus.)

freeloader [1930s+] (orig. US)

hum [1910s–30s] (Aus.)

hummer [1910s–40s] (Aus.)

knight of the scran-bag [19C]

lug [1920s+] (orig. US)

lug-biter [late 19C] (Aus.)

mump [early 18C]

mumper [late 17C+]

scadger [mid–late 19C] (i.e. 'cadger')

shirk/sherk [mid-17C–mid-18C]

snorer/snorrer [20C]

tapper [late 19C+]

thumber [1980s+] (US campus; someone who *thumbs* lifts)

tiger [mid-19C]

toucher [mid-19C+]

urger [1910s–60s] (Aus.)

MISERS

Cheap Charlie [20C]

cheapie [1970s+] (orig. US)

cheapo [1970s+]

dotties man [late 19C] (*dots* = money)

hog [20C] (US)

Jew [17C+]

love-penny [early 18C]

man with no hands [1940s+] (Aus.)

meany [1920s+] (usu. juv.)

minge bag [1990s]

moss dog [1910s] (*moss* = money)

near/nearbone [1930s+] (Ulster)

nickel nurser [1910s–70s] (US)

old flint [mid-19C]

old huddle (and twang) [mid-16C–mid-17C]

scrape-all [late 17C–18C]

screw [mid–late 19C]

Scrooge [mid-19C+] (Ebenezer *Scrooge*, the miserly figure in Charles Dickens' *A Christmas Carol*)

scurf [mid–late 19C] (a type of skin disease)

skate/skater [late 19C+] (cheap*skate*)

skinflint [late 18C+]

sting-bum [late 17C–early 19C]

vinegar pisser [late 18C–early 19C]

Yorkshire bite [19C]

zipper pockets [1970s] (US)

99 99 99 99 99 99 99 99 99 99 99 99 99 99 99 99 99 99 99 99 99 99 99

Clutchers, grippers and pinchers

clam [mid-19C+] (US)

clutch-fist [19C]

gripe-money [17C]

gripes [late 17C–18C]

gripper [late 19C]

penny-pincher [1930s+]

pinch-fart [late 16C–early 17C]

pinch-fist [late 16C–1900s]

pinch-penny [15C–mid-18C]

tight-arse/tight-ass/tight-butt [1980s+] (orig. US)

tight hand [1950s] (W.I.)

tightwad [late 19C+]

66 66 66 66 66 66 66 66 66 66 66 66 66 66 66 66 66 66 66 66 66 66 66

SOCIAL CLASSES

THE UPPER CLASSES

Algie/Algy [late 19C]

Astorbilt/Mr Astorbilt [20C] (US; the wealthy families *Astor* + Vander*bilt*)

bagel [1970s+] (S.Afr.; an upper-class young Jewish man)

big bug [19C] (US)

bit of posh [1970s+]

chinless wonder [1960s+]

high hat/high hatter [1920s+] (orig. US; a member of a social elite)

long-nose [1900s–30s] (US)

Miss Astor/Mrs Astor [1960s+] (US; an elite 'social leader' of a community)

nob [mid-18C+] (*nob*leman)

pinktea [1950s+] (US gay; an upper-class homosexual)

poshy [1990s+]

Rupert [1970s+] (orig. milit.)

Sloane (Ranger) [1970s+] (an upper-class southern Englishwoman, punning on *Sloane* Square + Lone *Ranger*)

stuffed shirt [1910s+] (orig. US; a pompous, aristocratic but ineffectual person)

stuff-jacket [1910s–30s]

title [1900s]

toff [mid-19C+] (i.e. 'tuft')

tuft [mid-18C–late 19C] (a titled undergraduate, from the *tuft* attached to a titled student's mortarboard)

upper [1950s–60s]

SOCIAL ELITES AND THEIR MEMBERS

Avenoodles/Fifth Avenoodles [mid–late 19C] (US; the elite residents of New York; *Fifth Ave*nue + *noodle,* a fool)

bong tong [late 19C–1900s] (Aus.; French *bon ton,* good taste/breeding)

99 99 99 99 99 99 99 99 99 99 99 99 99 99 99 99 99 99 99 99 99 99

Spurious and rowdy aristocrats

bit of haw-haw [late 19C–1900s] (a fop or dandy)

blood [mid-16C–late 19C] (an aristocratic rowdy)

Countess/Duchess of Puddle-dock [mid-17C–mid-19C] (a self-appointed but spurious aristocrat, from *Puddledock,* formerly a large stagnant pool off the River Thames)

Count No-account [late 19C–1910s] (a person posing fraudulently as an aristocrat)

haw-haw toff [late 19C] (a dandy or aristocrat)

hooray Henry/hoorah Henry [1930s+] (orig. US; a wealthy young man given to displays of public exhibitionism)

wellies [1980s+] (public-school educated upper middle-class students who play rather than work their way through university, from the green *wellington* boots worn to pursue rural pastimes)

66 66 66 66 66 66 66 66 66 66 66 66 66 66 66 66 66 66 66 66 66 66

brownstone front [mid-19C–1900s] (US; from their expensive *brownstone* houses)

carriage trade [20C]

cave-dweller [late 19C] (US; a member of the old New York aristocracy, from the old, dark mansions in which they live)

class [1950s+]

fancy pants [late 19C+]

five hundred [20C] (US)

green welly brigade [1970s+] (the rural upper classes)

hi si [1950s] (US; *hi*gh so*ci*ety)

silk stockings [late 18C–late 19C] (US)

straw hat push [1900s–30s] (Aus.)

t.o.m.s [1960s+] (Can.; *T*oronto, *O*ttawa and *M*ontreal, i.e. the Canadian urban elite)

upper crust [mid-19C+]

❞ ❞

'Vagina little-finger' and other snobs

la-di-dah [mid-19C+]

Lord Muck/Lady Muck [1930s+]

snoot [mid-19C+] (i.e. their 'snout' is in the air)

snotnose [1940s+] (orig. US)

snotty-nose [19C+]

toffee-nose [1940s+] (orig. milit.)

upways [1970s+] (US Black)

vagina little-finger [1950s–60s] (camp gay; *vagina* = Virginia, seen as an upper-class name + the *little finger* crooked while drinking)

❝ ❝

fish 'n' chip mob

THE LOWER CLASSES

beggar trash [20C] (US)

coppertail/coppertop [late 19C–1950s] (Aus; a person of little social standing)

donkey [1930s+] (a working-class Irish person)

droog/droogie [1990s] (US teen; a term coined by Anthony Burgess in *A Clockwork Orange*, where it meant 'friend')

fish 'n' chip mob [1970s] (society)

grit [1980s] (US campus; a working-class White student, from a type of food eaten in the South US)

janga-manga [1940s] (W.I.; lit. 'river-prawn eater')

linthead/lintbrain [1930s–60s] (US; orig. a worker in a cotton mill)

pleb/plebbie/plebby [1970s]

prole [1920s+]

rank and smell [late 19C]

sad vulgar [late 19C] (society)

schemie [20C] (someone who lives on a Scottish council estate or 'scheme')

scrubber [1950s+] (Irish; a common working-class woman)

yob [1920s+] (backslang, 'boy')

PARVENUS AND SOCIAL CLIMBERS

casual [1980s] (a working-class youth who dresses in designer-labelled *casual* clothing, but whose lifestyle remains resolutely proletarian)

codfish aristocracy [19C] (those nouveaux riches whose fortunes sprang from the Massachusetts cod industry)

dog-salmon aristocracy [19C] (US)

flash [early 17C–early 19C] (a nouveau riche)

gutter-blood [mid-19C] (a parvenu, a vulgar man who puts on airs)

99 99 99 99 99 99 99 99 99 99 99 99 99 99 99 99 99 99 99 99 99

Essex girls and boys

Kevin [1980s+] (upper and middle classes; a lower-middle- or working-class youth, seen as overly flashy and socially unacceptable)

Sharon/Shaz [1980s+] (middle class; Kevin's female equivalent, a lower-middle- or working-class young woman, seen as overly flashy and socially unacceptable)

Tracey [1980s+] (middle class; a type of a lower-middle- or working-class young woman identical to Sharon)

66 66 66 66 66 66 66 66 66 66 66 66 66 66 66 66 66 66 66 66 66

half-hour gentleman [late 19C] (society; a parvenu, one in whom breeding is at best an affectation)

Jack Gentleman [late 17C–18C] (a man of low birth or manners who has pretensions to be a gentleman)

mushroom [late 18C–early 19C] (a nouveau riche individual, from the propensity of the fungus to 'spring up overnight')

neecee princess [late 19C–1920s] (society; a nouveau riche young woman, from the London postal district *E*ast *C*entral, the City)

new nayga/new nigger [1940s] (W.I.; a parvenu, a nouveau riche)

recently struck it [late 19C] (US; a nouveau riche)

silvertail [late 19C–1950s] (orig. Aus.)

soc/soch/sosh [20C] (US teen; *soc*ial)

society-maddist [late 19C]

upjump [1910s+] (Aus.; an upstart, a nouveau riche)

uppities [late 19C] (US; social climbers)

zoot-suiter [1930s–40s] (US)

99 99 99 99 99 99 99 99 99 99 99 99 99 99 99 99 99 99 99 99 99

Three aspiring Aussies

Fitzroy Yank [1940s+] (Aus.; an unsophisticated person who tries to imitate the style of an American)

Pyrmont Yank [1950s+] (Aus.)

Woolloomooloo Yank/Woolloomooloo Frenchman [1950s+] (Aus.)

66 66 66 66 66 66 66 66 66 66 66 66 66 66 66 66 66 66 66 66 66

DRESSING UP AND DRESSING DOWN

TWO CENTURIES OF FLASHY DRESSERS

flash girl [19C]

tiger [19C]

tigress [early–mid-19C]

burerk/burick [mid-19C]
(Scot. *bure*, a loose woman)

leary bloke [mid-19C]

totty all colours [late 19C] (a
woman whose dress
resembles a 'coat of many
colours')

barber's block [late
19C–1920s] (an over-dressed
man, from the wooden
'head' on which a barber
placed a wig)

flash of light [late 19C+] (a
gaudily dressed woman)

Christmas tree [20C] (US; a
heavily over-made-up or
over-dressed woman)

lacy-pants [20C] (US)

**Mrs Astor's pet horse/billy
goat/cow/pet cow/plush
horse** [1920s+] (US; an
over-made-up or over-
dressed person)

Christmas tree

beetle [1930s–60s]

butterfly [1940s] (US Black)

clotheshorse [1940s+] (an over-dressed woman)

fancy pants [1940s+] (orig. US; an overdressed man, erring towards the effeminate in this preoccupation)

glamour puss [1950s+] (an ostentatiously well-dressed woman)

caution sign [1970s+] (US Black; anyone who dresses in an excessively gaudy and vulgar manner, with many clashing bright colours)

Santa Claus [1970s+] (US Black; a vulgar, gaudy and tasteless dresser)

99 99 99 99 99 99 99 99 99 99 99 99 99 99 99 99 99 99 99 99 99

Polyester princesses and other fashion criminals

bamma [1980s+] (US Black; Ala*bama*, the archetypal unsophisticated southern US state)

Barney [1980s+] (US campus; the *Flintstones* cartoon character *Barney* Rubble)

dag [1910s+] (Aus./N.Z.; orig. a piece of matted wool and excrement clinging to a sheep's backside)

fashion criminal/fashion mutant [1980s+] (US campus)

p.d.k. [1980s+] (US campus; *p*olyester *d*ouble *k*nit)

polyester princess [1990s] (US campus)

Zelda Gooch [1950s] (camp gay)

66 66 66 66 66 66 66 66 66 66 66 66 66 66 66 66 66 66 66 66 66

99 99 99 99 99 99 99 99 99 99 99 99 99 99 99 99 99 99 99 99 99

All dressed up...

all dolled up like a barber's cat [mid–late 19C] (Can.)

done up/dressed up/mockered up like a pox doctor's clerk [1950s+] (Aus.)

dressed/dolled/done up like a sore finger/thumb/toe [20C] (Aus./N.Z./US)

66 66 66 66 66 66 66 66 66 66 66 66 66 66 66 66 66 66 66 66 66

99 99 99 99 99 99 99 99 99 99 99 99 99 99 99 99 99 99 99 99 99

Trendoids and other fashion victims

esprit chick [1990s] (US teen; a girl who wears only designer clothing and looks down on others who dress differently)

fashion victim [1980s+] (anyone seen as being overly obedient to the fast-changing fluctuations of fashion, esp. those who unquestioningly adopt its more ludicrous excesses)

Ken [1980s+] (US campus; a painstakingly fashionably dressed and groomed man, from the popular toy and partner of Barbie)

trendoid [1980s+] (one who is slavishly devoted to following the latest trends, but never quite achieves the correct effect)

trendy [1960s+] (a devoted, if not always wholly successful, trend-follower)

66 66 66 66 66 66 66 66 66 66 66 66 66 66 66 66 66 66 66 66 66

99 99 99 99 99 99 99 99 99 99 99 99 99 99 99 99 99 99 99 99 99 99

Captain Queer-nabs and other tawdry dressers

bartholemew baby [late–mid-19C] (one who is dressed in tawdry finery from the dolls sold at the annual Bartholemew Fair)

Captain Queer-nabs [late 17C–early 19C] (a shabby, ill-dressed person)

Florence [late 17C–18C] (an untidily dressed young woman)

moggie/moggy [early 18C–late 19C] (an untidily dressed woman, a slattern)

rag bag/rag doll [late 19C+] (a sloppily-dressed woman, a slattern)

slummy [late 19C–1930s] (an ill-dressed, unattractive woman)

Sukey-Tawdry [mid-19C]

welfare mother [1960s+] (US Black; any woman, irrespective of status vis-à-vis welfare, who is poorly dressed and unkempt)

66 66 66 66 66 66 66 66 66 66 66 66 66 66 66 66 66 66 66 66 66 66

COUNTRY-DWELLERS

THE RUSTIC THROUGH FIVE CENTURIES

BACON AND CLUMPERTON: THE 16TH-CENTURY RUSTIC

clumperton [mid-16C–early 18C] (*clump* + simple*ton*)

bacon [late 16C–17C]

HOBNAILS AND LOBLOLLIES: THE 17TH-CENTURY RUSTIC

clod [17C]

loblolly [early 17C–late 19C] (lit. 'bubbling broth')

bacon-slicer [mid-17C]

country put [late 17C–late 18C]

hobnail [late 17C–19C]

hodge [late 17C–19C]

hick [late 17C+]

CLODHOPPERS AND MOSS-JUMPERS: THE 18TH-CENTURY RUSTIC

clodhopper [18C+]

country cokes [early 18C]

country hick [early 18C]

moss-jumper [mid-18C–mid-19C]

clouted-shoe/clout-shoe [late 18C]

BILLY TURNIPTOP: THE 19TH-CENTURY RUSTIC

cornthrasher [19C]

Toby Trot [19C]

hayseed [19C+] (Aus./N.Z./US)

milestone [early 19C]

chaw-bacon [early 19C+]

wool hat [early 19C+] (US)

Johnny [mid-19C]

whop-straw/Johnny Whop-straw [mid-19C]

bush-scrubber [late 19C] (Aus.)

barndoor savage [late 19C–1900s]

Billy Turniptop [late 19C–1900s] (an agricultural labourer)

punch clod [late 19C–1900s]

WOOLLY-BACKS AND CORNBALLS: THE 20TH-CENTURY RUSTIC

bacon-bonce [20C]

country-bookie/country boo-boo/country buck [20C] (W.I.)

road roller [1900s–30s] (N.Z.)

dad and dave [1930s+] (Aus.; the 1930s radio show *Dad and Dave*, set in rural Australia)

sod-buster [1930s+]

culchie [1940s+] (Irish *coillte*, woods)

hickey [1940s+] (Aus.)

boonie [1950s+] (i.e. one who lives in the *boondocks*, a rough country region)

cornball [1950s+]

woolly-back [1960s+]

swede [1970s+]

hickster [1990s]

🙶 🙶

A pair of rustic boobies

bitch booby [late 18C] (lit. 'female peasant')

dog booby [late 18C] (lit. 'male peasant')

🙸 🙸

BUSH HOGS AND COUNTRY JERKS:
A REDNECK LEXICON

barnyard savage [1900s–50s] (US)

boghopper [20C] (US)

briar-breaker/briar-hopper [1930s+] (US)

brush ape [20C] (US)

buckwheat [19C] (US)

bush ape [1940s] (US)

bush hog [1980s] (US)

bush rat [1930s–40s] (US)

canvasback [19C] (US)

clod-buster [1950s+] (US)

clod-crusher [late 19C] (US)

clod-jumper [1910s+] (US)

clod-knocker [20C] (US)

clod-masher [1960s–70s] (US)

cob [19C] (US; corn*cob*, from the supposed use of corncobs in place of lavatory paper)

corncobber [1970s] (US)

99 99 99 99 99 99 99 99 99 99 99 99 99 99 99 99 99 99 99 99 99 99 99

Animal-loving hicks

bull-driver [20C] (US)

cow jockey [20C] (US)

goat roper [20C] (US)

hog-rubber [early 17C]

possum-eater [1940s–50s] (Aus.)

squirrel-shooter/squirrel-popper [20C] (US)

66 66 66 66 66 66 66 66 66 66 66 66 66 66 66 66 66 66 66 66 66 66

cow jockey

corncracker [mid-19C+] (US)

cornfed [1910s] (US)

cornhusker [19C] (US)

country jerk [20C] (US)

ear of corn [1910s] (US)

farmer [mid-19C+] (US)

gully-jumper [20C] (US)

hilljack [20C] (US)

lane/lain [1930s–60s] (US Black; i.e. they live in a
country *lane*)

plow jockey [19C] (US)

redneck [early 19C+] (orig. US)

shitkicker [1960s+] (US)

stomp-jumper [19C] (US)

99 99 99 99 99 99 99 99 99 99 99 99 99 99 99 99 99 99 99 99 99

Fruit- and vegetable-loving hicks

acorn-cracker [1900s] (US)
apple-knocker [1910s+] (US)
apple-picker [1910s] (US)
apple-shaker [mid–late 19C] (US)
apple-squeezer [1930s] (US)
berry picker [20C] (US)
carrot cruncher [1960s+] (a visitor to
    London from the provinces)
cherry-picker [1920s–70s]
clover-kicker [1910s+] (US)
hay-pounder/hay-shagger/hay-shaker [20C]
    (Aus./N.Z./US)
pumpkin-roller [20C] (US)
swede-basher [1930s+]
turnip-snagger [20C] (Irish)

66 66 66 66 66 66 66 66 66 66 66 66 66 66 66 66 66 66 66 66 66

strawhead [1950s–60s] (US)
stump-jumper [19C] (US)
wood hick [19C] (US)

POLITICAL TYPES

LIBERALS AND LEFT-WINGERS

bolshie/bolshy [1920s+]
bagel baby [1950s+] (US; a young middle-class Jewish woman,
    active in liberal causes)

99 99 99 99 99 99 99 99 99 99 99 99 99 99 99 99 99 99 99 99 99 99 99

Naming the hick baby:
a short A–Z of 'rustic names'

Alvin [1940s+] (US)

Clem [20C] (US)

Clyde [1940s+] (orig. US Black)

Elmer [1920s–60s] (US)

Gomer [1960s+] (US; *Gomer* Pyle, a fictional TV yokel)

Hiram [20C] (US; an Old Testament name popular amongst Puritan immigrants)

Ike [late 19C+] (US)

Jasper [mid-19C+] (US)

Josh [mid-19C–1900s] (US)

Reuben [19C] (US)

Rube [late 19C+] (US; i.e. 'Reuben')

Rufus [1900s–50s] (US)

66 66 66 66 66 66 66 66 66 66 66 66 66 66 66 66 66 66 66 66 66 66 66

commie [1940s+]

commo [1940s+]

lefty [1930s+] (orig. US)

longhair [1960s+]

pink [1920s+] (orig. US)

pinkie [1970s] (Aus.)

pinko [1930s+] (orig. US)

red [1920s+]

red fed [1920s+] (N.Z.)

99 99 99 99 99 99 99 99 99 99 99 99 99 99 99 99 99 99 99 99 99 99

Champagne socialists

Band-Aid liberal [1980s]
Bollinger Bolshevik [1980s+]
cadillac commie [1990s]
champagne socialist [1980s+]
limousine liberal [1970s+]
parlour pink [1920s+]

66 66 66 66 66 66 66 66 66 66 66 66 66 66 66 66 66 66 66 66 66 66

red-ragger [1910s+] (Aus.)
splib [1940s–70s] (US Black; 'a liberal Black who looks angry
  but will not upset the status quo')
trendinista [1980s] (US campus; a political or social activist who
  combines heightened political consciousness with stylish
  clothing; *trend* + Sand*inista*)

STICK-IN-THE-MUDS

blimp [1930s+]
cube [1950s–60s]
dinosaur [1970s+]
dodo [late 19C+] (i.e. they are 'dead as a dodo')

99 99 99 99 99 99 99 99 99 99 99 99 99 99 99 99 99 99 99 99 99 99

Two capitalists
breadhead [1960s+]
nabob [mid–late 19C]

66 66 66 66 66 66 66 66 66 66 66 66 66 66 66 66 66 66 66 66 66 66

dug-out [1910s+]

dusty bread [1970s] (US Black; a conventional, conservative woman)

fart-head [1990s]

fogram/fogrum [late 18C–late 19C] (lit. 'out of date')

foozle/fuzzle [20C] (i.e. 'fossil')

fuddy-duddy/fud/fuddy-dud [20C] (dial. *duddy fuddiel*, a ragged fellow)

mouldy fig [1930s+] (orig. US; applied by modern jazz fans to fans of traditional New Orleans jazz)

old stick-in-the-mud [early 19C+]

old wigsby [late 19C] (middle class)

shell-back [1940s+]

square [1940s+] (orig. US Black)

square apple [20C] (US Und.)

stick-in-the-mud [early 18C+]

99 99 99 99 99 99 99 99 99 99 99 99 99 99 99 99 99 99 99 99 99 99

Right-wingers

hanger and flogger [20C] (a person who favours capital and corporal punishment)

hard-shell [mid-19C–1970s] (US)

moss-back/mossy-back [late 19C+] (i.e. they move so slowly that moss could grow on their back)

to the right of Genghis Khan [20C] (extremely right-wing)

66 66 66 66 66 66 66 66 66 66 66 66 66 66 66 66 66 66 66 66 66 66

PROFESSIONALLY INCOMPETENT AND CRIMINALLY DANGEROUS

THE POLICE

THE POLICE AS A UNIT

Babylon [1940s+] (orig. W.I., then UK/US Black; i.e. they are the sinful opposite of the Rastafarian 'promised land' of Africa)

big John [1950s+] (US Black)

the Bill [1960s+]

the boys [mid-19C] (US)

busters [1990s] (US Black)

chota [1960s+] (US)

cowboys [1950s+]

deputy do-right/do-right [1970s+] (US Black)

divine rights/divine right [1990s] (US Black)

fifty [1990s] (US Black; i.e. 'five-oh')

five-oh [1980s+] (US Black/teen; the TV police show *Hawaii 5-0*)

the fuzz [1920s+] (orig. US)

heat [1930s+] (US)

99 99 99 99 99 99 99 99 99 99 99 99 99 99 99 99 99 99 99 99 99 99 99

'The filth'

awful people [1940s–60s] (society)

crowbar brigade [mid–late 19C] (Irish)

the filth [1960s+] (UK Und.)

gestapo/gestaps [1950s+] (US Black)

hogs [1970s+] (US Black)

the swine [1970s+] (US Black)

66 66 66 66 66 66 66 66 66 66 66 66 66 66 66 66 66 66 66 66 66

Johnny-be-good [1970s–80s] (US Black)

the law [early 19C+] (orig. US)

nail 'em and jail 'em [1970s+] (US Black)

nailers [1960s] (US Black)

Old Bill [1950s+]

the plods [1970s+]

Sherlock Holmes [1960s+] (US Black)

POLICEMEN

bacon [1970s+]

beat-pounder [20C]

big eyes [20C] (US; police officers engaged in surveillance operations)

big hat [1960s+] (US)

bogey/bogy [1920s+] (lit. 'demon')

boogerman [20C] (US)

constab [20C] (W.I.; *constab*le)

cop [late 19C+] (orig. US)

copper [mid-19C+]

county mountie [1970s+] (US; a local policeman)

cozzpot [1960s]

creeper [1940s] (US Black)

dibble/dibb [1990s] (Officer *Dibble*, the policeman character in the TV cartoon series *Top Cat*)

dog-driver [1910s+] (W.I.)

door shaker [1940s–60s] (US)

flatfoot/flatheel [1910s+] (i.e. their *feet* are *flat* from pounding the beat)

fuzzy [1940s+]

gongers [1930s–40s] (police patrolling in cars; *gong* = the bell, which preceded the siren, on police cars)

gum heel [1960s+] (US prison; the rubber-soled shoes used for creeping around unheard)

Keystone [1910s+] (the comically inept *Keystone Cops* of the early cinema)

killjoy [1940s] (US Black)

limb (of the law) [1930s+] (Aus.)

loo [1960s+] (US; *loo*-tenant, i.e. lieutenant)

man who rides the screaming gasser [1930s–40s] (US Black; a policeman in a patrol car)

nod/noddy (men) [1960s+]

odd [1930s–50s]

peel [1920s+] (Aus.; *peel*er)

rad [1990s] (UK Black)

roller [1960s+] (US Black; a policeman who specializes in stopping and searching people on the street, lit. 'robber')

rozzer [late 19C+]

sidewalk snail [1940s–50s] (US)

sidewalk snail

99 99 99 99 99 99 99 99 99 99 99 99 99 99 99 99 99 99 99 99 99

Policemen in rhyming slang

RHYMING WITH COP

ginger-pop [late 19C]
greasy (mop) [20C] (Aus.)
hop [1910s+] (US)
John Hop/Johnny Hop [1910s+]
lemon (drop) [1980s+]
lollipop/lolly/lollypop [20C]
pork chop [20C]
string and top [20C]

RHYMING WITH COPPER

bottle and stopper [1950s–70s] (US)
grasshopper [late 19C–1950s]
Johnny Hopper [1910s+]

RHYMING WITH DICK

club and stick [20C]

RHYMING WITH JOHN

hot scone [1920s+] (Aus.)

RHYMING WITH OFFICER OF THE LAW

hammer and saw [1920s] (US)

RHYMING WITH POLICE

ducks and geese [20C] (Aus.)

RHYMING WITH SARGE

half of marge [1980s+] (UK Und.)

66 66 66 66 66 66 66 66 66 66 66 66 66 66 66 66 66 66 66 66 66

99 99 99 99 99 99 99 99 99 99 99 99 99 99 99 99 99 99 99 99 99 99

Butterboys and rusty guns

butterboy/butter-basher [1930s+] (a young policeman)

dupey-dupe [1970s+] (a foolishly naïve young policeman)

hairbag [1950s+] (US; a veteran police officer)

rusty gun [1960s+] (US; a veteran police officer)

savage [20C] (US; a young police officer keen to make arrests)

66 66 66 66 66 66 66 66 66 66 66 66 66 66 66 66 66 66 66 66 66 66

99 99 99 99 99 99 99 99 99 99 99 99 99 99 99 99 99 99 99 99 99 99

Policewomen

confidence-queen [late 19C] (US; a female detective)

Dickless Tracy [1960s+] (mainly US Und.; punning on the comic-strip detective *Dick Tracy*)

Goldie Locks [20C] (US; a uniformed policewoman, the 'locks' being those on handcuffs or police cells)

G-woman [1980s+] (US; a female FBI agent)

Smoky Beaver [1970s] (US; punning on 'Smoky Bear' + *beaver*, a woman)

66 66 66 66 66 66 66 66 66 66 66 66 66 66 66 66 66 66 66 66 66 66

town clown [1920s–40s] (US; a policeman working in a village or a small town)

weakheart [1970s]

woodentop [1980s] (a uniformed policeman)

woolly [1960s+] (a uniformed policeman)

BOYS IN BLUE

Alice Blue (gown) [1970s]

blue [mid-19C+] (US)

bluebelly [late 19C–1940s] (US)

blueberry (hill) [1960s+] (rhy. sl. 'the Bill')

bluebottle [mid-19C+]

blue boy [late 19C+]

99 99 99 99 99 99 99 99 99 99 99 99 99 99 99 99 99 99 99 99 99 99 99 99

A coterie of camp coppers

Alice [1970s] (camp gay)

Bobbsey twins [1950s–60s] (US camp gay)

Brenda (Bracelets) [1980s+] (camp gay)

Hilda Handcuffs [1980s+] (camp gay)

Lily Law/Lilly Law [1940s+] (orig. US gay)

Lucy Law [1960s+] (gay)

mother superior [1950s–70s] (camp gay; a police sergeant)

our friend with the talking brooch [1980s+] (gay; *talking brooch* = walkie-talkie)

sisters [1950s–60s] (camp gay)

Teresa Truncheon [1980s+] (camp gay)

66 66 66 66 66 66 66 66 66 66 66 66 66 66 66 66 66 66 66 66 66 66 66

99 99 99 99 99 99 99 99 99 99 99 99 99 99 99 99 99 99 99 99 99

Murphy and Muldoon:
Irish-American officers

Charlie Irvine [1970s+] (US Black)

Doolan [20C] (Aus.)

Gallagher and Sheehan [1910s] (US; the Irish
vaudeville stars)

Johnny Gallagher [20C] (US)

Muldoon [19C] (US)

Murphy [1960s] (US)

O'Malley [1990s]

Paddy [1940s+] (US Black)

shamrock [19C+] (US)

66 66 66 66 66 66 66 66 66 66 66 66 66 66 66 66 66 66 66 66 66

blue dangers [1960s+] (US Und.)

blue devils [19C]

blue-light special [1990s] (US Black)

Blue Meanies [1960s–70s] (the villains of the animated Beatles
film *Yellow Submarine*)

blues [20C] (Aus.)

John Bluebottle [20C]

little boy blue [1960s+] (US Black)

man in blue [late 19C]

raw lobster/unboiled lobster [early 19C]

MR PLOD AND OTHER 'NAMED' OFFICERS

Charlie Goon/Charlie Goons [1930s+] (US Black)

drack/drac [1960s+] (Aus.; *Dra*cula)

J. Edgar [1970s+] (US Black)

John Dunn [1930s+] (Aus.; mispron. of French *gendarme*)

John Elbow [20C] (i.e. they grab people by the *elbow*)

John Nabs [20C]

Johnny Law [1920s+] (US)

John Q. Law [1980s+] (US)

Mickey Mouse [1940s+] (US; equating the black and white colours of a police patrol car with those of *Mickey Mouse*)

Mr Plod [1970s+] (PC *Plod*, the policeman in Enid Blyton's *Noddy* books)

Penelope/penelopes [1990s] (US)

three-bullet Joey [1960s–80s] (US Black)

99 99 99 99 99 99 99 99 99 99 99 99 99 99 99 99 99 99 99 99 99 99

Feds and spooks

feebie [1940s+] (US; an agent of the FBI)

G-guy [1930s] (US; *G*overnment *guy*)

G-man [1930s+] (US)

hard John [1930s–40s] (US Black; an FBI agent)

spook [1940s+] (US; an agent of the CIA)

Uncle Whiskers [1920s+] (US Und.; a federal agent, from the facial hair traditionally adorning images of *Uncle* Sam)

66 66 66 66 66 66 66 66 66 66 66 66 66 66 66 66 66 66 66 66 66 66

ARRESTERS

body-snatcher [early 19C–1930s] (US)

catcher [mid-19C] (US)

collar [late 19C–1900s] (US; i.e. they *collar* criminals)

grab [mid–late 19C; 1950s]

hook [1990s] (US Black/Und.)

nabber [mid-19C–1960s] (US)

nailer [mid-19C]

nipper [mid–late 19C] (US)

pinch and padlock man [19C]

pincher [19C]

snatcher [19C+]

trap [early 18C+]

bulldog

THE MAN WITH A HEADACHE STICK

big stick [20C] (US)

bludger [1940s+] (Aus. Und.; i.e. 'bludgeoner')

headbeater/headbuster [1950s+] (US Black; a brutal police officer)

headknocker [1960s+] (US; a brutal police officer)

headwhipper [1950s+] (US Black)

man with a headache stick [1950s–60s] (US Black)

robocop [1980s] (US; a brutal or racist policeman)

skull-buster [1930s+] (US Black)

stickman [1950s–70s] (US Black)

walloper [1940s+] (Aus.)

whips [1960s+] (US Black)

whup-a-child [1970s+] (US Black)

PIGS, DOGS AND OTHER ANIMALS

animal [1910s+]

bear [1970s] (US)

the beast [1980s+] (W.I./UK Black teen)

beast-boy/beast-bwoy [1990s] (Black)

bull [late 19C+] (orig. US)

bulldog [1940s] (US)

dog [1960s] (US Black)

grunter [early 19C]

hog [1960s+] (US)

law dog/law hound [late 19C+] (US)

locust [mid-19C] (US)

oink [1960s+] (orig. US Black)

oinker [1980s+] (US)

99 99 99 99 99 99 99 99 99 99 99 99 99 99 99 99 99 99 99 99 99

The Vice Squad

crapper dick [20C] (US; i. e. they hang around
   public lavatories – *crappers* – to entrap gay men)
hoonchaser [1980s+] (N.Z.; lit. 'pimp chaser')
Mr Sin [1970s–80s] (US Black/LA)
mutton-shunter [late 19C] (*mutton* = prostitute)
pretender to the throne [1950s–60s] (US gay;
   a policeman who poses as gay to entrap
   homosexuals, punning on *throne*, a toilet)
pretty police [20C] (policemen specializing in
   the entrapment of gay men)
pussy posse [1960s+] (US police; officers who
   deal with prostitutes)
queer detail [1950s+] (US; officers who deal
   with homosexual crime)
rabbit pie shifter [19C] (*rabbit pie* = prostitute)
Vera Vice/Victoria Vice [1950s+] (gay)

66 66 66 66 66 66 66 66 66 66 66 66 66 66 66 66 66 66 66 66 66

pig [early 19C+]
porker [1970s]
Smoky (Bear) [1970s+] (a traffic officer, from the mascot of the
   US Forest Service *Smokey the Bear*)
vark [1950s+] (S Afr.; Akrikaans, 'pig')
weasel [1920s+] (US)

TRAFFIC POLICE AND PARKING WARDENS

bald-tyre bandit [1960s+] (UK Und.)

bloubaadjie [1970s] (S Afr.; a provincial traffic officer, lit. 'blue badge')

brown bomber [1980s] (Aus.; a parking policeman, from their brown uniforms)

gay gordon [20C] (US; rhy. sl. 'traffic warden')

grey ghost/grey meanie/grey bomber [1960s+] (Aus.; a parking policeman, from their grey uniforms)

Kojak with a Kodak [1970s] (US; a policeman manning a radar speed trap)

sticker-licker [1980s] (South Aus.; a parking policemen)

wasp [1960s+] (Irish; a traffic warden, from their black and yellow uniforms)

🗣 🗣

The Drugs Squad

the D.S. [1960s+]

gazer [1930s–50s] (US Und.; a federal narcotics agent)

knocko/knockman [1980s+] (US Black; i.e. they 'come knocking at the door')

narc [1950s+] (US)

narco [1950s+] (US)

people [1950s–60s] (US Black/drugs)

Sam [1980s+] (drugs; a federal narcotics agent, i.e. they work for Uncle *Sam*)

🗣 🗣 🗣 🗣 🗣 🗣 🗣 🗣 🗣 🗣 🗣 🗣 🗣 🗣 🗣 🗣 🗣 🗣 🗣 🗣

DETECTIVES

ace [1940s–50s] (US)

bear-tracker [20C]

big four/big foe [1980s+] (US Black; tough, élite detectives dealing with organized crime, often brutal and racially bigoted)

bishop [1950s–70s] (i.e. they 'search out sin')

busy(body)/bizzy [20C] (i.e. they rush around unlike uniformed policemen 'plodding' the beat)

deek [1930s+] (US; i.e. 'dick')

dick [late 19C+] (US; northern dial. *dick*, to look at)

gumshoe

Dick Tracy [1930s+] (the comic strip detective created by Chester Gould)

eye [1930s+] (US Und.)

gumshoe/gumboot/gumfoot/gumshoer [20C] (US; the rubber-soled shoes used for creeping around unheard)

ferret [late 19C–1920s]

fink [1910s+] (US Und.)

Johnny Ham [1930s] (US; playing on 'pig')

mouser [mid-19C]

nose [late 18C+]
plant [early–mid-19C]
private star [1940s–50s] (US)
snitcher [1900s–20s] (lit. 'tell-tale')
snoop [1920s+] (orig. US)
undercover [1960s+]

THE BRITISH BOBBY: A CHRONOLOGY OF ABUSE 1500–1900

FLOGGING-COVES
    bandog [15C–late 18C] (a bailiff)
    flogging-cove [16C–19C] (a beadle)
    muggill [late 16C–early 17C] (UK Und.; a beadle)

THE 17TH CENTURY: SCABS AND BOLLY DOGS
    bolly dog [17C] (a bailiff, lit. 'hobgoblin')
    bubble buff [17C] (a bailiff, lit. 'sham man')

99 99 99 99 99 99 99 99 99 99 99 99 99 99 99 99 99 99 99 99

Plain-clothes policemen

    clothes [1960s+] (US)
    gumshoe artist [1930s+] (US)
    mod squad [1970s] (plain-clothes police, usu.
      young and dressed in the prevailing teenage
      and early 1970s fashions, who looked for
      crime in colleges and local youth centres)
    squeaky shoe [20C]

66 66 66 66 66 66 66 66 66 66 66 66 66 66 66 66 66 66 66 66

99 99 99 99 99 99 99 99 99 99 99 99 99 99 99 99 99 99 99 99 99

The Flying Squad

heavy mob/heavy squad [1950s+] (UK Und.)

the Squad [1950s+] (Und.)

the Sweeney [1930s+] (rhy. sl. *Sweeney Todd*)

umbrella branch/umbrella brigade [1970s+]
(the Special Branch; i.e. they dress in the
bowler hat and rolled umbrella uniform of
their bureaucratic masters in Whitehall)

66 66 66 66 66 66 66 66 66 66 66 66 66 66 66 66 66 66 66 66 66

cull [17C] (a constable; *cull*ion, a contemptible person)

buckle-bosom [early 17C] (a constable, lit. 'grapple-chest')

scab [17C–18C] (a constable)

clap-shoulder [17C–early 19C] (a bailiff)

shoulder-clapper [17C–early 19C] (a bailiff)

bum [late 17C–early 18C] (a bum-bailiff)

catchpole [late 17C–late 18C] (a bum-bailiff, lit. 'chicken
catcher')

Charley/Charlie [late 17C–mid-19C] (a beadle)

THE 18TH CENTURY: ROBIN HOG AND MR THINGSTABLE

hawk [18C+] (a constable)

city bulldog [early 18C] (a constable)

cony-fumble [early 18C] (mispron. of 'constable')

counter-caterpillar [early 18C] (*counter* = court prison)

lurcher [early 18C] (lit. 'lurker')

Robin Hog [early 18C] (a constable)

town trap [early 18C] (a constable)

fool-finder [late 18C] (a bailiff, i.e. only fools are around when they come to call)

lurcher of the law [late 18C–early 19C] (a bum-bailiff)

member of the catch club [late 18C–early 19C] (a bailiff)

Mr Thingstable/thingstable [late 18C–early 19C] (a constable, euphemistically avoiding the first syllable, similar in sound to 'an indecent monosyllable')

shoulder-tapper [late 18C–early 19C] (a bailiff)

BLOOMING SIX FOOT OF TRIPE: THE GREAT VICTORIAN BOBBY

brass buttons [19C]

bugaboo [19C] (a bailiff, lit. 'bogeyman')

arm (of the law) [19C+]

bum-trap [early 19C] (a bailiff)

China Street pig [early 19C] (*China Street* = Bow Street)

conk [early 19C–1900s] (i.e. they 'sniff things out')

bloodhound [early 19C+]

crusher [early 19C+] (from their large feet)

griper/gripper [early 19C+] (Irish; a bailiff)

ossifer/occifer [early 19C+] (mispron. of 'officer')

99 99 99 99 99 99 99 99 99 99 99 99 99 99 99 99 99 99 99 99 99 99 99

Kitchen coppers

the cook's own [mid–late 19C] (from contemporary policemen's supposed affection for cooks working in London mansions)

cuddle-cook [1900s–10s]

66 66 66 66 66 66 66 66 66 66 66 66 66 66 66 66 66 66 66 66 66 66 66

gentleman of the short staff [mid-19C] (a constable, from his truncheon)

Jenny Darby [mid-19C] (*darbies* = handcuffs)

johndarm [mid-19C] (pron. of French *gendarme*)

red lobsters [mid-19C] (the Metropolitan Police; *lobster* = soldier, many policemen being ex-soldiers)

scarlet runner [mid-19C] (a Bow Street runner)

stop [mid-19C]

worm [mid-19C]

bang-beggar [mid–late 19C] (mainly Scot.; a constable, from his ill-treatment of beggars)

horney [mid-19C+] (UK Und.; lit. 'the Devil')

Johnny Darby [mid-19C+] (*darbies* = handcuffs)

nark [mid-19C+] (Romani *nak*, a nose)

99 99 99 99 99 99 99 99 99 99 99 99 99 99 99 99 99 99 99 99 99 99

Bobbies and peelers

bobby/bobbie [mid-19C+] (Sir *Robert* Peel, who founded the modern police force in the 19C)

Bobby Peeler [mid–late 19C]

peeler [mid-19C+] (Sir Robert *Peel*, who founded the modern UK police force in the 19C)

reeler [late 19C]

Robert/Roberto [late 19C] (punning on 'bobby')

66 66 66 66 66 66 66 66 66 66 66 66 66 66 66 66 66 66 66 66 66 66

conk

blooming six foot of tripe [late 19C] (a large policeman, lit. 'six feet of nonsense')

finger [late 19C] (i.e. they 'point the *finger*')

elbow [late 19C–1900s] (US)

peeper [late 19C+]

COPPER'S NARKS

belcher [20C] (US Und.)

bigmouth [1940s+] (orig. US)

bitch-squeak [1950s] (US)

blab [early 17C+]

carpark [1960s+] (rhy. sl. 'nark')

cheese-eater [1950s–60s] (US)

conk [early–mid-19C] (UK Und.)

copper's nark [late 19C+]

dobber(-in) [1950s+] (Aus./N.Z.)

dog [mid-19C+] (US/Aus)

dog's nose [1960s] (US Und.)

finger [1910s+]

fink [1910s+]

fizgig/phizgig [20C] (Aus.)

grass [1930s+]

grasser [1940s+]

grasshopper [1940s+]

grass in the park [20C] (rhy. sl. 'nark')

Hyde Park [20C] (rhy. sl. 'nark')

Miss Peach [1950s–60s] (camp gay)

mouthpiece [1900s–20s]

nark [mid-19C+]

Noah's ark [late 19C+] (rhy. sl. 'nark')

nose [late 18C+]

rat [early 19C+]

rat fink/r.f. [1960s+]

shopper [1920s–50s]

snitch [late 18C+]

snout [20C]

split [late 19C+]

99 99 99 99 99 99 99 99 99 99 99 99 99 99 99 99 99 99 99 99 99 99

Singing like a canary ...

canary [1930s+] (UK/US/S.Afr. Und.)

chirper [19C+]

nightingale [20C] (UK Und.)

singer [1930s–60s] (US Und.)

stool-pigeon [mid-19C+] (orig. US)

66 66 66 66 66 66 66 66 66 66 66 66 66 66 66 66 66 66 66 66 66 66

squeaker [late 19C+]
squealer [mid-19C+]
supergrass [1970s+] (UK Und.)
tip-off [1940s+]
Tom Slick [1950s–70s] (US Black)
tripe-hound [1920s]
weasel [1920s+] (US)
welcher/welsher [mid-19C+]
whistle-blower [1960s+] (US Und.)

PRISON WARDERS

babysitter [20C] (Can.)
badge [1920s+] (US prison)
big bull [20C] (US prison; the senior guard on a shift)

99 99 99 99 99 99 99 99 99 99 99 99 99 99 99 99 99 99 99 99 99 99

Bitch's bastards

bitch's bastard [1950s+] (UK prison; a severe,
possibly violent, warder)
caser [1940s+] (UK prison; a prison officer
notorious for excessive discipline)
crank [1950s+] (US prison; a veteran warder
who takes pleasure in persecuting younger or
newer inmates)
footballer [1910s] (UK Und.; an officer who
uses their feet on the inmates)
whip boss [1940s–50s] (US prison)

66 66 66 66 66 66 66 66 66 66 66 66 66 66 66 66 66 66 66 66 66 66

big six [1950s+] (US prison; the prison riot squad)

brass nuts [1960s] (US prison)

burglar [1960s+]

cage and key man [20C] (US prison; a prison guard responsible for a particular row of cells)

eye [1930s+] (US Und.)

clicker [18C] (UK prison)

hawk [20C] (US Black)

kanga [1950s+] (Aus.; rhy. sl. *kangaroo*, screw)

key/keys [20C] (US prison)

lockup [20C] (US prison)

the man [20C] (US)

99 99 99 99 99 99 99 99 99 99 99 99 99 99 99 99 99 99 99 99 99 99

Prison warders in rhyming slang

RHYMING WITH CHIEF

bully beef [1950s+] (UK prison)

corned beef [1950s+] (UK prison)

RHYMING WITH SCREW

flue [1940s–50s] (UK prison)

four by two [1930s+] (N.Z.)

kangaroo [1920s+]

little boy blue [20C]

scooby doo [1960s+] (UK prison)

RHYMING WITH WARDER

Harry Lauder [20C]

66 66 66 66 66 66 66 66 66 66 66 66 66 66 66 66 66 66 66 66 66

main man [1950s+] (orig. US Black; a chief prison officer)

redraw [late 19C] (backslang, 'warder')

screw [early 19C+] (UK prison)

screwdriver [1940s–50s] (UK prison; a chief officer who 'drives' their subordinates)

twirl [1930s+] (UK prison; lit. 'skeleton key')

twister [20C] (US prison)

white shirt [1950s+] (UK prison; a senior prison officer, i.e. they wear a white shirt as opposed to the blue shirts of the junior ranks)

yard bull/yard hack [20C] (US)

zombie [1940s–50s] (UK prison; a prison officer who looks permanently humourless)

THE LEGAL PROFESSION

JUDGES

Barnaby Rudge [20C] (rhy. sl.)

beak [mid-16C+]

beak-gander [late 19C] (*gander* = foolish old man)

bench-man [20C] (US Und.)

conjurer [late 17C–18C] (Und.; i.e. they pull sentences 'out of the hat')

fortune-teller [late 17C–18C]

inky smudge [late 19C–1930s] (rhy. sl.)

Joe Poke [late 19C] (*Justice of the Peace*)

lambskin man [late 17C–early 19C] (from their ermine-bordered robes)

man with the book of many years [1940s] (US Black)

monk [1920s–40s] (US Und.; a Supreme Court judge)

nob in the fur trade [mid-19C] (from their ermine-bordered robes)

smear and smudge [20C] (rhy. sl.)

thirteenth juryman [late 19C] (a biased judge)

SHYSTERS AND PETTIFOGGERS: LAWYERS

ambidexter [17C–late 18C] (a corrupt lawyer who takes fees from both plaintiff and defendant)

ambulance-chaser [late 19C+] (a lawyer who offers their services to victims of street and other accidents)

black box [18C–19C] (from their black-painted deed boxes)

cop a plea [1930s+] (US Und.)

councillor of the piepowder court [mid-18C–mid-19C] (a pettifogging lawyer; *Court of Piepowders* = the court of wayfarers or travelling traders)

fee-chaser [20C] (US)

green-bag [late 17C–late 19C] (from the *green bags* used to carry briefs)

jaw cove [mid-19C] (US Und.)

law sharp [late 19C–1930s] (US)

leg of the law [19C]

legal beagle [1940s+] (orig. US)

limb of the bar [early–mid-19C] (a barrister)

limb of the law [mid-18C–mid-19C] (a second-rate attorney)

lip [1920s+] (US; a lawyer in criminal practice, i.e. they 'talk back' in defence of his client)

loudmouth [1930s+] (orig. US)

mangsman [early–mid-19C] (lit. 'one who talks')

mouse [late 19C–1900s] (punning on 'rat')

mouth [1940s–60s] (US)

mouthpiece [19C+] (in the UK a solicitor, in the US an attorney)

penitentiary agent [1950s+] (US Und.; a lawyer who seems to be working more for the courts and police than for the defence of their client)

penitentiary despatcher [1960s+] (US Und.; a public defender whose clients end up in the *penitentiary*)

pettifogger [16C+] (a second-rate lawyer who deals only in minor cases, lit. 'little crook')

Philadelphia lawyer [mid-19C] (US; a shrewd or unscrupulous lawyer)

priest of the blue bag [mid-19C] (a barrister, from the traditional *blue bag* in which they carry their gown and wig)

puzzle-cause [late 18C–early 19C] (an ignorant, incompetent lawyer)

shista [1990s] (US Black)

shyster [mid-19C+] (orig. US; German *Scheisser*, shitter)

99 99 99 99 99 99 99 99 99 99 99 99 99 99 99 99 99 99 99 99 99 99

Fags and oilies: lawyers' clerks

fag [20C] (Aus.; in school use, a junior boy who performs (menial) tasks for his elders)

oily [1950s+] (prison; a solicitor's clerk, i.e. they visit their imprisoned clients to 'clean up' their pre-trial problems)

process-pusher [late 19C] (*process* = legal writ)

66 66 66 66 66 66 66 66 66 66 66 66 66 66 66 66 66 66 66 66 66

slicker [20C] (US; a predatory lawyer)

snipe [mid–late 19C] (i.e. like the game bird, they 'present a large bill')

son of prattlement [early 18C–early 19C]

split-cause [late 17C–18C] (i.e. they *split* hairs)

sublime rascal [mid-19C]

Tom Sawyer [late 19C+] (rhy. sl.)

tongue [20C] (US Und.; a public defender, a lawyer)

tongue-padder [late 17C–early 19C]

wig [1990s] (a barrister)

POLITICIANS

baby-kisser [1960s+] (US Black)

bigwig [early 18C+]

flapdoodler/flamdoodler [19C+] (US; lit. 'one who talks rubbish')

flesh-presser [1920s+] (orig. US)

gun-fighter [1960s+] (US; an aggressively forceful political candidate)

junkyard dog [1980s+] (US; a politician adept at investigating corruption)

palm-presser [20C]

peanut politician [mid–late 19C] (US; an underhand politician seeking minor personal gains)

postmaster-general [late 18C] (the prime minister)

quockerwodger [mid-19C] (a politician acting for an influential third party, rather than properly representing their constituents)

snollygoster [mid-19C+] (US; a shrewd, unprincipled politician)

baby-kisser

tyrekicker [1980s+] (N.Z.; a politician who discusses and debates, but takes no action; orig. from car sales, a person who examines a car at length, but does not buy it)

SERVICEMEN

boom-boom [1910s+] (juv.)

caterpillar [mid-18C–early 19C] (lit. 'rapacious person')

dogface [1930s+] (US; a soldier, an infantryman)

doggie [1930s+] (US; a soldier, an infantryman)

dough-boy [mid-19C+] (US milit.; a US soldier)

flag-flasher [mid-19C] (a soldier who wears their uniform despite being off duty and in civilian surroundings)

galoot [early–mid-19C] (a soldier or a marine, lit. 'lout')

gravel agitator [late 19C+] (US; an infantryman)

gravel-crusher [late 19C+] (US; an infantryman)

99 99 99 99 99 99 99 99 99 99 99 99 99 99 99 99 99 99 99 99 99 99

Fly-boys and throttle-jockeys: the Air Force

angel food [1950s–60s] (US gay)

chicken colonel [1940s+] (US; a full colonel in the US Air Force, from the silver eagles affixed to the uniform's shoulders that denote rank)

fly-boy [1940s+] (US)

throttle-jockey [1940s] (US)

66 66 66 66 66 66 66 66 66 66 66 66 66 66 66 66 66 66 66 66 66 66

99 99 99 99 99 99 99 99 99 99 99 99 99 99 99 99 99 99 99 99 99 99

Tin hats and top brass

brass button [mid-19C–1930s] (an officer)

curled darlings [mid-19C] (society; army officers, esp. those who had returned from fighting in the Crimean War, from their long beards and curled moustaches)

gold braid [1930s+] (senior military or prison officers)

tin hat [1910s] (a senior officer)

top brass [1930s+] (US; the highest-ranking officers)

toy soldier [1940s] (US Black; an officer cadet)

66 66 66 66 66 66 66 66 66 66 66 66 66 66 66 66 66 66 66 66 66 66

ground-pounder [1940s+] (US; an infantry soldier)

grunt [1960s+] (US; a combat soldier, a Marine soldier or a non-flying Airforce officer)

Her/His Majesty's bad/hard bargain [late 18C+] (a worthless soldier, i.e. his service does not justify his pay)

kiltie/kilty [mid-19C–early 20C] (a Scottish soldier)

old dig [1940s+] (Aus./N.Z.; a veteran soldier)

parish soldier [late 18C–mid-19C] (a militia-man)

pongo [1940s+] (Aus./N.Z.; a type of large anthropoid ape)

prancer [mid-19C] (a cavalry officer)

skin-merchant [late 18C–mid-19C] (a military recruiting officer)

stoushie [20C] (Aus./N.Z.) (a soldier; dial. *stashie*, a quarrel)

Tom [1980s+] (a British soldier)

✹✹ ✹✹ ✹✹ ✹✹ ✹✹ ✹✹ ✹✹ ✹✹ ✹✹ ✹✹ ✹✹ ✹✹ ✹✹

Privates and raw recruits

awkward squad [late 19C+] (orig. milit; new recruits who prove less than tractable when it comes to obeying orders)

boot [1910s+] (US milit.)

coolie [mid–late 19C]

square-basher [1950s+] (*square* = parade ground)

swadkin [early 18C–mid-19C] (lit. 'little bumpkin')

troopie/troepie [1970s+] (S Afr.; a soldier, esp. the lowest rank of national serviceman, lit. 'trooper')

❝❝ ❝❝ ❝❝ ❝❝ ❝❝ ❝❝ ❝❝ ❝❝ ❝❝ ❝❝ ❝❝ ❝❝

99 99 99 99 99 99 99 99 99 99 99 99 99 99 99 99 99 99 99 99

Deserters, conchies and part-timers

chocolate soldier [20C] (Aus.; a soldier who was drafted into the WW2 militia but never left Australia)

conchie/conchy [1910s+] (a conscientious objector)

concho [1960s] (US; a conscientious objector)

Cuthbert [1910s–30s] (a conscientious objector; *Cuthbert*, seen as a stereotypically 'weak' name)

Dad's Army [1940s+] (the Local Defence Volunteers, latterly the Home Guard)

draftnik [1950s–70s] (US campus; a person who has avoided the military service conscription)

flag-flapper [1910s+] (Aus.; a noisily patriotic person who ensures their ineligibility for active service)

Saturday night soldier [1910s+] (a member of the British Territorial Army)

Saturday soldier [late 19C] (a military volunteer)

trotter [1960s+] (Und.; a deserter)

Whitehall warrior [1960s+] (an officer seconded to administrative duties; *Whitehall*, the home of the UK government)

66 66 66 66 66 66 66 66 66 66 66 66 66 66 66 66 66 66 66 66

TOMMY AND FRITZ: SOLDIERS OF THE WORLD WARS

Abdul [1910s–40s] (Aus.; a Turkish soldier)

Boche [20C] (a German soldier; French *Alboche*, from *Allemand*, German)

Fritz [19C+] (a German soldier)

GI Jane [1940s+] (US; a female member of the US armed forces)

GI Joe [1930s+] (US; an American soldier)

gum-chum [1940s] (an American soldier stationed in the UK, from his plentiful supplies of chewing-*gum*)

Tommy (Atkins) [late 19C+] (a typical private soldier in the British army)

THE NAVY AND THE MARINES

blueberry pie [1980s+] (US gay; from their blue uniform)

canvas-climber [late 16C]

fish [late 18C–early 19C]

gob [late 19C+] (US; from their tendency to expectorate)

gobby [late 19C–1920s]

99 99 99 99 99 99 99 99 99 99 99 99 99 99 99 99 99 99 99 99 99

Three gay soldiers

dog food [1980s+] (US gay; a soldier as a potential sexual partner)

government-inspected meat [1990s] (US gay; a gay man in the US armed forces)

uniform [1950s+] (gay; a member of the armed or uniformed services)

66 66 66 66 66 66 66 66 66 66 66 66 66 66 66 66 66 66 66 66 66

otter [late 17C–early 18C]

salt [mid-19C+] (a veteran sailor)

salt water [mid-19C]

scaly fish [late 18C] (a rough, blunt sailor)

sea-crab [late 18C]

seafood [1930s+] (gay; sailors)

sea pussy [1980s+] (US gay; a gay sailor)

splicer [1910s–20s] (i.e. they '*splice* the mainbrace')

swab [late 18C–mid-19C] (a naval officer, from the washcloth used to clean the decks)

swab jockey [20C] (US; a merchant seaman, a sailor in the US Navy)

tar [mid-17C+]

tarpaulin [mid-17C–1900s]

Wavy Navy [1910s+] (the Royal Naval Volunteer Reserve, from the wavy braid worn by its officers on their uniform sleeves until 1956)

THE MEDICAL PROFESSION

DOCTORS

baby-catcher [1960s+]

Band-Aid [mid-20C+] (orig. US milit.)

clyster-pipe [early 17C–late 18C] (lit. 'enema-pipe')

corpse-provider [mid-19C–1920s]

croaker [mid-19C+] (US; lit. 'killer')

king's proctor [20C] (rhy. sl.)

medicine man [late 19C+]

medicine sharp [late 19C–1910s] (US)

needle man/needleman [1960s+] (US)

needle puncher/needle pusher [1960s+] (US)

physic-bottle [late 19C] (lit. 'medicine bottle')

pill/pills [mid-19C–1920s] (orig. milit.)

pill-peddler [20C]

pill-pusher [late 19C+]

pill-roller [20C]

pill-shooter [1920s–30s]

salts and senna [mid–late 19C] (from their common prescriptions)

99 99 99 99 99 99 99 99 99 99 99 99 99 99 99 99 99 99 99 99 99 99 99

Pox doctors and twat-scourers

cock doctor [20C] (a venerealogist)

pox doctor [1930s+] (a venerealogist)

scrape doctor [1960s+] (an abortionist)

twat-scourer [early 18C] (lit. 'vagina cleaner')

zit doctor [1960s+] (US teen; a dermatologist)

66 66 66 66 66 66 66 66 66 66 66 66 66 66 66 66 66 66 66 66 66 66

99 99 99 99 99 99 99 99 99 99 99 99 99 99 99 99 99 99 99 99 99 99 99

Knights of the pisspot

knight of the pisspot [late 19C] (a doctor who diagnoses on the basis of urine observation)

water scriger [late 18C–early 19C] (a doctor who diagnoses on the basis of urine observation)

66 66 66 66 66 66 66 66 66 66 66 66 66 66 66 66 66 66 66 66 66

squirt [mid-19C] (from their use of syringes)

the vet [1930s+] (orig. milit.)

DOCTOR FEELGOOD

Dr Feelgood [1960s+] (a doctor who obliges patients, often showbusiness or entertainment celebrities, with amphetamines or narcotics)

right croaker [1920s+] (US; a doctor who is willing to write prescriptions for narcotic drugs, patch up wounded villains and perform other illegal services)

writer [1930s+] (drugs; a doctor who will write prescriptions for narcotics and ask no questions about the user)

writing fool [20C] (drugs; a doctor who will write as many prescriptions for narcotics as there are people requesting them)

DR DRAW-FART AND OTHER QUACKS

cow-killer [late 19C] (US; i.e. they are barely safe with animals, let alone humans)

croakus [19C]

Dr Draw-fart [19C] (an itinerant quack doctor)

dog doctor [20C] (US; i.e. they are fit only to work with animals)

dog-leech [16C–18C]

horse-leech [late 16C–mid-17C]

quack [mid-17C+] (*quack*salver, someone who *quacks* mendaciously about the quality of their medicines and salves)

SURGEONS

bone-bender/bone-butcher [late 19C+] (US)
bone-carpenter/bone-chiseller [late 19C+] (US)
bones [19C]
butcher [mid-19C+] (US; an inefficient surgeon)
flesh-tailor [17C]
knife-man [1960s+]
lint-scraper [mid–late 19C] (a junior surgeon)
pintle-smith/pintle-tagger [late 18C–1900s] (lit. 'penis stitcher')
sawbones [mid-19C+]

PSYCHIATRISTS AND PSYCHOANALYSTS

bug doctor [mid-20C] (*bug* = insane person)
dome-doctor [1950s] (orig. US; lit. 'head-doctor')
head-candler [1950s–60s] (US; *candle* = test an egg for freshness)
head doctor [1950s+] (US)
head-feeler [1940s] (US)
head-peeper [1980s] (US)
head-shrinker/headshrink [1950s+] (orig. US)
head-tripper [1970s+] (US)
loony doctor [1910s+]
nutcracker [1950s+] (US)
nut doctor [1930s+] (US)
psych [20C] (US)
shrink [1960s+] (orig. US)
soul-doctor [1950s]
squirrel [1940s+] (US; i.e. they collect 'nuts')
trick cyclist [1940s+] (orig. milit.; mispron. of 'psychiatrist')
wig-picker [1960s+] (US; lit. 'brain-picker')

tooth carpenter

DENTISTS

fang-faker [late 19C] (lit. 'tooth-maker')

gum-digger [1930s+] (Aus./N.Z.)

gum-puncher [20C]

gum-smasher [mid-19C–1920s]

ivory-carpenter/ivory-picker/ivory-puller/ivory-snatcher
   [1940s–50s] (US)

jawbreaker/jawbone breaker/jawbone doctor [1930s+] (US)

jaw cracker/jaw puller [1930s+] (US)

jawsmith/jaw-smith [1930s–40s] (US)

snag-catcher [late 19C–1910s] (*snag* = stump)

tooth carpenter [1930s–40s] (US)

UNDERTAKERS

body-snatcher [late 19C+] (US)

carrion-crow man [20C] (W.I.)

carrion-hunter [late 18C–mid-19C]

cold cook [early 18C–late 19C]

death hunter [late 18C–20C]

ghoul [1930s+] (US)

overcoat maker [20C] (they make 'wooden *overcoats*', i.e. coffins)

TEACHERS

alphabet slinger [20C] (US)

beak [late 19C+]

Betty [20C] (US)

boy-farmer [late 19C]

bubble and squeak [late 19C+] (rhy. sl. 'beak')

chalk and talk/chalk-and-talker [1920s+] (Aus.)

chalkie [1940s+] (Aus.)

99 99 99 99 99 99 99 99 99 99 99 99 99 99 99 99 99 99 99 99 99 99

Grammatical traditionalists

gerund-grinder [early 18C–late 19C]

haberdasher of (nouns and) pronouns [late 17C–19C]

knight of the grammar [late 17C–mid-18C]

syntax [late 18C–early 19C]

verb-grinder [early 19C–1920s

66 66 66 66 66 66 66 66 66 66 66 66 66 66 66 66 66 66 66 66 66 66

99 99 99 99 99 99 99 99 99 99 99 99 99 99 99 99 99 99 99 99 99

Flaybottomists:
disciplinarian teachers

brusher [18C] (i.e. 'bum-brusher')
bum-brusher [18C]
bum-jerker [early–mid-19C]
flaybottomist [late 18C]
kid-walloper [late 19C–1940s]
nip lug [19C] (Scot.; lit. 'pinch ear')
whip-arse [early 17C]

66 66 66 66 66 66 66 66 66 66 66 66 66 66 66 66 66 66 66 66 66

learning shover [late 19C]
our Miss Brooks [1950s–60s] (camp gay; the name of a TV character)
schoolie [late 19C+] (Aus.)
scull/skull [early 18C–mid-19C] (the head, principal or master of a university college)
teach [1950s+] (US)

JOURNALISTS

Brenda [mid-20C] (*Brenda* Starr, a strip cartoon created by Dale Messick)
chaunter-cove [mid–late 19C]
Fleeter-Streeter [late 19C] ('a journalist of the baser sort')
hack [early 18C+] (*hack*ney carriage, i.e. he is 'for hire')
hackette [1970s+] (a female journalist)
ink-jerker [mid-19C–1910s] (US)

ink-slinger [mid-19C+] (orig. US)

ink-splasher [1900s–20s] (US)

journo [1960s+] (orig. Aus.)

news hawk/newshound [1910s+] (orig. US)

news hen [1940s–70s] (US; a female journalist)

newsie [1950s+] (US)

penciller [late 19C] (US)

penny-a-liar [late 19C] (punning on 'penny-a-liner')

penny-a-liner [mid-19C+] (a freelance literary or journalistic hack)

sniffer and snorter [20C] (rhy. sl. 'reporter')

snitcher [1930s–40s] (US Black; lit. 'tell-tale')

sob-reporter [1920s] (US; a journalist specializing in 'human interest' stories)

tripe-hound [1920s]

BOSSES AND WORKERS

OFFICE WORKERS

bludger [1910s+] (Aus.; a term used by manual labourers, who see white-collar work as idling)

brownbagger [1950s+] (US; from the *brown bag* used for carrying their lunch to work)

cackler [20C] (US; implying the group behaviour of a flock of hens)

chair-pounder [1910s] (US)

cuff-shooter [late 19C–1900s]

deskie/deskateer [1980s] (US)

Horace [1900s–30s] (an office-boy)

ink-bottle [late 19C]

❀ ❀

Dogsbodies

dogsbody [1920s+] (nautical jargon, 'midshipman', 'junior officer')

gnome [1950s+] (US)

grunt [1970s+] (US)

munchkin [1980s+] (US)

peggy [1970s+] (Aus.; nautical jargon, 'mess-steward')

❀ ❀

ink-spiller [late 19C]

knight of the pen [mid–late 19C]

nine-to-fiver [1960s+] (orig. US)

paper-collared swell [mid–late 19C] (N.Z.)

paper pusher [20C]

paper stainer [mid–late 19C]

pencil-pusher/pen-pusher [late 19C+] (orig. US)

pen-driver [late 19C]

ribbon clerk [1960s+] (US gay; a gay man with a desk job)

working stiff [20C]

BOSSES

big augur [mid-19C+] (US)

big bloke [late 19C–1910s] (Aus.)

big wheel [1930s+]

big white chief [1930s+] (orig. US)

gorger [mid 19C]

big vegetable

governor [early 19C+]
head devil [mid-19C–1910s] (US)
headknocker [late 19C+] (US)
high pressure [1920s] (US)
high-up [1920s+] (orig. US)
King Dick [20C] (Aus.)
main finger [late 19C–1920s] (US)
numero uno [1950s+] (US; Spanish, 'number one')
the old man [mid-19C+] (orig. US)
red light [late 19C–1930s]
scurf [mid–late 19C] (an employer who pays less than average wages)
top kick/top kicker [1920s+] (orig. US)

99 99 99 99 99 99 99 99 99 99 99 99 99 99 99 99 99 99 99 99 99 99

Big cheeses

big cheese [1910s+] (orig. US)
big potato [late 19C+]
big vegetable [1970s] (orig. US)
the cheese [1900s+] (Persian and Urdu *chiz*, thing)
the Stilton [late 19C] (playing on 'the cheese')
top banana [1950s+] (US)

66 66 66 66 66 66 66 66 66 66 66 66 66 66 66 66 66 66 66 66 66 66

99 99 99 99 99 99 99 99 99 99 99 99 99 99 99 99 99 99 99 99 99 99

Bosses in rhyming slang

Edmundo [1960s+] (i.e. *Edmundo* Ros)
Joe Goss [20C] (Aus./US)
lath and plaster [mid-19C] ('master')
pitch and toss [1940s+]

66 66 66 66 66 66 66 66 66 66 66 66 66 66 66 66 66 66 66 66 66 66

99 99 99 99 99 99 99 99 99 99 99 99 99 99 99 99 99 99 99 99 99 99

Bulls of the woods

bull-goose [20C] (US; the goose which maintains order among the rest of the flock)
bull moose [20C]
bull of the woods [19C] (US)

66 66 66 66 66 66 66 66 66 66 66 66 66 66 66 66 66 66 66 66 66 66

MANAGEMENT STOOGES

bagman [early 20C+] (orig. US; i.e. they 'carry the *bag*' for the actions of their employers)

company man/company stiff [1940s–50s] (US; a worker who is seen by his peers as loyal to the employers rather than the union)

flag-waver [20C] (US; i.e. they communicate the boss's orders)

flak catcher [1970s+]

hatchet man [late 19C+] (orig. US Und.; a man who is used to punish, or even murder, selected victims on the orders of his boss)

99 99 99 99 99 99 99 99 99 99 99 99 99 99 99 99 99 99 99 99 99

Finks and scabs

black-leg [mid-19C+] (a strike-breaker)

dung [mid-19C] (a strike-breaker)

fink [late 19C+] (a strike-breaker, a company policeman)

goon [1930s+] (US; non-union labour used for strike breaking, intimidation etc.)

hansom cab [20C] (Aus.; a non-unionist; rhy. sl. 'scab')

Jack [1940s+] (Aus.; a non-union labourer, a strike-breaker; rhy. sl. *Jack McNab*, scab)

knobstick [mid-19C] (a strike-breaker)

scab [late 18C+] (a strike-breaker)

scabby [1910s+] (Aus.; a non-union worker)

tit-for-tat [late 19C+] (Aus.; a non-trade unionist; rhy. sl. 'rat')

66 66 66 66 66 66 66 66 66 66 66 66 66 66 66 66 66 66 66 66 66

straw boss [late 19C+] (US; the image is of a threshing crew, where the chief deals with the grain, the subordinate with the straw)

FOREMEN

Adam [late 19C] (i.e. the 'first' man)

bear [1910s+] (US; a hard taskmaster)

big stick [20C] (US)

boss-boy [20C] (S Afr.; a Black foreman or overseer in charge of subordinate Black workers)

chief/head cook and bottle-washer [mid-19C+]

cowskin hero [late 18C] (W.I.; a plantation overseer, from his cowskin whip)

driver [mid-19C] (a manager or foreman who forces employees to work much harder than their wages demand)

head-beetler [mid-19C+] (*beetle* = any implement used in a variety of industrial processes for crushing, bruising, beating, flattening, or smoothing)

Joe O'Gorman [late 19C+] (rhy. sl. 'foreman')

Simon Legree [late 19C] (US Black; the name of the cruel slave-master in *Uncle Tom's Cabin* by Harriet Beecher Stowe)

MONEYLENDERS

cent per cent [late 18C] (i.e. they charge 100% interest)

gripe-fist/gripe-penny [19C]

Ikey-Mo [mid-19C+] (a Jewish moneylender; *Isaac* + *Moses*)

Jewman [20C] (Irish)

juice man [1950s+] (US Und.; the collector of loans for an illegal moneylender)

land-shark [19C]

note shaver [early 19C–1900s] (US; a promoter of bogus financial companies, a usurer)

Shylock/shy [20C] (the money-lender in Shakespeare's *Merchant of Venice*)

sixty-per-cent [mid–late 19C] (i.e. they charge 60% interest)

ten in the hundred [late 16C–late 18C] (i.e. they charge 10% interest)

gun

CRIMINALS

GANGSTERS

battler [late 19C+] (Glasgow; a violent gangster)

family man/family woman [late 18C–mid-19C] (a member of the criminal fraternity)

gun [1930s+] (US)

heat-packer [1940s+] (US Und.)

hound [1950s+]

mobster [1910s+] (orig. US)

off-brand [1990s] (US Black gang; a rival gangster)

rank [1990s+] (W.I./UK Black)

red hot [1970s+] (US; an aggressive, volatile person)

speng [1980s+] (W.I./UK Black teen; an urban gangster)

star(-bwai)/star-boy [1990s+] (W.I./UK Black)

THE BIG JUICE: GANGLAND BOSSES

big guy [1920s+] (US)
big juice [1960s–70s] (US Black; a White gang-boss)
ghetto star [1990s]
head bully (of the passage bank) [late 17C–early 19C]
head cully of the pass [late 17C–early 19C]

SMALL-TIME CROOKS

chicken thief [mid–late 19C; 1940s] (Aus./US; a petty thief)
doormat thief/doormat grafter [mid-19C+] (a petty or incompetent thief)
gas-meter bandit [1960s+]
gutter-prowler [19C] (a small-time thief)
Hugh Prowler [16C] (a small-time thief)
knickers bandit [1960s+]
louser [1940s–50s] (Aus.; a petty thief)
lurker [20C] (Aus.)
nibbling cull [19C] (a petty thief)
parking-meter bandit [1970s+] (a petty thief)

99 99 99 99 99 99 99 99 99 99 99 99 99 99 99 99 99 99 99 99 99 99 99

Gangsters' girls

gun moll [1900s–40s] (US Und.; a female gangster)
ponytail [1960s–70s] (S Afr.)
quacktail [1960s–70s] (S Afr.)
sheila [1960s–70s] (S Afr.)

66 66 66 66 66 66 66 66 66 66 66 66 66 66 66 66 66 66 66 66 66 66 66

pinch-gloak [19C] (a petty jewellery-thief)

prowler [19C] (US; a petty thief)

slag [1950s+]

snick fadger [mid–late 19C] (a petty thief)

streetman [20C] (a drug dealer or pickpocket)

tea and sugar burglar/tea and sugar bandit [late 19C+] (Aus.; a petty thief)

two-bit hustler [20C] (a second-rate confidence trickster)

wide-boy [1930s] (a minor villain, dabbling in 'get-rich-quick' schemes)

THIEVES

ball-buster [20C] (US Und.; a thief who grabs their victim by the testicles while an accomplice takes his wallet)

bird-lime [18C]

bludger [mid-19C–1950s] (i.e. 'bludgeoner')

bowman-prig [early 18C]

bubbler [late 17C–mid-19C] (a swindler)

cribbing cove [early–mid-19C]

cross-chap [mid-19C]

cross-cove [19C]

dangler [1990s+] (US Black)

tea and sugar burgler

dinger [19C] (a thief who throws away what they have stolen)

dromedary [late 17C–18C] (an incompetent thief)

dubber [late 17C–early 18C] (a lock-picker)

efter [mid-19C]

filcher [16C–late 18C; 1990s]

filching-cove [17C–18C]

flash cove/flash covess [early 19C]

fly-man [1920s] (an expert thief)

gazlon [20C] (UK Und.; Yiddish *gozlin*, a swindler)

getabit [late 19C–1900s]

gleaner [19C] (*glean* = steal)

grabber [mid-19C] (US Und.)

grasshopper [late 19C] (i.e. they 'hop' from theft to theft)

gumshoe/gumboot/gumfoot/gumshoer [20C] (US; a sneak thief or prowler)

high-topper [mid–late 19C] (a dandified thief)

iceman [1920s–50s] (US; a diamond thief; *ice* = diamonds)

in-and-out man [1950s+] (UK Und.; an opportunist thief)

"" ""

Backslang and rhyming slang thieves

corned beef [20C] (rhy. sl.)

fi-heath [mid-19C] (backslang)

hevethee [late 19C–1920s] (rearranging the constituent parts of the word 'thief')

leg of beef [20C] (rhy. sl.)

tea leaf/tealeaf [late 19C+] (rhy. sl.)

Ted Heath [1970s] (rhy. sl.)

66 66 66 66 66 66 66 66 66 66 66 66 66 66 66 66 66 66 66 66 66 66

99 99 99 99 99 99 99 99 99 99 99 99 99 99 99 99 99 99 99 99 99 99

Draw-latches and parlour-jumpers:
burglars

back-jumper [mid-19C+] (a thief who enters houses by the back door or window)

bafber [20C] (a thief who robs bedrooms when the occupant is asleep)

baster [mid-19C+] (Aus./US)

budge [late 17C–late 18C] (a thief who enters houses to steal coats and cloaks)

draw-latch [late 17C–18C]

drummer [1960s+] (a burglar who robs houses while the owners are out)

dwelling dancer [1940s] (Aus.)

evesdropper [18C] (a burglar who lurks outside houses waiting the chance to break in while the owners are out)

garreteer/garreter [19C] (a thief who enters houses via attics and skylights)

miller [mid-17C–mid-19C]

parlour-jumper [late 19C] (UK Und.)

rusher [late 18C–mid-19C]

screwer/screwman [1930s–50s]

second-storey man/second-storey worker [late 19C+] (US; a thief who climbs into building above the ground floor)

stair-dancer [1950s+] (a thief who steals from buildings and offices that have not been properly secured)

66 66 66 66 66 66 66 66 66 66 66 66 66 66 66 66 66 66 66 66 66 66

99 99 99 99 99 99 99 99 99 99 99 99 99 99 99 99 99 99 99 99 99 99

Finger-smiths and slip-gibbets: pickpockets

artist [mid-19C+] (US Und./Irish; an adroit pickpocket)

buzz [18C+]

cloy/cloye [late 17C–18C] (UK Und.)

conveyance/conveyancer [mid-19C]

cutter [19C]

dipper [19C]

dipping-bloke [19C]

finger-smith [19C]

gallows(-bird) [late 18C–19C] (a thief or pickpocket)

grafter [mid-19C+] (orig. US)

hook [late 19C+] (Aus.)

knockabout man [1930s+] (Aus.)

knuck [early 19C–1900s]

natty lad [late 18C–early 19C] (a young pickpocket)

nipper [late 19C] (Und.)

shoot-flier [late 19C–1930s] (UK Und.)

slip-gibbet [late 18C–19C]

snatch cly [late 18C–early 19C] (UK Und.; a thief who specializes in stealing from women's pockets)

66 66 66 66 66 66 66 66 66 66 66 66 66 66 66 66 66 66 66 66 66 66

jilter [mid-19C] (orig. US; a sneak thief)

kink [1910s–50s] (US Und.; a car thief)

klep/klepper [late 19C–1970s] (*klep*tomaniac)

lobby-sneak [mid-19C+] (UK Und.)

nabber [late 19C] (US)

nicker [mid–late 17C]

pitch-fingers [19C]

possum [1940s+] (Aus.)

prigster [late 17C–mid-18C] (UK Und.)

puggard [early 17C] (UK Und.)

racket man [mid-19C] (US)

rip-off artist/rip-off merchant [1970s+]

rolling kiddy [early–mid-19C] (UK Und.; a dandified thief)

rum dab [late 17C–early 18C] (UK Und.; a successful thief)

stair-dancer

sneaking budge [late 17C–late 18C] (a sneak thief)

snelt [20C] (Aus./N.Z.; a sneak thief)

snib [early 17C–mid-19C] (Scot.; a sneak thief)

snudge [late 17C–early 18C] (UK Und.)

tiefin tief [1950s] (W.I.; lit. 'thieving thief')

yegg [late 19C+] (US Und.; a safe-cracker)

YOUNG CRIMINALS

bad bwoy [1970s+] (W.I./UK Black teen)

bad-head [20C] (W.I./Belz.)

bad-john [1960s–70s] (W.I.)

diddly-bopper/diddy-bopper/dittybopper [1950s+] (orig. US Black; a young street thug)

eriff [late 18C–19C] (lit. 'two-year-old canary')

ferret [late 19C] (a young thief who steals coal from barges)

flash kiddy [early 19C] (a dandified young thief)

kidling [late 19C] (a young thief with a father 'in the trade')

kinchin cove [late 17C–18C] (a child brought up as a thief)

punk [1910s+] (US)

rum kiddy [late 18C–early 19C] (UK Und.; a successful young thief)

scuttler [mid–late 19C] (Manchester; a young street thug)

Tyburn blossom [late 18C–early 19C] (a young thief or pickpocket)

ziff [mid-19C] (a young thief)

CONMEN

bat-fowler [late 16C–early 17C]

beat [late 19C–1900s]

bite [18C–1900s]

bluff artist [1930s] (US)

brass man [1930s+] (Aus.)

chiseler/chiseller [mid-19C+] (orig. US)

chizzer [1930s]

clipster [1940s–60s] (US)

con artist [20C]

coneroo/conneroo [1930s–40s] (US)

con-man [late 19C+] (orig. US)

QUALITY WATCHES FULLY WATERPROOF

shark

con-merchant [1960s+] (US)

crossbiting cully [mid-17C–late 19C]

crossman/cross-man [mid-19C]

diddler [early 19C]

dingo [1920s+] (Aus.)

eel [20C] (orig. US)

fake [late 19C–1960s] (US)

fast-talker [1930s+]

fiddler [mid-19C+]

flat-catcher [early 19C+]

fleecer [20C]

flimflammer [late 19C+] (US)

fool-monger [late 16C–early 18C]

fool trap [late 16C–early 18C]

goose shearer [18C–19C] (UK Und.)

grifter [1910s+] (US Und; a small-change swindler or conman)

gyp artist [20C] (*gyp*sy *artist*)

gyp moll [20C] (US; a female swindler)

hooker [late 17C–early 18C]

jeff artist/jeff hat [1930s+] (US)

Jeremy Diddler [early 19C]

lurkman [1930s+] (Aus.)

mace-gloak [early 19C]

piker [1930s+] (Aus.)

purse-bouncer [1900s]

rook [late 16C+] (an allegedly larcenous bird)

rorter [1920s+] (Aus.)

rum bite [early 19C] (UK Und.)

scammer [1980s+] (US campus)

💬 💬

Oil merchants

bounce [early 19C] (a well-dressed swindler)

fastidious cove [late 19C] (a fashionable swindler)

flash [early 17C–early 19C+] (an ostentatious swindler)

high-flyer/high flier [mid-19C] (a genteel beggar or swindler)

long-shoe [1950s–80s] (US Black; an urbane swindler, from a style of footwear worn by Black US pimps of the 1960s and 1970s)

oil merchant [1930s–50s] (US; *oil* = flattery)

slick [mid-19C+] (orig. US Black)

slick-boy [1990s] (US Black)

slicker [20C] (US)

slick-'em-plenty [1970s] (US Black; a smooth-talking confidence trickster)

66 66 66 66 66 66 66 66 66 66 66 66 66 66 66 66 66 66 66 66 66

scamp [mid-19C]

shark [16C+]

sheep-shearer [16C–mid-18C]

sheg-up [1940s] (W.I.)

tiddlywinker [late 19C]

tongue pad [early 18C]

twicer [late 19C+] (Aus.; a 'double-dealer')

wheadle/wheedle [late 17C–early 19C] (UK Und.)

THUGS AND MUGGERS

basher [mid-19C+]

big dog [19C] (US)

blaster [1930s+]

blood tub [mid–late 19C] (US; a street gangster)

boko-smasher [late 19C–1900s] (*boko* = nose)

bottler [1940s+] (N.Z.)

bozo [1910s+] (orig. US)

bruiser [late 16C+]

cutter [mid-16C]

ding-boy [late 17C–18C] (UK Und.; a villain's accomplice)

flash captain [mid-18C]

flimper [mid-19C] (a mugger)

goon [1930s+] (orig. US)

hard [late 19C+]

hard ticket [late 19C+] (US)

heavy man [1920s+]

hood [late 19C+] (US; a gangster or thug)

hoodlum [late 19C+] (orig. US; a gangster or thug)

keelie [mid-19C+] (Scot.; a street thug)

mouth-breather [1980s+] (a particularly stupid thug)

nut [late 19C] (Aus.)

pug [mid-19C+] (*pug*ilist)

ragster [19C]

ramper [late 19C] (a street thug)

roughneck [mid-19C+] (orig. US)

rush buckler [19C] (lit. 'rush sword')

smacko [1940s] (US Black)

spoilers [1940s+] (S Afr.; a township thug)

thugette [1990s+] (a female thug)

99 99 99 99 99 99 99 99 99 99 99 99 99 99 99 99 99 99 99 99 99 99

Hard-arses and cold-deckers: practitioners of extreme violence

ball-breaker [1950s+] (orig. US)

cold-decker [20C] (US Und.)

gouger [1960s+] (Irish)

hard-ass/hard-arse [1970s+] (orig. US)

hardrocker [1980s+] (US)

muzzler [mid-19C] (US; a strong-arm robber)

plug-ugly [mid-19C+] (orig. US; a violent thug)

ruffian [late 17C–18C] (an assassin)

slasher [mid-16C–19C]

tearcat/tearer [16C]

twibill [17C] (lit. 'two-edged axe')

66 66 66 66 66 66 66 66 66 66 66 66 66 66 66 66 66 66 66 66 66

99 99 99 99 99 99 99 99 99 99 99 99 99 99 99 99 99 99 99 99 99 99

Baboons and mad dogs

ape [20C] (a thug or hoodlum)

baboon [early 16C+] (from the animal's aggression)

dead rabbit [mid-19C] (US; from the name of a street gang)

gorilla [mid-19C+] (US)

gorill [mid-19C–1940s] (US)

hawk [1970s+] (US; a mugger)

mad dog [1970s+] (US Black)

66 66 66 66 66 66 66 66 66 66 66 66 66 66 66 66 66 66 66 66 66

SEX CRIMINALS

RAPISTS

booty bandit [1920s+] (US Black; a homosexual rapist)

granny-dodger [1960s+] (US prison; a rapist of elderly women)

Jack Roller [1990s] (S Afr.; an individual, usu. one of gang, who abducts and rapes women)

junior jumper [1990s] (US Black; a juvenile (under 16) who commits rape and robbery)

rape-o [20C] (US Und.)

short-arm bandit [20C] (*short-arm* = penis)

short-arm heister [20C] (US Und.)

skinner [20C] (US Und.)

tree-jumper [20C] (US prison; a rapist or sexual molester)

CHILD MOLESTORS

asoc/asocial [20C] (US Und.)

baby-raper [1960s+] (a man who commits statutory rape)

bacon bonce [1990s+] (rhy. sl. 'nonce')

beast [1980s+]

Chester Molester [20C]

diddler [20C] (US Und.)

nonce [1970s+] (lit. 'nothing')

Pamper pirate/Pamper sniffer [20C] (US Und.)

short eyes [1960s+] (US prison)

Uncle Lester [1990s] (rhy. sl 'molestor')

gorilla

NATIONALLY
DISGRACEFUL

WHITE PEOPLE

WHITES: A (MOSTLY) BLACK AMERICAN LEXICON

anglo [19C] (*Anglo*-Saxon)

baldhead [1950s+] (W.I.)

ballface [mid–late 19C] (US Black)

ballhead [1950s+] (Black)

beast [1960s+] (US Black)

blanco [1980s+] (US Black; Spanish, 'white')

blank [late 19C–1910s] (Anglo-Ind.; French *blanc*, white)

cave [1990s] (US Black; from the belief that the early *cave* dwellers were White, while Black Africans lived on the plains)

caveboy [1990s] (US Black)

chalk [1970s–80s] (US Black)

cracker-ass [20C] (US Black; *crack* = boast)

devil [1920s+] (US Black, esp. Black Muslim)

fade [20C] (US Black)

ghost [1970s+] (US Black)

gray boy/grey boy [1950s+] (US Black)

gunjie [1990s] (Native Aus.)

honkie/honk/honkey/honky [1940s+] (US Black; *hunky*, the original name for Poles who worked in Chicago stockyards)

hunkamo [1990s] (US Black)

ice-cream [1970s] (Black teen)

lily [1960s+] (US Black)

lilywhite [20C] (US Black; a White person who claims superiority on the grounds of their colour)

maggot [1980s+] (US Black)

Mickey Mouse [1930s–60s] (US Black)

Mr Cracker [1950s+] (US Black; lit. 'Mr Boaster')

mlungu [1980s+] (S Afr. Black; Nguni *umlungu*, a White man)

pale [1900s–40s] (US Black)

paleface [1940s+] (orig. US Black)

pink [late 19C+] (US Black)

pinkie [1960s+] (US Black)

pink whoogie [20C] (US; *whoogie* = White Black)

plain people [19C] (US Black; reversing the White term 'coloured people')

roundeye [1960s+] (reversing the White term 'slant-eye', an East Asian person)

sabana [20C] (US Hispanic; Spanish, 'sheet')

snow [1950s+]

soda cracker [1990s] (US campus; a type of light-coloured biscuit)

swine-eater [1950s+] (US Black Muslim; the eating of pork being unlawful in Islam)

vanilla [1930s+] (US Black)

99 99 99 99 99 99 99 99 99 99 99 99 99 99 99 99 99 99 99 99 99 99

Super-honkies: White bosses

great white father [1930s–40s] (US Black; any White authority-figure, esp. the US president)

master-dog [20C] (US Black; the supreme authoritarian figure within an institutional hierarchy)

super-honkie [1960s] (US Black; an exceptionally authoritarian White person)

66 66 66 66 66 66 66 66 66 66 66 66 66 66 66 66 66 66 66 66 66 66

white-eyes [1970s+] (US Black)

whitey [1940s+] (Black)

whoogie [20C] (US Black; *wh*ite + b*oogie*, lit. 'White Black')

wit ou [1970s+] (S Afr. Indian; lit. 'white fellow')

WHITE MEN

Charles [mid-19C+] (US Black)

Charley/Charlie [1960s+] (US Black)

Chuck/Mr Chuck [1960s–70s] (US Black)

grayboy/gray boy [1950s+] (US Black)

99 99 99 99 99 99 99 99 99 99 99 99 99 99 99 99 99 99 99 99 99 99

Yo-boys

jig-chaser [20C] (US; a White person who pursues the company of Blacks)

kaffirboetie/kafferboetie [1930s+] (S Afr.; a White sympathizer with Black causes, lit. 'Black brother')

niggerlover [mid-19C+] (orig. US; a White who fails to display the supposedly necessary loathing of Blacks)

wigga/wigger [1990s] (orig. US; a White person who adopts a Black lifestyle; *w*hite + n*igger*)

yo-boy [1980s+] (US Black; a White youth who apes his Black contemporaries)

zebra [1990s] (US Black teen; a White person who poses as Black)

66 66 66 66 66 66 66 66 66 66 66 66 66 66 66 66 66 66 66 66 66 66

gub [1970s+] (Aus. Aborigine; i.e. 'garbage')

man with (the) fuzzy balls [1960s–80s] (US Black)

Mr Charlie [1920s+] (US Black)

Mr Eddie [1900s–30s] (US Black)

Mr Gub [1960s+] (Aus.)

Mr Peanut [1960s] (US Black)

pink boy [1960s+] (US Black)

Sylvester [1950s] (US Black)

WHITE WOMEN

Ann [1990s]

bale of hay/bale of straw [1920s+]

blondie [20C] (US Black)

French vanilla [1990s] (US Black teen; a white woman seen as a sex object)

grey gal [1950s+]

gringa [20C] (US Hispanic)

Miss Amy [1960s+] (US Black; a young White woman)

Miss Ann/Miss Annie [1920s+] (US Black; a White woman considered to be hostile or patronizing to Blacks)

Miss Lillian [1960s–70s] (US Black; an older White woman)

silk (broad) [1930s–50s] (US Black; from the silky texture of White female hair)

snow [1950s–60s] (US Black)

Susan B. Anthony [1990s] (US Black teen; a conventional White woman, from the 19C US feminist pioneer)

white satin [1950s] (Aus.; a white woman seen as a sex object)

WHITE TRASH AND OTHER LOW-DOWNERS

bama chukker [1940s+] (US Black; lit. 'Alabama corncob-husker')

che-che [20C] (W.I.)

clay-eater [19C] (US)

corncracker [mid-19C+] (US)

dirt-eater [mid-19C–1940s] (US)

ecky-becky [20C] (W.I.; Ijo *beke*, a European)

grit-sucker [19C+] (US)

low-downer [mid–late 19C] (US Black)

mong-mong [20C] (W.I./Gren.)

paleface nigger [1940s+] (US; a highly unpopular White person, whose skin colour does not save them from the opprobrium usu. heaped on Blacks)

p.w.t. [1990s] (US; *p*oor *w*hite *t*rash)

grit-sucker

trailer trash/trash [1990s] (US; poor Whites living in trailers)

walk and nyam [early 19C+] (W.I.; lit. 'walk and eat')

white kaffir [mid-19C+] (S Afr.; a badly behaved White person, so-called by their peers, lit. 'White Black person')

white nigger [mid–late 19C] (a White person who does menial labour)

white trash/trash [late 18C+] (orig. US Black; the poor White population of the Southern US)

99 99 99 99 99 99 99 99 99 99 99 99 99 99 99 99 99 99 99 99 99 99 99

Rednecks

cracker [1920s+] (orig. US Black; lit. 'boaster')

good old boy/good ole boy [19C+] (US)

grit [1960s+] (US orig. Black; a type of food eaten in the Southern US)

Jeff [1930s+] (*Jeff*erson Davis, president of the Confederate States during the American Civil War)

mean White [late 19C] (US Black; an extremely unpleasant White person)

pecker(wood) [1920s+] (orig. US Black; the red woodpecker used as a symbol of Whites)

red [20C] (US; i.e. 'redneck')

redneck [early 19C+] (orig. US; from their sunburnt necks)

white white [1990s] (US Black)

yacoo/yakoo [1960s+] (US Black; *Yacub*, the white devil-figure of Black Muslim theology)

66 66 66 66 66 66 66 66 66 66 66 66 66 66 66 66 66 66 66 66 66 66

BLACK PEOPLE

A PRE-20TH-CENTURY CHRONOLOGY

nigger/naygur/neeger/nigga/niggur [late 16C+] (lit. 'black')
kaffir [early 17C+] (orig. S Afr.; Arab *kefir*, an infidel)
lilywhite [late 17C–early 19C]
Hottentot [late 17C+] (S Afr.; lit. 'stammerer')
monkey [late 17C+]
Sambo/Sambie [18C+] (Foulah, 'uncle')
snowball [late 18C–early 19C]
darkie/darky [late 18C+]
curlyhead [early 19C] (US)
guinea bird [early 19C] (W.I.; an African-born Black person)
salt-water negro [early 19C] (W.I.; an African-born Black person)

99 99 99 99 99 99 99 99 99 99 99 99 99 99 99 99 99 99 99 99 99 99

Black people in rhyming slang

RHYMING WITH COON
  harvest moon [20C]
  silvery (moon) [1950s+]

RHYMING WITH DARKIE
  Feargal Sharkey [1990s+]
  Greville Starkey [1990s+]

RHYMING WITH NIGGER
  mechanical digger [20C]
  square rigger [20C]

66 66 66 66 66 66 66 66 66 66 66 66 66 66 66 66 66 66 66 66 66

99 99 99 99 99 99 99 99 99 99 99 99 99 99 99 99 99 99 99 99 99

Black-on-black

black nigger [19C–1950s] (US Black)

black nigger in charge [1930s+] (a Black authority figure)

boot [1950s+] (US/UK Black)

nagah [1950s+] (W.I. Rasta; i.e. 'nigger')

nap [1900s–60s] (US Black; i.e. someone with *nappy* hair)

66 66 66 66 66 66 66 66 66 66 66 66 66 66 66 66 66 66 66 66 66

African ape [19C+] (US)

ape [19C+] (US)

black ape [19C+] (US)

unbleached American [mid-19C] (an African-American)

shade [mid–late 19C] (US)

dark [mid-19C–1910s] (US)

kink(head) [mid-19C–1940s] (US)

coolie [mid-19C+] (S Afr.)

coolie boy [mid-19C+] (S Afr.)

coon [mid-19C+] (orig. US; rac*coon*, typified as a cunning creature)

jigwalker/jigwawk [late 19C–1930s] (US)

shadow [late 19C+] (US)

shine [late 19C+] (US; a person with a very dark, smooth complexion)

squasho [late 19C+] (US; *quashie*, a peasant)

A 20TH-CENTURY (MOSTLY AMERICAN) LEXICON

ace (of spades) [1980s+]

af/aff [1960s+] (S Afr.; *Af*rican)

afro [1930s–70s] (US; an English or American person of African descent)

Bongo [20C] (orig. US; a supposedly typical African name)

bongo lips [20C] (US)

boogie/boogey [1920s+] (i.e. 'bogey')

boothead [1980s+] (US)

burrhead [20C] (US)

cloud [20C]

coconut-dodger [1920s] (US Black; an African Black)

cotton picker [1930s+] (the typical role of the Black slave in the southern US)

dark cloud [1900s–30s] (usu. Aus./US)

eggplant [20C] (US; from the shiny purple-black skin of the aubergine)

eightball [1910s+] (US; an African-American, from the black eightball in pool)

99 99 99 99 99 99 99 99 99 99 99 99 99 99 99 99 99 99 99 99 99 99

Black women

bit of ebony [mid-19C+]

coolie girl [19C+] (S Afr.)

ethy meat [20C] (*Eth*iopean *meat*)

gin [19C+] (Dharuk *diyin*, a woman)

nigette [1990s] (US; lit. 'female nigger')

66 66 66 66 66 66 66 66 66 66 66 66 66 66 66 66 66 66 66 66 66

Black children

alligator bait [late 19C–1960s] (US)

coon jigger [mid-19C–1920s] (US; lit. 'black gadget')

dewbaby [1960s] (US Black; a very dark skinned male child)

piccaninny/pickaninny [late 18C+] (orig. W.I.; Spanish *pequeño*, small)

spadelet [1920s+] (orig. US; lit. 'little spade')

66 66 66 66 66 66 66 66 66 66 66 66 66 66 66 66 66 66 66 66 66

Enoch [1970s] (*Enoch* Powell, the UK anti-immigration politician)

golly [1960s+] (*golli*wog)

goon [1940s] (US; lit. 'stupid person')

groe [1990s] (US; ne*gro*)

hunky/hunkie [1920s+] (US; *bohunk*, an unsophisticated person)

j.b. [1940s+] (US; *j*et *b*lack)

jig/jigg [1910s+] (orig. US)

jigaboo [1920s+] (orig. US)

jungle bunny [1950s+]

moreno [1980s+] (US; Spanish, 'dark-skinned')

nig-bo [1990s+]

oogie [1970s+] (Southern US campus; Black students collectively)

orangutan [20C] (US)

pongo [1960s–70s] (a type of large anthropoid ape)

porch monkey [1970s+] (US)

rughead [1960s+] (US)

shad mouth [1930s–40s] (US; *shad* = a type of thick-lipped fish)

spade [1920s+] (orig. US; from the phrase 'black as the ace of *spades*')

spearchucker [1960s+] (US)

spook [1940s+]

sunburned Irishman [20C] (alluding to the shared low social position of immigrant Irish and Black people)

velcro head [1970s+] (US)

Zulu [20C] (US)

SHIT-SKINS AND SMUT-BUTTS

chimney chops [late 18C] (from the blackness of a chimney)

choco [1970s+]

chocolate [20C]

chocolate baby [1900s] (US)

chocolate bunny [1980s] (US)

chocolate drop [late 19C+]

dinge [mid-19C+]

inkbug [mid-19C] (US)

inkspot [1910s–60s] (US)

mud flap [20C] (US)

scuttle [1900s] (US; coal*scuttle*)

shit-skin [20C]

smoke [late 19C+]

smokestack [late 19C+] (US Black)

smudge [1940s+] (US)

smut-butt [1970s] (US campus)

sooty [1950s+]

tar baby [1940s+] (US)

INKY-DINKY: VERY 'BLACK' BLACK PEOPLE

black bird [late 19C+]
blackout/black-out [1940s]
blue [19C+] (US Black)
coal [1940s]
congo [19C+] (a slave bought from the *Congo* nation)
Crow Jane [1900s–20s] (US Black; a very dark-skinned woman)
dust [19C–1950s] (US Black)
ink [1910s–30s] (US)
inky-dinky [1900s–40s] (US Black)
lampblack [1930s–40s] (US Black; a type of carbon residue used as a pigment)
midnight [1950s–70s] (US Black)
midnight the cat [1950s–60s] (US Black)
park ape [1930s–40s] (US Black; an extremely unattractive and very dark-skinned person)
suede [1940s–50s] (Black)
zombie [1970s+] (US Black; a supposedly very African-looking person, short of stature, with a dark complexion and broad features)

CAFÉ AU LAIT: LIGHT-SKINNED BLACK PEOPLE

beige [1930s–40s] (US Black)
bright [1940s–50s] (US Black)
bright-skin [mid-19C–1950s] (US Black)
brown man [1950s+] (W.I.)
buckwheat [19C+] (US Black)
café au lait [1920s–30s] (US Black; a light-skinned Black woman)
Casper [1950s] (US Black; from the cartoon character *Casper the Friendly Ghost*)

cocoa [20C] (US)

headlight [1930s–40s] (US)

pinkie [late 19C+]

pinktoe/pinktoes/pinky [late 19C+] (US Black; a light-skinned Black woman)

pumpkin-seed/pumpkin skin [19C–1920s] (US Black)

spotlight [1940s–60s] (US Black; a light-skinned Black woman)

wholewheat bread [1970s+] (US Black)

ALBINOS

freckle-nature [1950s] (W.I.)

grey-nayga [1960s] (W.I.)

Norwegian [1950s] (W.I.)

puss-eye [1950s] (W.I.)

ripe banana [1950s] (W.I.)

speckle [1950s] (W.I.)

white kaffir [1930s+] (S Afr.)

white man [1950s] (W.I.)

white-nayga [1960s] (W.I.; lit. 'white nigger')

whitey-whitey [1950s] (W.I.)

BAD-ASS NIGGERS

bad-ass nigger [20C] (US Black; an aggressive young black man)

bad boy [1970s+] (US Black)

bad nigger [early 18C+] (US Black)

Bigger Thomas [1960s] (US Black; the hero of Richard Wright's novel *Native Son*)

blue gum [20C] (US; a Black person viewed by Whites as particularly dangerous and believed to have a poisonous bite)

blue lips [20C]

Caledonia [1920s–50s] (US Black; a rebellious Black woman)

dog nigger [1970s] (US Black)

field nigger [1960s] (US Black; from the slavery-era distinction between the rougher, less refined field-workers and those who worked as house servants)

no-account (nigger) [early 19C+] (US Black)

uppity nigger [mid-19C+] (orig. US)

UNCLE TOMS

choirboy [1970s+] (US Black)

handkerchief-head [20C] (US Black; a subservient Black woman)

jeff artist/jeff hat [1930s+] (US Black; *jeff* = racist White)

Jim Crow [mid-19C+] (US; from the plantation song 'Jump *Jim Crow*')

mammy [19C+] (US Black; the stereotypical Black nanny or cook)

Mister Tom/Mister Thomas [1960s+] (US Black)

pork chop [1970s+] (US)

Sam [1940s–50s] (US Black)

shuffle [1900s–60s] (US Black; from the gait of a stereotypically subservient Black person)

stepinfetchit [1930s+] (US Black; lit. 'step and fetch it')

Tom/Tommy [1950s+] (orig. US Black)

Tomette [1960s] (US Black; a Black woman criticized for being too fond of White society)

Uncle Thomas [1960s] (US Black)

Uncle Tom [1920s+] (orig. US Black; the hero of Harriet Beecher Stowe's antislavery novel *Uncle Tom's Cabin*)

99 99 99 99 99 99 99 99 99 99 99 99 99 99 99 99 99 99 99 99 99 99

Apples in the white folks' yard

apple in the white folks' yard [1900s–20s] (US
Black/South; a Black person who is very well
thought of by Whites)

bap [1980s+] (US; an upwardly mobile Black
achiever; *B*lack *A*merican *P*rince/*P*rincess)

Dr Thomas [1970s+] (US Black; a middle-class
Black aspiring to White status)

e-light [1990s] (US Black; an elitist African-
American, with insufficient regard for his
less well-off peers and their causes; pron.
of 'élite')

pink chaser [late 19C+] (US Black; a Black
person who pursues the company and
friendship of Whites)

play-White [1950s+] (S Afr.; a Black person
who attempts to 'pass' as White)

showcase nigger [1960s–70s] (US Black; a
token Black employee, hired to parade the
liberal racial attitudes of a White-owned
organization)

window man [1950s+] (S Afr.; a Black person
who is trying to pass as White, i.e. they
pretend to be gazing into shop windows when
their darker friends or relations appear)

66 66 66 66 66 66 66 66 66 66 66 66 66 66 66 66 66 66 66 66 66 66

99 99 99 99 99 99 99 99 99 99 99 99 99 99 99 99 99 99 99 99 99 99

Bounty bars: 'White on the Inside'

apple [1980s+] (a Native American who is seen as insufficiently nationalistic)

banana [1980s+] (a Chinese person who adopts Western values)

bounty bar [1980s+] (a Black person who has 'sold out')

choc-ice [1990s] (US Black; a Black person who adopts White attitudes and values)

coconut [1980s+] (US; a Black person who has 'sold out')

cookie [1950s+] (US Black; a Black person who espouses White values)

fudgsicle [mid-20C] (US; a Black person who espouses White values)

Oreo (cookie) [1960s+] (US Black; a Black person who espouses White values)

pancake [late 19C–1940s] (US Black; a Black person seen as imitative of Whites)

Twinkie [1990s] (US campus; an Asian person who identifies with Whites)

66 66 66 66 66 66 66 66 66 66 66 66 66 66 66 66 66 66 66 66 66 66

yard nigger [20C]

yes-baas [1960s+] (S Afr.; lit. 'yes boss')

zip coon [1980s] (US Black; from the song 'Ole *Zip Coon*')

99 99 99 99 99 99 99 99 99 99 99 99 99 99 99 99 99 99 99 99 99

Five obsequious aunts

Aunt Jane [1960s] (US Black)
Aunt Jemima [1960s+] (US Black)
Aunt Mary [1960s]
Aunt Sally [1960s] (US Black)
Aunt Thomasina [1960s] (US Black)

66 66 66 66 66 66 66 66 66 66 66 66 66 66 66 66 66 66 66 66 66

PEOPLE OF MIXED RACE

black-and-tan [mid–late 19C] (US)

blueskin [late 18C–early 19C] (the offspring of a White man and a Black woman)

boogerlee [20C] (US; a person of mixed Black and White ancestry)

brindle [20C] (Aus.; lit. 'streaked')

brownie [20C] (US)

brown polish [late 19C–1900s] (orig. US)

chop suey [20C] (US; Chinese *shap sui*, a dish of stir-fried meat and vegetables, lit. 'mixed bits')

colora [1960s+] (S Afr. gay; a mixed-race gay man; Spanish, 'coloured' + feminine suffix -*a*)

dingey Christian/dingy Christian [late 18C] (the 'true' Christian being fully White)

fly-in-the-milk [20C] (US)

ginger-cake/gingerbread [19C+] (US)

half-and-half [19C+] (US)

high brown [1900s–60s] (US; a woman or girl of half-Black, half-White ancestry)

high yellow/high yaller/deep yellow [1920s+] (US; a woman or girl of half-Black, half-White ancestry)

hound dog [20C] (US; playing on 'mongrel')

pumpernickel [20C] (a mixed-race Black prostitute, from a type of dark wholemeal rye bread)

redbone [mid-19C–1970s] (US Black; a pale-skinned Black person with native American blood)

spotlight [1940s–60s] (US Black; an African-American of mixed ancestry)

EURASIANS

blackie-white/blacky-white [1930s–40s] (Anglo-Ind.)

chillicracker [1930s–50s] (Anglo-Ind.)

four annas in the rupee [late 19C–1900s] (a Eurasian quadroon, *four annas* being one-quarter of a *rupee*)

snuff and butter (maiden) [1920s–40s] (Anglo-Ind.; a Eurasian woman)

MIXED-RACE AUSTRALIANS

bronzewing [20C] (a Native Australian of mixed ancestry)

creamie [20C] (Aus.; a mixed-race child)

creamie piece/creamy piece [1970s] (Aus.; a half-Aboriginal woman)

Darwin blonde [1940s] (Aus.; *Darwin*, the capital of the Northern Territory of Australia)

magpie [1980s] (Aus.)

piebald [late 19C+] (Aus.)

Rainbow queens: mixed-race relationships

beachcomber [1910s–50s] (Can.; a White man living with an Inuit woman)

coal burner [1970s+] (a White man or woman who enjoys sexual relations with a Black man or woman)

combo/kombo [late 19C+] (Aus.; a white man who cohabits with or marries an Aborigine woman)

gin-jockey [1950s+] (Aus.; a White man who enjoys sexual relations with Aborigine women)

love chocolate [1980s+] (a White person who specializes in Black partners)

love vanilla [1980s+] (a Black person who specializes in White partners)

rainbow queen [1980s+] (US Black/gay; anyone who is involved in a Black/White sexual relationship)

salt and pepper [1950s+] (US Black; an inter-racial couple)

salt-and-pepper queens [1970s+] (gay; a mixed-race gay couple)

spic and span [1950s+] (US Black; a mixed-race Puerto Rican and Black couple)

66 66 66 66 66 66 66 66 66 66 66 66 66 66 66 66 66 66 66 66 66

yellow fellow/yeller feller [20C] (Aus.; a half-White, half-Aborigine man)

yellow girl/yaller gal/yellow broad [mid-19C+] (a half-White, half-Aborigine woman)

MIXED-RACE WEST INDIANS

dark-sambo [1950s+] (W.I.; a person who is one-quarter White and three-quarters Black)

grey-white nigger [1950s] (W.I.)

liver-spot [1940s+] (W.I.)

no-nation [20C] (W.I.; a dark-skinned person of more than two racial mixtures)

red nigger [20C] (W.I.; a person both of whose parents are of mixed African/White descent)

yellow snake [late 18C] (W.I.)

BRITONS

THE ENGLISH

beefeater [20C] (US)

bug [late 18C] (Anglo-Irish; from the belief that English settlers brought insects to Ireland)

bull [mid-19C–1920s] (mainly US)

hardhead [20C] (US)

John Bull/Johnny Bull [late 18C+] (coined in John Arbuthnot's *The History of John Bull*, 1712)

John Bull's bastard [1940s–50s] (Irish)

kipper [1940s+] (Aus.; i.e., like the processed herring, they are 'two-faced with no guts')

lemon-eater/lemon-pelter/lemon-sucker [1960s+] (US; i.e. they are 'sour')

lime-juicer [mid-19C–1950s] (Aus./US; from the lime juice drunk by English sailors to prevent scurvy)

limey [late-19C+] (orig. Aus.)

over-'omer [20C] (Can.; an English person whose conversation centres on the advantages of living *over home*, i.e. in England)

pock-pudding/poke-pudding/pock-pud [early 18C–late 19C] (Scot.; lit. 'glutton')

pommie/pom/pommy [1910s+] (Aus.; i.e. 'pomegranate')

soutpiel [1970s+] (S Afr.; an English person who retains their colonialist mentality, lit. 'salt-dick', because he has one foot in South Africa, one in England and his penis dangling in the ocean in between)

whinging pom [20C] (Aus./N.Z.; from the perceived propensity of the English for complaining)

99 99 99 99 99 99 99 99 99 99 99 99 99 99 99 99 99 99 99 99 99 99

Britain

Fogland [1910s] (Aus.)
Pomgolia [1970s+] (N.Z.)

66 66 66 66 66 66 66 66 66 66 66 66 66 66 66 66 66 66 66 66 66 66

99 99 99 99 99 99 99 99 99 99 99 99 99 99 99 99 99 99 99 99 99 99

Expat Brits

Benny [1980s] (British Army usage, an inhabitant of the Falkland Islands, from an intellectually deficient rural character in the UK TV soap opera *Crossroads*)

pomegranate/pommygranate/pommygrant [1910s–20s] (Aus; playing on the similarity of the sound of *pomegranate* and *immigrant*)

redneck [20C] (S Afr.; from the effects of unwonted exposure to sun)

rock scorpion [mid–late 19C] (orig. milit.; a civilian inhabitant of Gibraltar)

to-and-from [1940s+] (Aus.; rhy. sl. 'pom')

66 66 66 66 66 66 66 66 66 66 66 66 66 66 66 66 66 66 66 66 66 66

A MOSTLY INSULTING TOUR OF
THE ENGLISH COUNTIES

beanbelly/bean-belly [mid-17C–19C] (a native of
Leicestershire, a major producer of beans)

Bristol hog [late 18C–mid-19C] (a native of Bristol)

Brummagem button [mid-19C+] (a native of Birmingham)

Cambridgeshire camel [late 17C–early 19C] (a native or
established resident of Cambridgeshire, from the stilt-walkers
once found in the fens)

cat [late 19C] (a native of Cheshire)

Dicky Sam [mid-19C] (a native of Liverpool; Lancashire dial.)

dumpling [late 19C] (a native of Norfolk)

Essex calf [late 19C] (a native of Essex, as used by those of
Suffolk)

Essex lion [17C–mid-19C] (a native of Essex, as used by those
of Kent)

Hampshire hog [early 18C+] (an inhabitant of Hampshire)

hardware bloke [late 19C–1910s] (a native of Birmingham,
known for its manufacture of pots, pans and other hardware)

loiner [1940s+] (an inhabitant of Leeds)

malt-horse [early 17C–1900s] (a native of Bedford, from the
high-quality malt extracted from Bedfordshire barley)

〝 〝

England

Home for lost frogs/fogs [1930s+]

Limey land [1910s–70s] (US)

Old Dart [late 19C+] (Aus./N.Z.)

〝 〝

Middlesex clown [mid-17C–early 19C] (an inhabitant or native of Middlesex)

Middlesex mongrel [18C] (an inhabitant or native of Middlesex)

moon-raker [late 18C–early 19C] (a native of Wiltshire)

Norfolk dumpling/Norfolk turkey [late 17C+] (a native of Norfolk)

Plym [1910s] (an inhabitant of Plymouth)

web-foot [late 19C] (a native of Lincolnshire)

yellow belly [late 18C+] (a native of Lincolnshire, esp. of the southern or fenland part of the county, from the yellow-stomached frog that abounds there)

THE WELSH

leek/leak [early 18C]

riff-raff [20C] (rhy. sl. 'Taff')

sheep-shagger [20C]

Shinkin-ap-Morgan [mid-17C–mid-18C] (lit. 'Jenkins son of Morgan')

Taff [19C+]

Taffy [late 17C+] (Welsh *Dafydd*, David)

Welsh goat [mid-18C–mid-19C]

Welshie/Welshy [1950s+]

99 99 99 99 99 99 99 99 99 99 99 99 99 99 99 99 99 99 99 99 99

Wales

Itchland [late 17C–early 19C] (from the supposed abundance of lice)

Leekshire [18C–19C]

66 66 66 66 66 66 66 66 66 66 66 66 66 66 66 66 66 66 66 66 66

Scotland

Haggisland [late 19C+]

Land o' Cakes [18C–late 19C]

Louseland [late 17C–18C]

Marmalade Country [late 19C] (orig. music-hall)

Scratchland [late 18C–early 19C]

🙷 🙷

THE SCOTS

Geordie [1940s+] (Aus./N.Z.)

Jock/Jockey [18C+]

no rats [late 19C] (from the supposed power of bagpipes to drive away rats)

porridge wog [1990s+]

Scotchie/Scotchy [mid-19C+]

sweaty sock [20C] (rhy. sl. 'Jock')

THE IRISH

bark [19C]

boghopper [20C] (US)

boglander [17C+]

bog-rat [20C]

bogtrotter [late 17C+]

bog-wog [1990s+]

flannel mouth/flannel face [19C+] (US; from the 'flannel' supposedly spoken by the Irish)

Gaelick [1980s+] (US gay; a gay Irishman)
Greenlander [mid–late 19C] (US)
green nigger [20C] (US)
lace-curtain Irish [1920s+] (US; genteel, petit-bourgeois Irish-Americans)
Mulligan [late 19C–1940s] (US)
Murphy [late 19C–1930s] (orig. UK)

99 99 99 99 99 99 99 99 99 99 99 99 99 99 99 99 99 99 99 99 99

Micks and Paddies

Gashouse Mick [1900s–30s] (US; from their living near the gasworks and other insalubrious areas)
goodie and baddie [20C] (rhy. sl. 'Paddy')
Mick [mid-19C+] (orig. US)
Mickey/Mickie [mid-19C+] (US)
Mickser [1950s+]
Mikey [mid-19C+] (US)
Pad [late 18C+]
Paddy [late 18C+]
Paddywhack [late 18C–early 19C]
Pat [early 19C+]
Patlander [19C]
Patrick [1940s+]
Plastic Paddy [1980s+] (a second-generation Irish immigrant to the UK)
shovel and pick [20C] (rhy. sl. 'Mick')

66 66 66 66 66 66 66 66 66 66 66 66 66 66 66 66 66 66 66 66 66

nipplie [1990s] (someone living outside Ireland who makes tenuous claims to Irish nationality; *n*ew *I*rish *p*atriot *p*ermanently *l*iving *in* *e*xile)

potato-eater [late 19C+] (US)

shanty Irish [20C] (US; lower-class Irish)

Teaguelander [late 17C–mid-19C] (*Teague* = Catholic)

thatched head [early 17C] (from the stereotypically unkempt appearance of the Irishman)

wog [1960s] (US)

Patrick [1940s+]

Plastic Paddy [1980s+] (a second-generation Irish immigrant to the UK)

shovel and pick [20C] (rhy. sl. 'Mick')

🙿 🙿

Ireland

Barkshire [19C] (Ireland; from the 'barking' of the Irish)

Greenland [mid–late 19C] (US)

Murphyland [mid-19C–early 20C] (US)

Paddyland/Paddy's land [mid-19C]

Patland [19C]

Teagueland [late 17C–mid-19C]

Urinal of the planets [late 17C–mid-19C] (from the country's high rainfall)

❝ ❝

CONTINENTAL EUROPEANS

FRENCHMEN

crappo [19C] (French *crapaud*, a toad)

Frenchie/Frenchy [mid-19C+] (US)

French peasoup [19C+] (US/Can.; a French immigrant)

frog [late 18C+]

frogeater [late 18C+]

froggie/froggy/froggee [mid-19C+] (orig. US)

Frogolian [1970s+] (N.Z.)

frog-swallower [late 19C]

froncey [late 19C]

grape-stomper [mid-20C]

Jean Potage [19C] (US; a French-born immigrant, lit. 'John Soup')

jiggle and jog [1970s] (rhy. sl. 'frog')

Jimmy Rounds [early 19C] (French *je me rends*, 'I surrender', the cry supposedly offered by hapless French sailors when faced with the might of the Royal Navy)

oui-oui [1940s] (French, 'yes yes')

frog-swallower

parleyvoo/parlay-voo [early 19C+] (French *parlez-vous*, do you speak)

peasoup/peasouper [19C+] (US; a French-born immigrant)

wee-wee/wi-wi/wewi [mid-19C] (orig. Aus./N.Z.; i.e. 'oui-oui')

wooden shoes [late 17C–mid-18C] (the *wooden* sabot, the traditional French footwear)

GERMANS

Boche [20C] (French *Alboche*, from *Allemand*, German)

cabbage-eater [19C] (US)

Dutchman [mid-19C–1920s] (US; German *Deutsch*, German)

flapdragon [17C] (i.e. they are all display but no substance)

Fritz/Fritzie [19C+]

Hans [late 16C+]

Heinie [20C]

Hun [late 19C+] (Scot.)

Jerry [1910s+]

kraut [mid-19C+] (orig. US; sauer*kraut*)

kraut-eater [mid-19C–1930s] (US)

kraut stomper [1910s+] (US)

Limburger [late 19C–1950s] (US; a popular cheese which is nevertheless made in Belgium)

metzel [19C] (US; German *Metzelsuppe*, a type of soup made with sausage)

Otto [20C]

pretzel [1940s]

sauerkraut [mid–late 19C] (US; a dish of shredded, pickled cabbage)

sauerkraut-eater [1910s]

sausage [late 19C–1920s]
sausage-eater [1910s]
sourcrout [mid-19C] (US; i.e. 'sauerkraut')

THE DUTCH

butterbag [mid-17C] (from the stereotype of the Dutch *butter* maker)
buttermouth [mid-16C–19C]
cloggite [1990s] (i.e. they wear *clogs*)
frog [17C] (implying merely 'despicable person', the term was transferred to the French in the following century as the focus of British national enmity changed)
Hans [late 16C+]
hogan-magan/hogen-mogen/hogan [late 17C–early 18C] (Dutch *Hoogmogendheiden*, lit. 'High Mightinesses', the official title of the States-General)

SCANDINAVIANS

cottontop [20C] (US; lit. someone with with white or blonde hair)
dumb sock [1930s+] (US)
herring choker [late 19C+] (US; a Scandinavian-born immigrant)
herring destroyer [late 19C+] (US; a Scandinavian-born immigrant)
herring snapper [late 19C+] (US; a Scandinavian-born immigrant)
Norski [20C] (US; a person of Norwegian origin)
Scandahoovian/Scandanoovian [late 19C+] (US)
Scowegian [1920s+]

99 99 99 99 99 99 99 99 99 99 99 99 99 99 99 99 99 99 99 99 99

The crowned 'heads' of Europe

beerhead [1940s] (US; a German)

boxhead [1920s–40s] (US; a Scandinavian)

flathead [mid-19C+] (US; a German or Lithuanian)

hardhead [20C] (US; a German or Dutchman)

hop-head [20C] (US; a German, from the stereotyped German liking for beer)

kaaskop [1970s+] (S Afr.; a Dutchman, lit. 'cheese-head')

krauthead [1910s+] (US; a German)

marblehead [19C] (a Greek, from the association of Greece with classical statuary)

panzer head [1980s] (a German, from the Panzer tanks used by the German forces in WW2)

roundhead [late 19C+] (US; a Swedish immigrant)

squarehead [20C] (US; a German or Scandinavian, from the severe 'Prussian' haircut)

66 66 66 66 66 66 66 66 66 66 66 66 66 66 66 66 66 66 66 66 66

ITALIANS

Dino [1910s] (US; an Italian or Hispanic labourer)

eytie/itie/I-Tie [1920s+] (orig. US)

eyeto [1940s+] (Aus.)

garlic-eater [mid-19C–1940s] (US)

garlic-snapper [1940s] (US)

Gina la Salsa [1950s+] (camp gay; an effeminate male Italian homosexual)

grocer's shop [1970s] (rhy. sl. 'wop')

Guido [1960s–70s] (US)

ice-creamer [1930s+]

macaroni [mid-19C+]

Marco Polo [1980s+] (US gay; a gay Italian man)

meatball [1930s+] (US)

spaghetti bender

mountain wop [1960s+] (US)

pasta-breath [20C] (US)

Roman candle [1940s+]

spag/spaggie [1960s+] (Aus.)

spaghetti [1930s+] (orig. US)

spaghetti bender [20C]

spaghetti head [20C] (US)

Taliano [20C]

wop/woppe [19C] (Spanish *guapo*, a dandy)

THE SPANISH AND PORTUGUESE

don [19C]

garlic-eater [mid-19C–1940s] (US)

oil slick [20C] (rhy. sl. 'spic')

Porra [1970s+] (S Afr.; a Portuguese)

South County Indian [20C] (US; from the many Portuguese immigrants to the US who settled in *South County*, Rhode Island)

spic/spick/spik [1910s+] (orig. US)

GREEKS

bubble (and squeak) [1950s+] (rhy. sl.)

dimmo/dimo [20C] (from the generic Greek forename *Demosthenes*)

grik [1970s+] (US)

grill [1950s+] (Aus.; from the near-monopoly of Greeks on the running of small cafes)

Werris [1960s+] (Aus.; rhy. sl. *Werris Creek*)

Zorba [1980s] (Aus.; from the novel and film *Zorba the Greek*)

CENTRAL AND EASTERN EUROPEANS

Balt [1940s–50s] (Aus.; any European refugee or immigrant; lit.
one from the Baltic states)

bear [early 19C+] (a Russian)

bohunk/bohak/bohawk [late 19C+] (US; *Bo*hemian
+ *Hung*arian)

cabbage-eater [19C] (US; a Russian)

Chesky [20C] (US; a Czech immigrant)

flannel mouth/flannel face [19C+] (US; a Pole)

Hunyak [20C] (US; an immigrant from Central Europe)

Polack/Polak/Pollacky [20C] (a Pole)

Russki/Rusky/Rooskie [1910s+] (a Russian)

sausage roll [1940s+] (rhy. sl. 'Pole')

99 99 99 99 99 99 99 99 99 99 99 99 99 99 99 99 99 99 99 99 99 99

Romanis

bush-cove [19C] (from their supposed habit
sleeping under *bushes*)

fair gang [19C] (alluding to the stereotype of
the gypsy fairground worker)

gippy [1910s]

gypo/gyppo/gyppy/gippo/jippo [20C]

gypper [late 19C+]

piker [19C] (*pike* = highway)

rag-head [20C]

66 66 66 66 66 66 66 66 66 66 66 66 66 66 66 66 66 66 66 66 66

AMERICANS

NORTH AMERICANS

board and plank [1940s+] (rhy. sl. 'Yank')
hamshank [1940s–60s] (rhy. sl. 'Yank')
septic/seppo [1970s+] (orig. Aus.; rhy. sl. 'Yank')
sherman [1940s+] (rhy. sl. 'Yank')
Widow Twankey [20C] (rhy. sl. 'Yankee')
wooden plank [20C] (rhy. sl. 'Yank')
Yank [late 18C+]

A MOSTLY INSULTING TOUR OF THE AMERICAN STATES

ALABAMA
lizard [mid-19C+]

ARKANSAS
Arky/Arkie [1920s+] (US)
goober [mid-19C+] (US; lit. 'peanut')
goober-grabber/goober-grubber [19C+] (US)
gopher [mid-19C] (US)
toothpick [late 19C] (US; the Arkansas *toothpick*, a type of large knife)

sherman

COLORADO
Rover [late 19C] (US)

CONNECTICUT

  nutmeg (maker) [early–late 19C] (US; from Connecticut's nickname, '*Nutmeg* State')

  wooden nutmeg [late 19C] (US; i.e. they are 'false')

DELAWARE

  musk-rat [19C+] (US)

FLORIDA

  alligator [late 19C+] (US)

  conch [19C+] (US; a poor white native of the Florida Keys)

  fish-head [20C] (US; a native of the West Florida coast)

  fly-up-the-creek [late 19C+] (US; a popular name of the small green heron, a native of Florida)

  gator [20C] (US)

  gopher [mid-19C] (US)

  rosin heel [19C] (US)

GEORGIA

  buzzard [mid-19C+] (US)

🙶 🙶

Three Canadians

  canuck/canucker/cannock [19C] (US; a French Canadian)

  potato [1950s] (Can.; a native of New Brunswick)

  Spud Islander [1950s+] (a native or inhabitant of Prince Edward Island)

🙶 🙶

clay-eater [19C] (US)

corncracker [mid-19C+] (US)

HAWAII

pineapple princess/pineapple queen [1960s+] (gay)

ILLINOIS

flathead [mid-19C+] (US; an inhabitant of the Illinois–Ohio lowlands)

sucker [mid-19C+] (US; poss. from the name of the state fish, or from the gullibility of the state's early settlers)

INDIANA

hoosier [19C+] (US; 'a rustic simpleton')

hoosieroon/hoosheroon [mid–late 19C] (US)

IOWA

hawk-eye [mid-19C+]

KANSAS

jayhawker [mid-19C+] (US; from the alleged similarity of the state's inhabitants to the *jay*, noted for its bullying of other birds)

KENTUCKY

crack-corn [19C+] (US; a white native of Kentucky)

hardhead [mid-19C–1950s] (US; a White native of rural Tennessee or Kentucky)

LOUISIANA

boogerlee [20C] (US; a Cajun)

coon-ass [19C+] (a Cajun; French *conasse*, the female genitals, thus *conassière*, sl. for French *femelots*, the gudgeon; the *coon-asses* were fishers of gudgeon)

pelican [mid-19C+] (US; the *pelican* on the state flag)

MAINE
fox [late 19C+] (US)
Mainiac [mid-19C+] (US)

MARYLAND
craw-thumper [late 18C+] (US; orig. a Catholic)

MIDDLE AMERICA
fly-over people [20C] (US; i.e. they inhabit those states over which one passes in an aeroplane flying from coast to coast)

MINNESOTA
gopher [mid-19C] (US)

MISSISSIPPI
mudcat [late 19C+] (US)
tadpole [late 19C] (US)

NEBRASKA
bug-eater [19C] (US; from an attempt in the 19C to persuade impoverished country-people to eat locusts when the state was overrun by them)

NEVADA
desert rat [19C+] (US)
sage hen [late 19C] (US; from the abundance of prairie fowl in the state)

NEW HAMPSHIRE
granite-boy [mid-19C+] (from the state's *granite* quarries)

NEW JERSEY
   clam-catcher [mid-19C–1900s] (US)

NORTH CAROLINA
   goober [mid-19C+] (US; lit. 'peanut')
   goober-grabber/goober-grubber [19C+] (US)
   tarheel/tar-boiler [mid-19C+] (from the *tar* produced in the state)

NORTH DAKOTA
   flickertail [20C] (US; the ground squirrel, the state's best known native animal)

OHIO
   buckeye [early 19C+] (US; from the *buckeye* tree)
   flathead [mid-19C+] (US; an inhabitant of the Illinois–Ohio lowlands)

OREGON
   lop-ear/flop-ear [mid-19C+] (US; lit. 'rabbit')

PENNSYLVANIA
   leatherhead [mid–late 19C] (US)
   penance [mid-19C+] (US; punning on the religious fervour of the state's inhabitants)

RHODE ISLAND
   gun-flint [late 19C] (US)

SOUTH CAROLINA
   weasel [mid-19C+] (US)

TENNESSEE
   buckshine [mid-19C+]

corncracker [mid-19C+] (US)

hardhead [mid-19C–1950s] (US; a white native of rural Tennessee or Kentucky)

mud-head [mid-19C+] (US)

whelp [mid-19C+]

VERMONT

Green Mountain boys [late 19C] (US; from the lit. meaning of Vermont, French *verts monts*, green mountains)

VIRGINIA

beagle [mid-19C] (US; from the popularity of fox-hunting in the state)

buckskin [late 18C–early 19C]

clover-eater [19C] (US)

hit-your-back [20C] (US; from the supposed hospitality of Virginians, i.e. they are constantly slapping one another's *backs* in camaraderie)

soreback [20C] (US)

WISCONSIN

badger [mid-19C+] (US; from the early Wisconsin lead-miners who lived in subterranean diggings alongside the seams of lead they were mining)

99 99 99 99 99 99 99 99 99 99 99 99 99 99 99 99 99 99 99 99 99 99

New Englanders

clam-digger [20C] (US)

eel [19C+] (US West; i.e. they are 'slippery')

66 66 66 66 66 66 66 66 66 66 66 66 66 66 66 66 66 66 66 66 66 66

NATIVE AMERICANS

biscuit beggar [20C] (US)
black duck [18C]
blanket-ass/blanket-head [1970s+] (US)
bow and arrow [20C] (US)
brunette [1940s]
copper/copperhide/copperskin [late 18C–late 19C] (US)
copperhead [late 18C–late 19C]

99 99 99 99 99 99 99 99 99 99 99 99 99 99 99 99 99 99 99 99 99 99

Bostonians

bean-eater [late 19C–1940s] (US)
bow-wow [19C] (US)
pumpkin/pompkin [late 18C–early 19C]
stars and stripes [late 19C] (from their traditional Sunday meal of baked beans (*stars*) and pork belly (*stripes*))

66 66 66 66 66 66 66 66 66 66 66 66 66 66 66 66 66 66 66 66 66 66

99 99 99 99 99 99 99 99 99 99 99 99 99 99 99 99 99 99 99 99 99 99

White Southerners

chiv [mid–late 19C] (US West; *chiv*alry, a supposed obsession in the White South)
Reb/Rebel [mid-19C+] (US; from the Southern 'rebellion' that triggered the American Civil War)

66 66 66 66 66 66 66 66 66 66 66 66 66 66 66 66 66 66 66 66 66 66

featherhead [mid-19C+] (US)

gut-eater [1920s–60s] (from the Native American's supposed taste for offal)

Injun/Injin [early 19C+] (US; pron. of 'Indian')

leatherskin [mid–late 19C] (US)

redbone [mid-19C–1970s] (US Black)

Tonto [20C] (a Native American regarded as insufficiently nationalistic, from the name of the Lone Ranger's Native American sidekick)

bean bandit

Uncle Tomahawk [1960s+] (US; a Native American who is condemned as insufficiently nationalistic, punning on *Uncle Tom*, a subservient Black person + *tomahawk*, the traditional Native American weapon)

HISPANICS

SPANISH-AMERICANS

bean-choker [1980s+] (US)

burrito [1980s+] (US)

chacha queen [1980s+] (US gay; a Hispanic homosexual)

Pedro [1940s–50s] (US)

spic/spick/spik [1910s+] (US)

PUERTO RICANS

butter pecan [1990s] (US Black teen; an attractive Puerto Rican woman)

dago [mid-19C+] (orig. US)

hick [1960s+] (US)

island nigger [1980s+] (US)

Jose [1970s+] (US)

mujer [1970s+] (an attractive Puerto Rican woman; Spanish, 'wife')

niggerican [1970s] (US)

Rican [1970s+] (US)

MEXICANS

adobe maker [20C] (US)

Chico [1960s+] (a lower-class Mexican or one of mixed blood)

chile bean/chili bean/chile-bean [1960s+]

chilli-belly/chilli-gut [1960s+] (US)

chilli-choker [1950s+] (US)

chilli-eater/chilli-chomper/chilli-picker [20C] (US)

chilli-head [1970s+] (US)

99 99 99 99 99 99 99 99 99 99 99 99 99 99 99 99 99 99 99 99 99 99

Bean bandits

bean [1940s+] (US)

beanbag [1970s] (US)

bean bandit [1950s–70s] (US)

bean-eater [1910s+] (US)

beano [late 19C–1920s]

frijole-eater [20C] (US; Spanish *frijole*, bean)

66 66 66 66 66 66 66 66 66 66 66 66 66 66 66 66 66 66 66 66 66 66

dago [mid-19C+] (orig. US)

engabachado [1960s] (US; a Mexican who attempts to pass as white, lit. 'rendered white')

frito [1950s–60s] (US)

greaser [mid-19C+] (orig. US)

greaserita [mid-19C] (US; a Mexican woman)

lubricator [mid–late 19C] (US)

oiler [1900s–60s] (US)

pepper belly/pepper gut [20C] (US)

spiggoty [19C] (US; i.e. 'spikka da English', a supposed Mexican pron. of 'speak English')

taco [1960s+] (US)

taco-bender/taco-eater/taco-head [1960s+] (US)

Tio Taco [20C] (US; lit. 'Uncle Taco')

ANTIPODEANS

AUSTRALIANS

Aussie [late 19C+]

digger [mid-19C+]

dinkum [late 19C+] (Aus.)

gum-sucker [mid–late 19C+] (Aus.)

kangaroo [mid-19C+] (US)

tothersider [mid-19C+] (Aus.; a mainlander as viewed by a Tasmanian, i.e. they live on 'the other side')

AUSTRALIANS STATE BY STATE

QUEENSLANDERS

Bananalander [late 19C+] (Aus.)

banana man [mid-19C+] (Aus.)

bananaskin [late 19C] (Aus.)

VICTORIANS

cabbage gardener/cabbage patcher/cabbage stater [late 19C+] (Aus.)

Mexican [1980s+] (Aus.; a Victorian as seen from New South Wales, or Queensland)

mudlark [20C] (Aus.)

NEW SOUTH WELSHMEN

cockroach [20C] (Aus.)

cornstalk [late 19C–1940s] (Aus.; a European native of New South Wales)

crow-eater [late 19C+] (Aus.; a White inhabitant of South Australia)

Mexican [1980s+] (Aus.; a native of New South Wales viewed from Queensland)

Parra [1970s+] (Aus.; an inhabitant of the western suburbs of Sydney, from *Parra*matta, New South Wales)

Waler [late 19C+] (Aus.)

Welshie/Welshy [1920s] (Aus.)

TASMANIANS

fly specker [20C] (Aus.; referring to Tasmania's relative size compared to Australia)

gum-sucker [mid–late 19C+] (Aus.)

mountain devil [20C] (Aus.; a type of Tasmanian lizard)

mutton-bird/mutton eater [late 19C+] (Aus.; a native of northern Tasmania, from an edible species of Puffin)

groper [1920s+] (Aus.)

Groperlander [1920s+](Aus.)

sand-groper [late 19C+] (Aus.)

NATIVE AUSTRALIANS

abo [20C] (Aus.)

bitumen blonde [1930s+] (Aus.; an Aboriginal woman)

blackbird [mid–late 19C] (Aus.)

boog [1930s+] (Aus.; i.e. 'bogey')

crow-bait [mid–late 19C] (Aus.)

dark cloud [1900s–30s] (usu. Aus./US)

din [19C] (a Native Australian woman; Dharuk *diyin*, woman)

jacky (jacky) [mid-19C+] (Aus.)

murky [20C] (Aus.)

nigger [mid-19C+]

stud (gin) [1920s+] (Aus.; an Aboriginal woman viewed as a sex object)

unbleached Australian [20C]

whistlecock [late 19C+] (Aus.; from the practice of slitting open the penis as part of an initiation ritual or as a prophylactic measure)

NEW ZEALANDERS

Kiwi [1910s+]

Pig Islander [20C] (Aus./N.Z.)

Rangitoto Yank/Rangitoto Yankee [1960s+] (N.Z.; an Aucklander, from *Rangitoto*, an island in Auckland harbour)

MAORIS

brown velvet [1930s] (a Maori woman viewed as a sex object)
dago [1900s–50s] (N.Z.)
smoky/smokey [1980s+] (N.Z.)
tar baby [1950s] (N.Z.)
tarpot [1940s] (N.Z.)

ASIANS AND EAST ASIANS

INDIANS AND PAKISTANIS

banana split [1990s] (US Black teen; a sexy Asian woman)
brownie [mid-19C+] (US)
camel chaser/camel jockey/camel jock [1960s+] (US)
coolie/koelie [mid-19C+] (S Afr.; lit. 'labourer')
dothead [1980s+] (US; from the Hindu caste mark worn by married women)
f.o.b. [1970s] (N.Z.; an Asian immigrant; *f*resh *o*ff the *b*oat)
goo-goo [1900s–50s] (US)
halal [1990s] (a Pakistani immigrant, from the ritually slaughtered meat eaten by Muslims)
nuprin [1990s] (US campus)

99 99 99 99 99 99 99 99 99 99 99 99 99 99 99 99 99 99 99 99 99 99

Asians in rhyming slang

half-ounce of baccy [1970s+] ('paki')
hedgehog [20C] ('wog')
Joe Daki [1980s+] ('paki')
ounce of baccy/ouncer [20C] ('paki')

66 66 66 66 66 66 66 66 66 66 66 66 66 66 66 66 66 66 66 66 66 66

ou-di-du-dat [1950s] (W.I.; pron. of 'how does he do that?')
pak [1950s+]
paki/pakki [1960s+]
sand scratcher [20C] (US)
wog/woggy [1920s+]

EAST ASIANS

buddhahead [20C] (US)
pie-face [1980s] (Aus.; from the supposed resemblance of the eyes of East Asians to cuts in a pie-crust)
Ping [1980s+] (N.Z.)
Pong [20C] (Aus.)
rice man [1930s+] (US Black)
Rice Paddy Hattie [1980s+] (US gay; a gay East Asian man)
slant(-eye) [1950s+]
slit [1940s+]
slope/slopehead/slopy [1940s+]
Suzie Wang/Suzie Wong [1960s] (camp gay; an East Asian homosexual, punning on the film *The World of Suzie Wong* + *wang*, the penis)
tight eyes [1960s–70s] (US Black)
yellow peril [20C]

99 99 99 99 99 99 99 99 99 99 99 99 99 99 99 99 99 99 99 99 99 99

East Asians in rhyming slang

kitchen sink [20C] ('Chink')
tiddleywink/tiddlywink [1970s+] ('Chink')
Wee Willie Winky [1990s+] ('chinky')
widow's wink [1970s] ('Chink')

66 66 66 66 66 66 66 66 66 66 66 66 66 66 66 66 66 66 66 66 66 66

CHINESE PEOPLE

Charlie Chan [1930s] (US; the fictional Chinese detective)
China boy [mid-19C+]
chinee [19C]
Chink [late 19C+] (orig. Aus.)
chinki-chonks/chinky-chonks [1970s+]
chinko [late 19C] (orig. N.Z.)
chinky [1970s+]
chopstick [1960s+] (US Black)
laundryman [late 19C+] (US; the stereotypical Chinese occupation)
paddy [20C] (Aus.; from the *paddy* fields in which rice grows)
rice-belly [20C] (US)
rice-eater [1990s] (Aus.)
squeeze-eye [1940s] (W.I.)

🙿 🙿

Four Vietnamese and one Filipino

dink [1920s+]
filipinyok [20C] (US)
gook [1920s+] (orig. US milit.; i.e. 'goo-goo', an imitation of the speech sound)
nog [1960s+] (Aus.)
plate-face [1980s+] (Aus.; from the perceived flatness of some East Asian faces)
zip [1950s+] (US; lit. 'nothing', from their supposed lack of intelligence)

❝ ❝

yap [1950s] (W.I.)

yellow face [late 19C–1900s]

yellow fish [20C] (US; an illegal Chinese immigrant)

yellow peril [20C] (the Communist Chinese)

JAPANESE PEOPLE

Jap [late 19C+]

Japanee [mid-19C+] (US)

Jappo/Jappy [1940s–50s] (US)

micro-chip [20C] (rhy. sl. 'Nip')

Mr Moto [1930s–70s] (US; the fictional Japanese detective)

moose [1950s–80s] (US; a Japanese woman, esp. the wife of a US serviceman; Japanese *musume*, daughter, girl)

Nip/Nippo [1940s+] (orig. US; *Nip*ponese)

orange pip [20C] (rhy. sl. 'Nip')

rat trap [1940s+] (rhy. sl. 'Jap')

yellow belly [1940s] (Aus.)

ARABS

Abdul [1980s+] (US)

Ayrab/A-rab [1960s+] (US)

camel chaser/camel jockey/camel jock [1960s+] (US)

dune coon [1990s]

'Ghan [20C] (Aus.; Af*ghan*)

handkerchief-head [1990s] (US)

rag-head [1920s+] (US)

sand-hopper [20C]

sand nigger [1980s+] (US)

towel-head [1980s+]

SPIRITUALLY IMPOVERISHED

GOD

the big boss [1920s] (US)
big guy [1920s+] (US)
head knock [1930s–40s] (US Black; God, Jesus)
Jerusalem slim [1920s–70s] (US tramp; Jesus Christ)
the man [1970s+] (US)
the man upstairs [1960s+]
the old man [1900s–50s] (US)
Tommy Dodd [late 19C–1950s] (rhy. sl.)

PROTESTANTS

bible-backed [20C] (US; conspicuously anti-Catholic)
black Irish [20C] (US; an Irish Protestant)
black Protestant [20C] (US; an anti-Catholic Protestant)
narrowback [1930s+] (US)
Paris bun [20C]

99 99 99 99 99 99 99 99 99 99 99 99 99 99 99 99 99 99 99 99 99 99 99

Apron and gaiters: five bishops

apron and gaiters [late 19C–1910s] (from
  their vestments)
Archbishop of Cant [1930s+] (an Anglican
  archbishop)
the bip [1920s+] (society)
magpie [early 17C–1920s] (an Anglican
  bishop)
pair of lawn sleeves [mid-19C] (from their
  vestments)

66 66 66 66 66 66 66 66 66 66 66 66 66 66 66 66 66 66 66 66 66 66

Prod [1940s+] (esp. in Northern Ireland)

Proddo [20C] (Aus. Catholic use)

Proddy (dog) [1950s+] (Irish Catholic use)

proddyhopper [20C] (N.Z. juv.)

Proddywoddy/Proddywhoddy [1940s+] (esp. in Northern Ireland)

soapdodger [20C]

ANGLICANS HIGH AND LOW

amener [late 19C–1900s] (a devout Anglican)

bells and smells [20C] (high-church Anglicanism, from the use of altar *bells* and incense in the Eucharist)

broad and shallow [mid-19C] (the Anglican Church as a liberal '*broad* church', tolerant of different doctrinal viewpoints)

C and E man [20C] (US; someone who attends church only rarely; *C*hristmas *and E*aster *man*)

high and dry [mid-19C] (a *high*-church Anglican)

low and slow [mid-19C] (a *low*-church Anglican)

BAPTISTS

bappo [1920s+] (Aus.)

Crying Willie [20C] (US; referring to their religious lamentations)

dipper [late 17C+] (US)

footwasher [19C+] (US; a fundamentalist Baptist)

hardhead [20C] (US; a primitive Baptist)

wet-wash Baptist [20C] (US; from their method of baptism which involves total immersion)

METHODISTS

chicken-eater [20C] (US; from the habit of members of the congregation inviting the preacher home for a lunch of roast *chicken*)

dry-clean Methodist [20C] (from their method of baptism which involves sprinkling rather than immersing)

99 99 99 99 99 99 99 99 99 99 99 99 99 99 99 99 99 99 99 99 99

God-hoppers and happy-clappies

bead-counter [19C]

Christer [1920s+] (US; an overtly religious person, esp. a proselytizing teetotaller)

God-botherer [1970s+] (Aus.)

God-hopper [1940s–50s] (US)

gospel-grinder [mid-19C–1940s] (US)

gospel-slinger [mid-19C–1940s] (US)

happy-clappies [1980s+] (orig. S Afr.)

hell-robber [1930s+] (US)

holy roller [1970s+] (US; a sanctimonious person or religious fundamentalist)

hoot-and-holler [20C] (US; the nickname of a Pentecostalist sect)

Jesus freak [1960s+] (orig. US)

mission squawker [1920s] (US tramp; a mission evangelist)

mission stiff [late 19C+] (US; a missionary worker)

psalm-singing muzzler [20C] (US Und.)

66 66 66 66 66 66 66 66 66 66 66 66 66 66 66 66 66 66 66 66 66

metho [1940s+] (Aus.)

methodist measure [1940s+] (US; a short *measure* of alcohol, from the traditional teetotallism of Methodists)

Methody [mid-19C+] (Irish)

swaddler [mid-18C–19C]

PRESBYTERIANS

blackmouth [20C] (Ulster)

blueskin [18C–early 19C]

crop [late 18C] (from their traditional short, cropped hairstyles)

pressed beef [1950s+] (Catholic use)

pressie [1950s+] (Aus.)

99 99 99 99 99 99 99 99 99 99 99 99 99 99 99 99 99 99 99 99 99 99 99

Campus Christians

bible-beater [1970s] (US campus; an evangelizing, fundamentalist Christian)

crusader [1990s] (US campus; an evangelistic, fundamentalist Christian)

donkey [mid-19C] (US campus; a notably religious student)

lap-ears [mid-19C] (US campus; a notably religious student, lit. 'donkey')

long ear [mid–late 19C] (US campus; a sober, religious student)

66 66 66 66 66 66 66 66 66 66 66 66 66 66 66 66 66 66 66 66 66 66

PURITANS AND PI-MEN

bible-basher [1950s+] (Aus.)

bible-puncher [1930s+] (orig. milit.)

bible-walloper [19C]

bluenoser [1970s]

blue stocking [18C] (US)

Holy Joe [mid-19C+]

Nicodemus [late 17C] (a religious fanatic)

pi-man [20C] (*pious man*)

tight-arse/tight-ass/tight-butt [1980s+] (orig. US)

Tipper Gore [1990s] (US teen; the wife of US politician
Al Gore, apostrophised by her critics as a byword for
narrow-mindedness)

wowser [late 19C+] (Aus./N.Z.;
dial. *wow*, to howl like a dog)

CATHOLICS

bead-jiggler/bead-mumbler [1960s]
(US)

bead-puller [20C] (US)

breast fleet [late 18C] (Catholics
as a group)

cat-licker [20C] (US)

cattle ticks [20C]

chest-pounder [20C] (US)

fish-eater

Fenian [1910s+] (Ulster Catholics/
nationalists, from the *Fenian* Brotherhood, a militant Irish
nationalist group of the second half of the 19C)

99 99 99 99 99 99 99 99 99 99 99 99 99 99 99 99 99 99 99 99 99

Guppy-gobblers and minnow-munchers

fish [1950s+] (US; from the Catholic tradition
of abstaining from meat on Fridays)
fish-eater [1950s+] (Can.)
guppy-gobbler [1960s] (US)
mackerel-snapper/-eater/-gobbler/
-smacker/-snatcher [mid-19C; 1920s+]
(orig. US)
minnow-muncher [1960s+] (US)
tatty muncher [1980s+]

66 66 66 66 66 66 66 66 66 66 66 66 66 66 66 66 66 66 66 66 66

Jack Papish [early 18C]
left-footer/left-hander [1930s+]
popehead [1990s] (Ulster)
red-letter man [late 17C–18C] (from the *red letter* used to mark
saints' days)
rockchopper [1940s–50s] (Aus.; orig. Irish immigrants to
Australia, who were mainly convicts and as such were
condemned to hard labour)
Roman candle [1940s+]
statue-lover [20C] (US)
Taig/Teague [17C+] (from the Irish name *Tadhg*, rendered in
English as Thaddeus)

PREACHERS

amen-bawler [19C]

amen-snorter [late 19C] (mainly Aus.)

ballocks/bollocks/bollox [18C–early 19C] (i.e. they talk nonsense)

dodger [mid–late 19C] (i.e. 'devil-dodger')

fire-escape [mid-19C–1920s] (the *fire* being that of hell)

gospel-cove [1900s–10s] (Aus.)

humdrum [early 18C–19C] (i.e. they are dull and monotonous)

Jesus screamer [1950s+] (US)

Mr Prunella [late 18C–early 19C] (*prunella*, a strong fabric used for clergymen's gowns)

mumble-matins [mid-16C–early 17C]

parish bull/parish prig [mid-19C] (UK Und.)

parish stallion [late 19C]

99 99 99 99 99 99 99 99 99 99 99 99 99 99 99 99 99 99 99 99 99 99 99

(Clergy-)Men in black

black boy [17C–mid-19C]

black fly [18C]

body of divinity bound in black calf [mid-18C–early 19C]

chimney sweep [late 19C]

crow [late 18C–1900s]

pudding-sleeves [late 18C–early 19C] (from the voluminous *sleeves* of his vestments)

white-choker [late 19C–1910s]

66 66 66 66 66 66 66 66 66 66 66 66 66 66 66 66 66 66 66 66 66 66

devil-chaser

Parson Trulliber [mid-19C] (a rude, vulgar country clergyman)

postilion of the gospel [late 18C–early 19C] (a parson who rushes through the service)

puzzle-text [late 18C–early 19C]

sin-buster [1930s] (US)

sin-shifter [1910s+]

skypilot [late 19C+]

soul-doctor [late 18C–19C]

spiritual flesh-broker [late 17C–18C]

spoil-pudding [late 18C–early 19C] (a long-winded parson, i.e. their sermons last so long as to spoil their parishioners' Sunday lunch)

tickle-text [late 18C–1900s]

tub-man/tub-preacher [mid-17C]

ungrateful man [late 18C–early 19C] (he 'at least once a week abuses his best benefactor, i.e. the devil')

wet parson [late 18C–early 19C] (a parson with a taste for liquor)

99 99 99 99 99 99 99 99 99 99 99 99 99 99 99 99 99 99 99 99 99

Devil-dodgers

devil-chaser [20C] (US)
devil-dodger [mid-19C]
devil-scolder [mid-19C]
devil-teaser [1910s] (US)
haul-devil [mid-19C–1900s]
snub devil [late 18C–late 19C]

66 66 66 66 66 66 66 66 66 66 66 66 66 66 66 66 66 66 66 66 66

HELLFIRE PREACHERS

bible-basher [1950s+] (orig. Aus.)
break-pulpit [late 16C–17C]
brimstone buster [19C] (US)
cushion-smiter [mid–late 19C]
cushion-thumper [mid-17C–late 19C]
gospel-shooter [19C+] (US)
gospel-whanger [19C+] (US)
pound-text [late 18C–late 19C]
psalm-smiter [mid-19C]
pulpit-banger [20C] (US)
pulpit-drummer [20C] (US)
table-tapper [20C] (US)
tub-thumper/tub-drubber [late 18C+]

JEWS

Bronx Indian [1940s] (US; from the *Bronx* area of New York, which once had a large Jewish population)

Brooklyn Indian [20C] (US; from *Brooklyn*, New York, which is home to many Jews)

Christ-killer [mid-19C+] (US)

Hebe/Hebie/Heeb [1920s+] (orig. US; *Heb*rew)

iddy (boy) [20C] (i.e. 'Yid')

Israelite [1940s] (US Black)

Izzy/Issey [late 19C+]

Jew-boy [late 18C+]

Jewie [late 19C+] (Anglo-Irish)

Red Sea pedestrian

Judaic superbacy [late 19C] (a Jew dressed in 'all the glory of his best clothes')

kike [late 19C+] (orig. US; poss. rhyming with the common Jewish name *Ike*, i.e. Isaac, or from the Yiddish *kikel*, a circle, the mark used by some illiterate Jewish immigrants when signing papers at Ellis Island, New York)

Mr Money [1960s+] (US Black)

oi yoi yoi [1900s–30s] (US)

oven-dodger [1980s+] (referring to the crematorium ovens of the Nazi death camps)

piebald mucker sheeny [late 19C] (a dirty, aging Jew)

Red Sea pedestrian [20C] (Aus.; from the Israelites' crossing of the Red Sea)

refujew [1930s–40s] (US; a Jewish refugee from Germany or Central Europe)

sheeny/sheeney/sheenie [19C]

slick-'em-plenty [1970s] (US Black)

snide and shine [late 19C] (a Jew living in London's East End)

Yehudi [20C] (US; Hebrew, 'Jew')

Yid/Yit/Yitt [mid-19C+] (German *Jude*, a Jew)

Yiddle [20C]

99 99 99 99 99 99 99 99 99 99 99 99 99 99 99 99 99 99 99 99 99 99

Three circumcised penises

clip [1940s]

clipdick [1940s+]

snipcock [1960s+]

66 66 66 66 66 66 66 66 66 66 66 66 66 66 66 66 66 66 66 66 66

99 99 99 99 99 99 99 99 99 99 99 99 99 99 99 99 99 99 99 99 99 99

Lox jocks and bagel-benders

bagel bender [1970s+] (US)

baloney bender [1930s] (US)

lox jock/lox jockey [20C] (US; *lox* = smoked salmon)

motzer [late 19C–1900s] (US; Hebrew *matze*, unleavened bread traditionally eaten at the Jewish festival of Passover)

noodle soup drinker [1900s–30s] (US)

porker [late 18C+] (the Jewish laws of *kashrut* forbid the consumption of pig flesh)

66 66 66 66 66 66 66 66 66 66 66 66 66 66 66 66 66 66 66 66 66 66

JEWS IN RHYMING SLANG: PART I

RHYMING WITH JEW

box of glue [1950s] (US)

buckle my shoe [late 19C+]

fifteen and two/fifteen-two [1940s+] (US)

five to two [20C]

four by two [1930s+] (N.Z.)

half past two [20C]

kangaroo [20C]

pot of glue [20C]

pull-through [1970s]

quarter to two [20C]

Sarah Soo [1920s+]

ten to two [1930s+]

Four noses

eagle beak [1920s+] (US)

hook [1960s+] (US Black)

hooknose/hookface [mid-19C]

nickelnose [1970s+] (US; combining the
stereotypes of the large-nosed Jew and the
money-obsessed Jew)

❝ ❝

JEWS IN RHYMING SLANG: PART II

RHYMING WITH YID

Cisco Kid [1960s+]

four-wheel skid/three-wheel skid [1930s+]

front-wheel skid/back-wheel skid [1960s+]

saucepan lid [1950s+]

slippery (Sid) [1980s+]

teapot (lid) [20C]

tin lid [20C]

JEWS BY NAME

Abe [19C+] (*Ab*raham, the biblical patriarch)

Abie [1950s–60s] (US Black)

Abie Kabibble [1910s–30s] (US; Yiddish *ish kabibble*, 'who cares?')

Goldberg/Goldstein [1930s+] (US Black)

Hoggenheimer [1910s] (S Afr.; the stereotypical Jewish capitalist)

Hymie [20C] (orig. US; *Hym*an)

ikey-mo [early 19C+] (*Isaac* + *Moses*)
Solly [late 19C+] (*Solo*mon)
Solomon Isaac [late 19C–1910s]

JEWISH TRADESMEN

Mr Three Balls [1940s–50s] (from the *three* brass *balls* that hang
  outside a pawnbroker's shop)
nunky [1920s–30s] (*uncle* = pawnbroker)
shonk [19C]

99 99 99 99 99 99 99 99 99 99 99 99 99 99 99 99 99 99 99 99 99 99

Jewish quarters

Abrahamstead [1970s+] (Hampstead,
  North London)
Hymietown [1980s+] (US; New York City)
Jerusalem the golden/-by-the-sea/-on-sea
  [1950s+] (Brighton)
Jewburg [1900s–50s] (S Afr.; Johannesburg)
Jewish Alps [20C] (US; Washington
  Heights, New York)
Jew York [20C] (society; New York City)
Yiddish highway [20C] (US; US30, the route
  from New York to Miami, supposedly the
  migratory route of retiring Jews)
Yidney [1970s+] (society; Sydney, Australia)
Yidsbury [1970s+] (Finsbury, North
  London)

66 66 66 66 66 66 66 66 66 66 66 66 66 66 66 66 66 66 66 66 66

shonnicker [mid-19C+] (Yiddish, 'small trader')
three balls [1930s+] (US Black)

GENTILES

flour mixer [20C] (a non-Jewish woman; rhy. sl. 'shiksa')
goy [late 19C+] (Hebrew, 'nation')
goyisher [late 19C+]
shakester/shickster [mid-19C] (a Gentile woman, i.e. 'shicksa')
shaygets/sheygets [late 19C+] (a young male gentile; Hebrew, 'rascal')
shicksa/chickster/shakester/shickse/shickster/shikster [mid-19C+] (Jewish; a gentile woman)
yenta [1920s+] (orig. US; a gentile woman)
yock/yok [20C] (backslang, 'goy')